Camouflage Uniforms of the German Wehrmacht: Manufacturers • Zeltbahnen • Headgear • Fallschirmjäger Smocks • Army Smocks • Padded Uniforms • Leibermuster • Tents • Non-Regulation Clothes • Post War *Werner Palinckx with Dr. J.F. Borsarello.* An indispensable guide for historians, collectors and military modelers, this book finally resolves the confusion surrounding many of the World War II Wehrmacht (both Army and Luftwaffe) patterns and garments and establishes a complete and concise system of identification and terminology. A comparative section with post-war fabrications is added as a tool for authentication. More than 10 different camouflage patterns are covered, including the super rare carbon overprint and Leibermuster. Authentic zeltbahns, helmet covers, caps, smocks, winter clothing, anti-gas outfits, body aprons, tents and more.
Size: 9"x12" • over 580 color & b/w photos • 288 pp. • ISBN: 0-7643-1623-0 • hard cover • $79.95

Afrikakorps: Tropical Uniforms, Insignia & Equipment of the German Soldier in World War II *Robert Kurtz.* The ultimate visual guide for collectors of World War II German tropical uniforms! Using actual items from top Afrikakorps collections – tunics, headgear, insignia, documents, field gear – as well as many World War II era photographs, this book covers it all in color. From mint issue items, to rare sun-bleached tunics and caps, the wide variety of tropical uniforms used by the Army, Luftwaffe, Kriegsmarine and Waffen-SS are illustrated in superb large format photography, including up-close detail.
Size: 9"x12" • over 730 color, b/w photographs • 300 pp. • ISBN: 0-7643-1920-5 • hard cover • $79.95

We are always interested in working with authors or collectors on wonderful book ideas. Contact us at **www.schifferbooks.com**, and page down to "For Authors – Submit a Book Proposal." Or call or write to us about your proposal.

Talk with your local bookseller. Their knowledge is one of the best tools in finding the correct book, and we all need to support them.

** Peter Schiffer and Team **
Designed & composed in America.
Printed in China.

FLAMETHROWER TROOPS OF WORLD WAR I

FLAMETHROWER TROOPS
OF WORLD WAR I: THE CENTRAL AND ALLIED POWERS

Thomas Wictor

Schiffer Military History
Atglen, PA

Acknowledgments

The following people were instrumental in the completion of this book. Without their generous help, this project would simply not have been possible. My deepest gratitude is extended to all.

Dimitar Boikov (Bulgaria); Michael Constandy (United States); Nik Cornish (Russia); Thierry Ehret (France and Germany); Ventsislav Gramatsky (Bulgaria); Simon Jones (Great Britain); Gaetano Nieddu (Italy); Antonio Rosetto (Italy and Austria-Hungary); Marco Pellegrini (Bulgaria and Ottoman Empire); Dr. Mikhail Supotnitskiy (Russia and Great Britain); and Mesut Uyar (Ottoman Empire).

Thanks also to Andi Lucas, Jack Sheldon, and Andrew Heaton for their contributions and assistance. Thanks especially to my patient editor, Robert Biondi.

Dedication

For the men and women of the United States armed forces.

All photos from the author's collection unless otherwise credited.

Book design by Robert Biondi.

Library of Congress Catalog Number: 2010930662.

Printed in China.
ISBN: 978-0-7643-3526-6

We are always looking for people to write books on new and related subjects. If you have an idea for a book, please contact us at the address below.

Published by Schiffer Publishing Ltd.
4880 Lower Valley Road
Atglen, PA 19310
Phone: (610) 593-1777
FAX: (610) 593-2002
E-mail: Info@schifferbooks.com.
Visit our web site at: www.schifferbooks.com
Please write for a free catalog.
This book may be purchased from the publisher.
Please include $5.00 postage.
Try your bookstore first.

In Europe, Schiffer books are distributed by:
Bushwood Books
6 Marksbury Ave.
Kew Gardens, Surrey TW9 4JF
England
Phone: 44 (0)20 8392-8585
FAX: 44 (0)20 8392-9876
E-mail: info@bushwoodbooks.co.uk
www.bushwoodbooks.co.uk

Contents

Introduction

In 1909 the German army officially embraced flamethrowers as a replacement of "fire tubes" *(Brandröhren),* incendiary devices used by pioneers to attack bunkers, fortresses, and other strong points. Three years later pioneer siege trains *(Pionier-Belagerungstrain)* were issued the first portable flamethrowers.[1] This move was the culmination of seven years of research by the Prussian Engineer Committee *(Preussisches Ingenieur-Komitee),* the Pioneer Experimental Company *(Pionier-Versuchs-Kompagnie)* of the Guard Pioneer Battalion *(Garde-Pionier-Bataillon),* and mechanical engineer Richard Fiedler of Berlin, inventor of the flamethrower.

Another seminal figure in the development of the flamethrower was Bernhard Reddemann, a German firefighter, inventor, and soldier, who in 1907 converted hand pumps and steam pumpers into flamethrowers.[2] He met with Fiedler and may have collaborated with him on flamethrower development. Soon after the outbreak of war in 1914, Reddemann persuaded the German Supreme Command to create a flamethrower detachment that eventually grew into a full regiment.

All the major combatants of the war established flamethrower units, all of which saw combat. This book is the first attempt to document these troops. Part I covers the Central Powers, Part II the Allies. Within the two sections, the nations are arranged by the comprehensiveness and influence of their flame-warfare efforts. For the Central Powers, the dominant force was Germany; for the Allies France took the lead, although Great Britain, Russia and the United States developed their own weapons as well.

Not generally known among western historians is the Russian interest in flame warfare, which began in 1898 with the experiments conducted by the 1st Field-Engineer Brigade under the supervision of the Chief Military Engineering Directorate (GIU) of the War Ministry.[3] Static kerosene flamethrowers designed by a Captain Ziger-Korn were tested and found to be too vulnerable to artillery. In 1909 Richard Fiedler used his connections to Tsar Nicholas II to arrange for a demonstration of his small, medium, and large flamethrowers at an artillery proving ground at Izhora, 20 miles south of Petrograd.

Despite the impressive display, the GIU deemed the weapons inaccurate, too complicated to use and supply, and too exposed to enemy fire. In 1911 the irrepressible Fiedler invited Russian officials to Berlin for another demonstration; this time he offered them ten small flamethrowers, 100 automatic igniters, and 360 lbs. each of regular and smokeless oil, for the price of 10,000 rubles. For more money Fiedler would provide personal instruction on the use of his flamethrowers and reveal the composition of his oils and the mechanism of his igniters. Again, the Russians declined. During the early part of the war German flamethrowers created panic among the allies, inducing the Russians to begin a crash course in flame warfare that came close to matching the efforts of the French and Italians.

Much of the information in this book has been drawn from official sources. For quick reference the chapters are presented as time lines, followed by a description of the tactics used. Select flamethrower attacks are briefly described, while data on weapons is found in Appendix 1. For the most part, only weapons used in combat are featured. When the record is unclear, as in the case of Britain and the United States, flamethrowers are included even though they may not have been developed beyond the prototype stage.

Unit names are translated into English, usually followed by the name in the original language, and ranks are abbreviated after their first usage for each individual.

Part One: The Central Powers

German small-flamethrower squad (Kleiftrupp) and hand-grenade throwers of the Guard Reserve Pioneer Regiment (Garde-Reserve-Pionier-Regiment), training in 1917. A four-man squad served the late-model Kleif M.1915 flamethrower.

GERMANY

1914

August – At the beginning of position warfare, individual pioneer formations received flamethrowers as offensive weapons[1] kept in pioneer parks.[2] Each platoon of selected pioneer companies, battalions, or regiments was issued a *kleine Flammenwerfer (Kleif) M.1912,* operated by a two-man squad. Pioneer officers consulted with regimental and battalion infantry commanders to formulate orders for the flamethrower squads, which were not given direct supervision by pioneer NCOs.

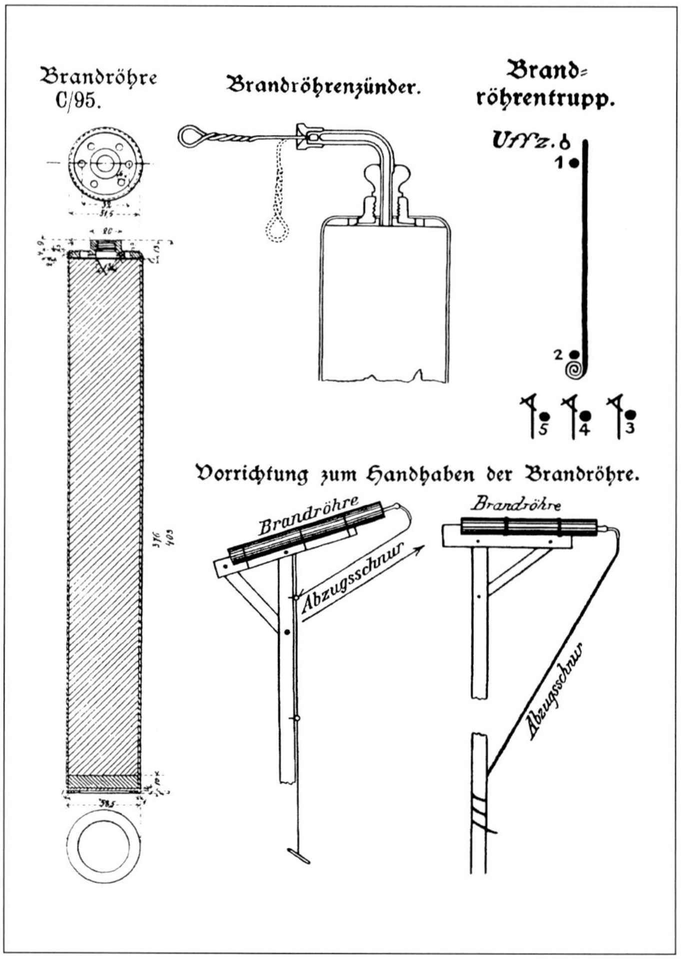

August 25 – According to United States Minister to Belgium Brand Whitlock, the Germans who burned the Belgian city of Louvain were equipped with "apparatus for the purpose of firing dwellings, incendiary pastils, machines for spraying petroleum, etc."[3]

September 7 – Reichstag Deputy Matthias Erzberger wrote to General Erich von Falkenhayn, Minister of War, suggesting that Richard Fiedler's flamethrowers be mounted on dirigibles to attack Britain.[4] The idea was rejected as impracticable.

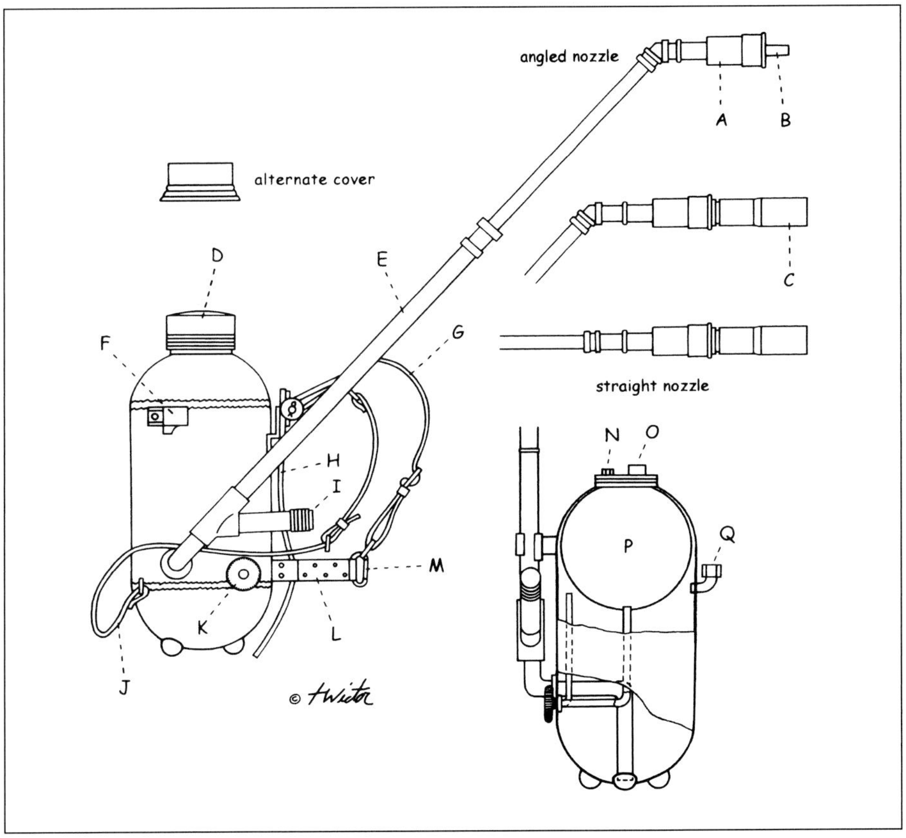

Opposite

Right: Fire tube (Brandröhre M.95), an incendiary weapon of the pioneers. In 1909 flamethrowers were designated the official replacement of fire tubes, although the latter remained in the pioneer arsenal and were used extensively in World War I. Clockwise from left: fire tube; fire-tube igniter, which was screwed into a threaded socket in the celluloid top of the tube; six-man fire-tube squad (Brandröhrentrupp) consisting of NCO squad leader, two pole carriers, and three men armed with one fused fire tube each; devices for handling fire tubes, which were mounted on long poles. To activate the fire tube, the pioneer pulled on the lanyard attached to the ring of the igniter.

Left: The kleine Flammenwerfer (Kleif) M.1912, the first production-model portable flamethrower. Designed by Richard Fiedler, it was adopted by the German army in 1912 and deployed in the first months of the war. The telescoping lance – here fitted with the angled nozzle – was fixed to the oil tank by a swiveling joint. A two-man squad (Flammenwerfertrupp) operated the weapon: a Kleif carrier (Kleifträger) wore the flamethrower and aimed the lance, while the assistant (Hilfsmann) fired the oil by opening the block valve at the base of the lance. The oil-filling tube is visible on the left side of the tank. Courtesy Russian State Military-Historical Archives.

Left: Right side of Kleif M.1912: (left) and cutaway front view without the carrying harness: A) igniter holder; B) lance nozzle; C) igniter with protective cover in place; D) threaded cover; E) telescoping lance attached to flamethrower by swiveling universal joint; F) clamp for holding lance during transportation; G) leather shoulder strap; H) steel carrying frame; I) block valve; J) lance strap for containing recoil; K) oil-pressurization valve; L) steel waist support; M) carabiner; N) propellant-filler cap; O) pressure gauge; P) propellant chamber; Q) oil-filler tube. Most models of Kleif had an internal propellant chamber instead of an external bottle.

Below: A pioneer Unteroffizier armed with a Kleif M.1912 in 1914. Note the facemask, worn by Austrian Kleif operators as well. The lance is fitted with the straight nozzle and a live igniter in the holder. The oil-filler tube and threaded relief plug – features of the Kleif M.1914 and M.1916 as well – can be seen on the left side of the weapon. Note that the flamethrower lacked a waist belt so that the operator could quickly drop the weapon if it was punctured or began to leak fuel.

Above, Left: Grosse Flammenwerfer (Grof) M.1912 captured by the British at St. Pierre Divion in 1915. The first production-model large flamethrower, it was fitted with two tanks for the nitrogen propellant and served by a five-man squad (Groftrupp) consisting of lance operator (Rohrführer), two assistants and two Grof staff (Grofleute), who operated the various valves. Note the damaged telescoping lance, which is missing the nozzle and igniter holder. File #T70628, Record Group 175, U.S. National Archives.

Right: A) Oil-release valves; B) socket for connecting a second oil tank; C) nitrogen propellant tank; D) threaded socket for pressure gauge; E) safety valve for bleeding off pressure; F) oil discharge pipe. File #T70628, Record Group 175, U.S. National Archives.

October 4 or 5 – Flamethrowers were deployed at Bagatelle-Pavillon in the Argonne, the first combat use of the devices.[5] The 4th Company of Pioneer Battalion No. 29 *(Posensches Pionier-Bataillon Nr. 29)*, attached to the 27th Division, launched the unsuccessful attack against emplaced French troops.[6]

October 10 – *Hauptmann* Bernhard Reddemann, commander of the 2nd Company of Pioneer Battalion No. 29, traveled to Berlin to lobby the Supreme Army Command (*Oberste Heeresleitung* or *OHL*) for the creation of a flamethrower unit.[7]

October 16 – Headquarters of the German Second Army issued Note 32, "Arms Available to the Pioneers for Close Combat: Projectors for Flame and Smoke-producing Liquid."

The Commander-in-Chief provided flamethrowers and flamethrower pioneers to individual army corps as needed. These specialists trained line pioneers to use the weapons and serve as reinforcements. Flamethrowers were employed mainly in house and street fighting and were held at the position from where the assault was launched.[8]

November 11 – The War Ministry ordered that special weapons of the pioneers such as trench mortars and ammunition, flamethrowers, hand grenades, rifle grenades, and smoke charges be exclusively at the disposal of the *OHL*.[9] Flamethrowers and accessories would be held by the Acting Engineer Committee *(stellvertretendes*

Gefreiter of Pioneer Battalion No. 29 (Posensches Pionier-Bataillion Nr. 29), the 4th Company of which was the first unit to use flamethrowers in combat. The action took place October 4-5, 1915, in the Argonne. This pioneer wears the M1910 field-gray service jacket (Waffenrock) and M1910 peaked service cap (Dienstmütze), also called the visor cap (Schirmmütze) with the black band of the pioneers. A hand-written notation on the back of the postcard identifies the soldier as an "FW," an official abbreviation for "Flammenwerfer." The term referred to both the weapon and the men who used it.

War volunteers of the Guard Pioneer Replacement Battalion (Garde-Pionier-Ersatz-Bataillon) in October of 1914, wearing the M1895 dark-blue service jacket (Dunkelblau) with white Guard lace (Garde Litzen) on the collars and cuffs. Flamethrower Detachment Reddemann (Flammenwerfer-Abteilung Reddemann), the first German flamethrower detachment, was composed of firefighters of the Posen Fire Brigade and war volunteers, likely members of the Guard Pioneer Replacement Battalion.

Ingenieur-Komitee) in Berlin. The *OHL* determined which pioneer units received flamethrowers and were sent into combat and/or trained other pioneers.

End of 1914 – Flamethrowers were mostly recalled from service, although some line-pioneer formations retained them well into 1915. The *OHL* reported to the War Ministry that the apparatuses were unusable.[10] They were completely new weapons that required extensive training and understanding of their capabilities.[11] Also, the *Kleif M.1912* was too fragile, too unwieldy, and did not maintain pressure.[12]

1915

January 18 – The War Ministry and the Acting Engineer Committee ordered the establishment of Flamethrower Detachment Reddemann *(Flammenwerfer-Abteilung Reddemann),* the first unit armed exclusively with flamethrowers.[13] The commander, *Haupt.* Bernhard Reddemann, would develop the weapon technically and create new tactics. Flamethrower Detachment Reddemann consisted of a Posen Fire Brigade *Feldwebel* as *Offizier-Stellvertreter* and 48 Posen firefighters and war volunteers.[14] The unit was formed in Berlin and assigned to the Fifth Army.[15]

February 1 – Flamethrower Detachment Reddemann accompanied the VI Reserve Corps to Romagne sous Montfaucon to prepare for battle.[16]

February 26 – Flamethrower Detachment Reddemann carried out its first attack at Malancourt, using 12 small hand-pumped flamethrowers and two *grosse Flammenwerfer (Grof) M.1912* to drive the French from their trenches.[17] After a reserve officer of the Leipzig Fire Brigade and two NCOs and 20 men of an unidentified unit were assigned to Flamethrower Detachment Reddemann, a second flame attack was launched at Vauquois, near Verdun.[18]

Firefighters, some of whom also served in the Guard Pioneer Replacement Battalion.

Right: The Ebersbach Fire Brigade displays a small hand pump. Flamethrower Detachment Reddemann used 12 such devices as flamethrowers at Malancourt on February 26, 1915, the first mass flame attack of the war.

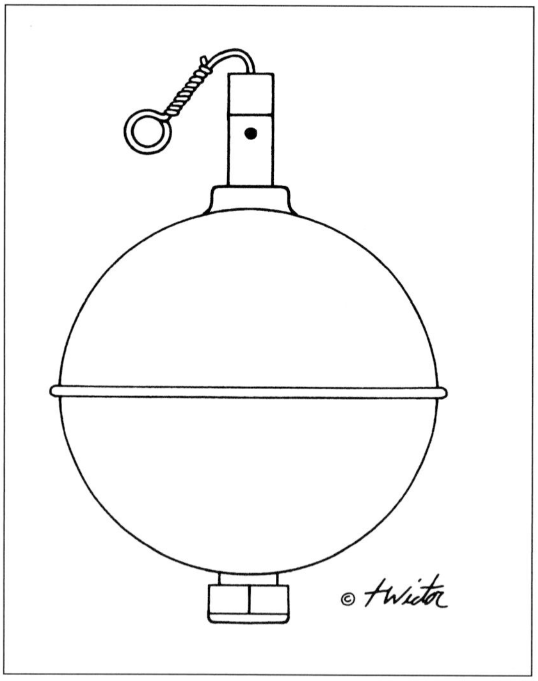

Left: German incendiary grenade (Brandgranate or Brand-Handgranate), also called the "flame ball" (Flammenkugel). Used by flamethrower pioneers to ignite oil sprayed on the ground, it had a five- or seven-second friction fuse activated by pulling the wire ring.

March 8 – Kurhessian Pioneer Battalion No. 11 *(Kurhessisches Pionier-Bataillon Nr. 11)* used *Kleif M.1912* against the Russians at Hill 10, Rawa, Poland.[19] The weapons were deployed defensively in trenches by two-man squads which engaged in close-quarter combat during massed Russian infantry attacks. It was the first time Russian troops were exposed to flamethrowers.

March 15 – The *OHL* ordered that a flamethrower battalion be established under the command of *Haupt.* Reddemann. Raised in Berlin around a core of men from the Guard Pioneer Replacement Battalion *(Garde-Pionier-Ersatz-Bataillon),*[20] the 3rd Guard Pioneer Battalion *(III. Garde-Pionier-Bataillon)* was comprised of the 9th through 12th Companies and the Experimental Company *(Versuchs-Kompagnie).*[21]

The 3rd Guard Pioneer Battalion had an initial strength of 800.[22] NCOs and men were drawn from the Guard Pioneer Replacement Battalion, fire brigades, 16 different pioneer battalions, and most other branches of the service, volunteers from all over the empire.[23] The battalion was under the direct control of the *OHL*. Reddemann was ordered to present written reports every two or three months, describing the organization and state of the unit, its engagements, new experiences and extensions of this form of attack, and new experiments and equipment. At the end of each month he delivered an oral report to the Operations Detachment *(Operationsabteilung)* of the *OHL*.

The four field companies of the battalion had 139 men each. A field company contained three combat platoons *(Kampfzüge),* each armed with four to six *Grof* and six *Kleif.*

March 28 – A Russian newspaper reported that every German infantry company in Poland was being armed with a portable flamethrower that "looks like a copper bucket and is swung over the shoulder like a knapsack. A hose is attached."[24] This weapon was said to burn all the flesh off of bodies, leaving only the bones.

May 15 – The 9th Company of the 3rd Guard Pioneer Battalion was sent to Douai to reinforce Flamethrower Detachment Reddemann; the three remaining companies soon followed.

Spring of 1915 – Some German divisions on the western front began deploying assault squads *(Sturmtrupps),* ad-hoc units created to overcome French strong points

Pioneer of Pioneer Battalion No. 11 (Kurhessisches Pionier-Batallon Nr. 11), which used flamethrowers extensively on the eastern front in 1915. This soldier wears his walking-out uniform of M1910 service jacket, black trousers, lace-up shoes, and M1910 service cap. Pioneer Battalion No. 11 retained its flamethrowers after the weapons were formally withdrawn from service.

Five members of the Workshop Detachment (Werkstatt Abteilung) of the 3rd Guard Pioneer Battalion (III. Garde-Pionier-Bataillon), the flamethrower battalion established on March 15, 1915. Four wear the field-gray M1910 service jacket, and one is uniformed in the simplified service jacket (vereinfachte Waffenrock) with plain cuffs. Note the large oil stain on the chest of the young pioneer standing on the left.

Shock Troop (Stosstrupp) 11 of the Guard Pioneer Battalion. Flamethrower commander Major Bernhard Reddemann coined the term Stosstrupp for small groups of pioneers who spearheaded infantry assaults. Hand-grenade throwers of the flamethrower battalion were uniformed and equipped identically as these men with M1916 steel helmets, grenade bags, M1917 stick grenades, and 7.92mm Mauser Kar 98AZ carbines. They wear the M1910 service jacket, the simplified service jacket, and the M1915 blouse (Bluse), all in field gray. Note the leather-reinforced knees of the trousers.

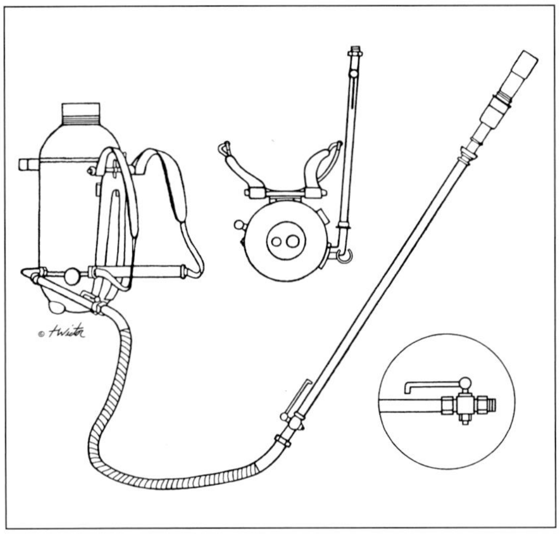

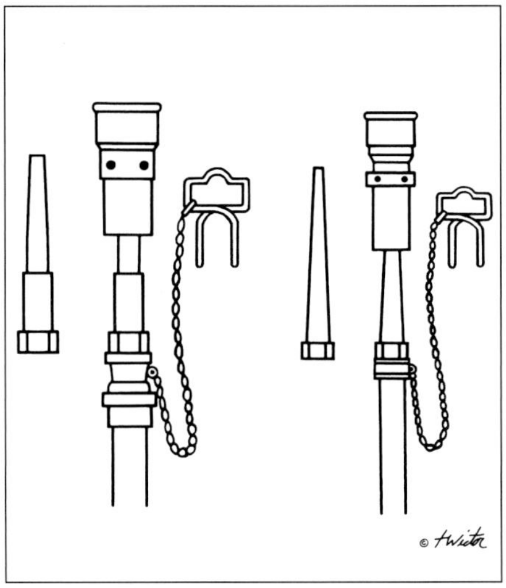

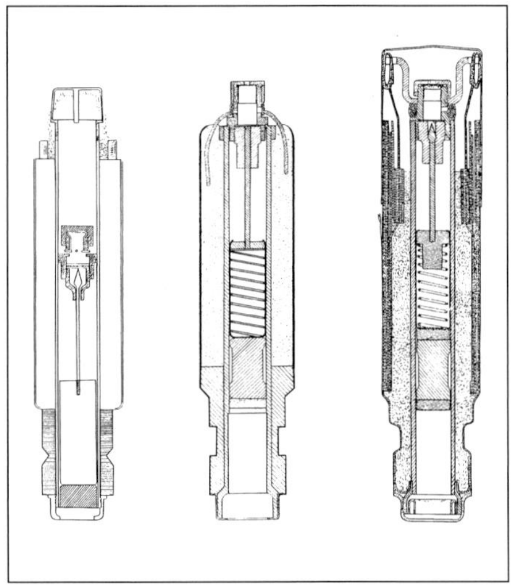

Left: Kleif M.1914, a conversion of the Kleif M.1912. The rigid, swiveling lance of the former was replaced with a swiveling outflow pipe and a rubber hose attached to an M1914 lance with stopcock. A four-man squad (Kleiftrupp) consisting of lance operator, Kleif carrier, assistant, and squad leader (Truppführer) served the device. Note the igniter in the M1912 holder, fitted over the lance nozzle. The disk-like oil-pressurization valve can be seen on the right side of the tank, while the overhead view shows the oil-filling tube on the left side and the propellant-filler cap and pressure gauge on the top, exposed by the removal of the threaded protective lid. Inset: detail of stopcock on oil-outflow pipe, operated by the flamethrower carrier.

Center: M1914 igniter holders for the large lance (left) and the small lance. Beside each are the brass lance nozzles. The igniter fork was attached to a length of chain; the fork tines held the igniter in place by slipping into a groove at its base. When the fork was withdrawn, springs inside the holder ejected the spent igniter.

Right: Three types of large and small flamethrower igniters; only the M.1917 (right) is identified by model number. All three were doubled-walled metal cylinders that operated on the same principle: When the lance operator opened the oil-release stopcock, the rush of oil left the nozzle and struck a block of gelatin inside the igniter. The gelatin block rammed a firing pin into a percussion cap, which detonated and in turn ignited combustible material inside the double walls of the igniter shell. As soon as the percussion cap detonated, the spent percussion cap and firing-pin assembly were ejected, leaving a clear passageway for the oil. At the base of each igniter was a groove for the tines of the igniter fork. Igniters burned for up to two minutes.

Opposite
Top left: Flamethrower post of Pioneer Battalion No. 11 at Hill 10 in Rawa, Poland, 1915. The pioneer demonstrates how the Kleif M.1912 was used to spray poison gas at the Russian line. Pioneers and cavalrymen who operated the weapons wore firefighters' breathing apparatuses with oxygen tanks.

Top right: Pioneer of Assault Battalion No. 5 (Rohr) (Sturmbataillon Nr. 5 [Rohr]), the first assault battalion, uniformed in the M1915 blouse with black shoulder straps mandated on September 21, 1915. On October 17, 1915, the assault detachment that later became Rohr's battalion was assigned a 26-man flamethrower platoon armed with six small devices. These troops were officially transferred from the 3rd Guard Pioneer Battalion, but some confusion exists as to their actual origin.

such as shelters and blockhouses hidden in woods. Assault squads were typically comprised of one to three infantry groups and one line-pioneer group armed with machine guns, trench mortars, and *Kleif M.1912*.[25]

May 22 – The 3rd Guard Pioneer Battalion saw its first action at Neuville, west of Douai. Although the mission was successful, the flamethrower pioneers suffered relatively high casualties, leading *Haupt.* Reddemann to pull the battalion from the field and create more effective assault tactics.[26]

June 1 – A Replacement Company *(Ersatz-Kompagnie)* was added to the 3rd Guard Pioneer Battalion.

June 6 – The 1st Company of Pioneer Battalion No. 11 used flamethrowers to spray an unidentified poison gas – possibly hydrogen cyanide – against the Russians at Hill 10, Rawa, Poland.[27] A major from *Armee-Oberkommando 9* in Lodz organized the attack and supervised the training of pioneers and cavalrymen to serve as flamethrower operators. At 8:20 P.M. the Germans sprayed the gas toward the Russian trenches, killing 600.

July 13 – The Germans resumed large-scale flamethrower assaults after retraining the men of the 3rd Guard Pioneer Battalion.[28]

July 30 – At 3:25 A.M. the 9th Company of the 3rd Guard Pioneer Battalion launched a flamethrower attack against the British at Hooge, using nine *Grof* and 11 *Kleif*. This was the first time the British faced flamethrowers. They retreated from their front-line trenches but gained back the lost ground by August 9.[29]

September 9 – During a flamethrower attack against the French at the *Hartmannsweilerkopf*, carried out by the 9th and 10th Companies of the 3rd Guard Pioneer Battalion, five large "gasoline sprayers" were used in addition to *Grof* and *Kleif*. Designed by *Leutnant* Schlayer of Cavalry Motor-transport Column 24 *(Kavallerie Kraftwagen-Kolonne 24)*, the sprayers each consisted of one tank that held 69 gallons of gasoline connected to two propellant bottles. A nozzle sprayed the gasoline 115 feet; it was ignited with a thrown fire tube. Men of the 1st Landwehr Pioneer Company XIV Army Corps *(1. Landwehr-Pionier-Kompagnie XIV. Armee Korps)* operated the weapons.[30]

September 13 – *Hauptmann* Willy Martin Rohr took over as commander of the Assault Detachment *(Sturmabteilung)* of Army Detachment Gaede *(Armee Abteilung Gaede)*. On October 17 he was assigned a flamethrower platoon of one officer, three NCOs, and 20 men armed with six *Kleif*. The personnel were from either the 3rd Guard Pioneer Battalion[31] or Pioneer Replacement Battalion No. 36 *(Pionier-Ersatz-*

Bottom: Men of the 16th Company, 3rd Guard Pioneer Battalion, established in December of 1915. All wear either the M1910 service jacket or the simplified service jacket. The shabbiness of their uniforms and the "crusher" shape of their M1910 peaked caps give them a rough, world-weary look. Flamethrower pioneers kept two uniforms, one of which they wore during training and in combat. Note the wine and liquor bottles sardonically arranged at the feet of the Unteroffiziere in front.

Pioneer of Pioneer Replacement Battalion No. 36 (Pionier-Ersatz-Bataillon Nr. 36), replacement battalion for Pioneer Regiments 35 and 36, the two gas regiments. According to the former adjutant of Assault Battalion Rohr, the unit's first flamethrower operators may have come from Pioneer Replacement Battalion No. 36. As gas troops, they may not have been adequately trained in flame combat.

Bataillon Nr. 36),[32] the replacement battalion of the two poison-gas units, Pioneer Regiments 35 and 36. Replacements for the flamethrower platoon came from the 3rd Guard Pioneer Battalion. The flamethrower platoon of Assault Detachment Rohr saw action throughout the war; members were transferred into the flamethrower battalions and later regiment.

October 6 – The 13th and 14th Companies and a recruit depot were added to the 3rd Guard Pioneer Battalion.[33]

Late December – The 15th and 16th Companies were added to the 3rd Guard Pioneer Battalion.[34] In 1915, the 3rd Guard Pioneer Battalion launched a total of 32 attacks on the Meuse, in the Priesterwalde, the Argonne, Flanders, the Vosges, and the Champagne. Two of the attacks were not successful.[35]

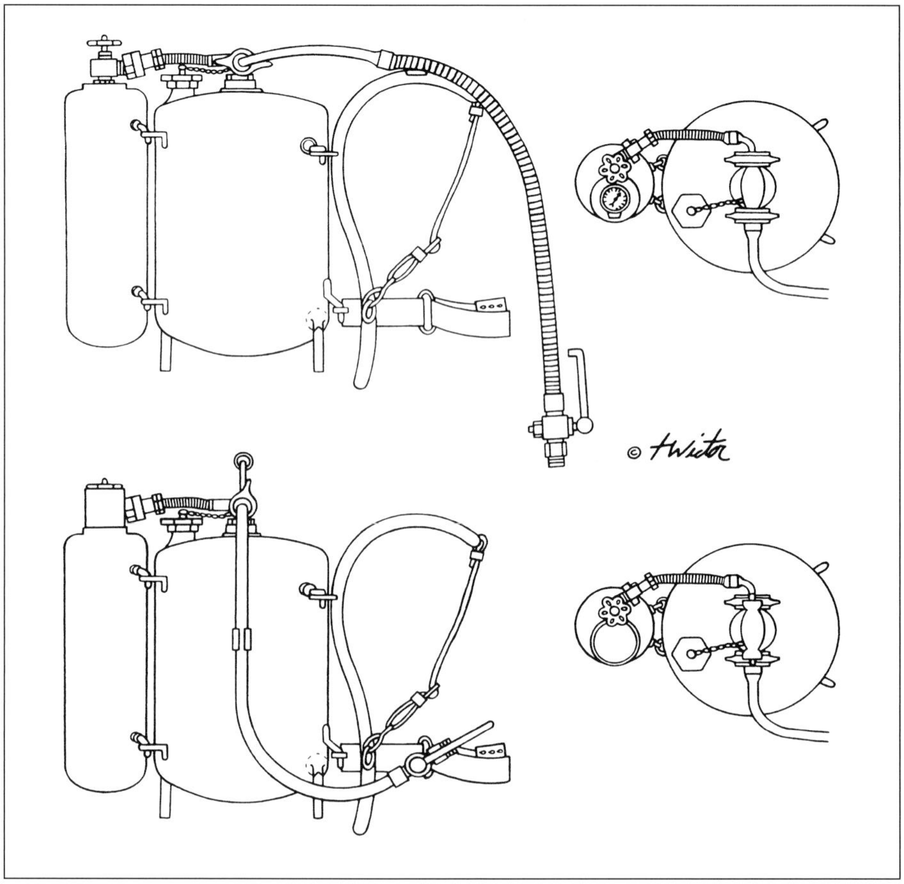

Kleif M.1915, early model (top) and late model. Designed and built by the 3rd Guard Pioneer Battalion, the Kleif M.1915 had an external propellant bottle instead of the internal chamber found in all Fiedler portable flamethrowers. The rubber oil-outflow hose of the early model was replaced with a rigid steel pipe in the late model. In addition, the late model incorporated a protective steel cover for the propellant gauge and a handle on top of the oil tank. Both models had a carrying frame with a waist belt that made the weapon difficult for the operator to drop in the event of a puncture or leak.

1916

Early 1916 – A Reserve Company was formed in the 3rd Guard Pioneer Battalion from the battalion recruit depot and the Guard Pioneer Replacement Battalion in Berlin. The plan for the Verdun offensive required that the 3rd Guard Pioneer Battalion provide a flamethrower company for each of the six infantry divisions taking part. In addition, two companies armed with large and small flamethrowers would attack in the woods of Consenvoye, and another company would assault in the Champagne. Nine companies altogether were required.[36]

Early February – The number of *Kleif* in each flamethrower company was tripled from 18 to 54, and the personnel of each field company were increased from 139 to 200. More officers and men of the battalion recruit depot and the Guard Pioneer Replacement Battalion were brought in, along with 360 handpicked infantrymen.

Captured German equipment that includes a Kleif M.1914 on the far left and two late-model Kleif M.1915. In the case of the latter, the igniter holders have been removed from both lances. The Kleif on the right is missing its carrying harness, and it has been fitted with a second propellant tank for curved-trajectory firing.

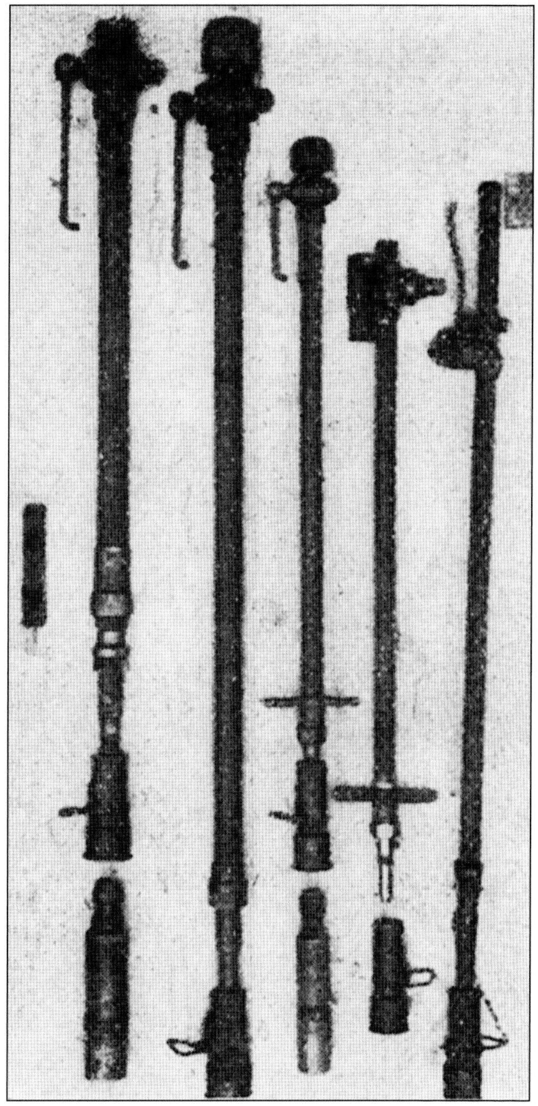

Each of the three combat platoons of a flamethrower field company were organized into five flame detachments, one machine-gun detachment on loan from the infantry, and one replacement detachment; each flame detachment was armed with two *Kleif*.[37] The number of *Grof* per company remained unchanged at 22.

February 6 – Each of the 62 infantry companies that would attack in Verdun formed a shock troop composed of 16-20 infantrymen with one rifle and three hand grenades each; one pioneer group equipped with axes, hatchets, saws, wire cutters, and concentrated and elongated charges; and one *Kleif* squad armed with two flamethrowers, incendiary grenades, and hand grenades.[38] A total of 372 *Kleif* were used by infantry shock troops.

February – The 4th Guard Pioneer Battalion *(IV. Garde-Pionier-Bataillon)* was established. It consisted of a staff, a workshop detachment, and the 1st and 2nd Companies.[39]

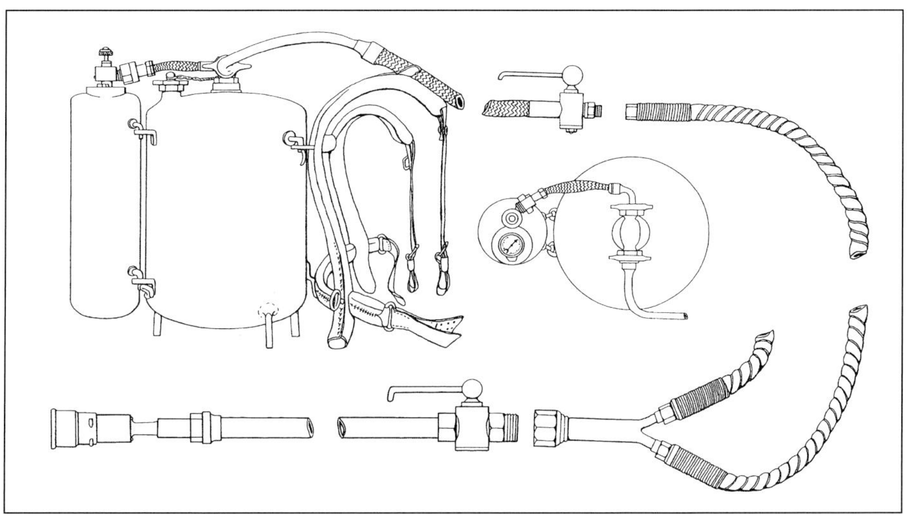

Left: Double small flamethrower (Doppelkleif) consisting of two early model Kleif M.1915 connected by 1.5m and 3m hoses to a single large 1.5m lance. All models of double Kleif used the forked coupling and were operated by seven-man squads. The double Kleif had a duration of about 22 seconds and was used against barricades in trenches and to cover the advance of flamethrower troops.

Above: German flamethrower lances. From left: telescoping 1.75m large lance in retracted position, with igniter; 1.5m large lance; 1m small lance with igniter; 1m small lance with early-model self-closing valve and 8mm nozzle painted with red band; 1.4m small lance with late-model self-closing valve. Small lances were issued with both 6mm and 8mm nozzles, the latter painted with a red band. It increased the range of the flame jet at the expense of duration. Courtesy Thierry Ehret

February 21 – Beginning of the Battle of Verdun. Between February 21 and April 27, ten flamethrower companies armed with 400 devices carried out 57 attacks, 33 of which were judged to be successful.

February 25 – The 2nd Guard Pioneer Replacement Battalion *(II. Garde-Pionier-Ersatz-Bataillon)*, was established to provide replacement flamethrower operators for the 3rd and 4th Guard Pioneer Battalions.[40] It was based in Berlin.

March 11 – Assault Detachment Rohr officially became Assault Battalion Rohr *(Sturmbataillon Rohr),* its flamethrower troops drawn directly from the 2nd Guard Pioneer Replacement Battalion. After serving with the assault battalion, these pioneers were transferred into the 3rd and 4th Guard Pioneer Battalions.

April 20 – The 3rd and 4th Guard Pioneer Battalions were merged into the Guard Reserve Pioneer Regiment *(Garde-Reserve-Pionier-Regiment).* It consisted of the 1st-4th Companies in the 1st Battalion, the 5th-8th Companies in the 2nd Battalion, the 9th and 10th Companies, an Experimental Company *(Versuchs-Kompagnie),* a recruit depot, and three battalion staffs and workshops.[41] Individual flamethrower companies were initially attached to various army corps. However, this was soon abandoned, as some companies became degraded through too much combat, while others saw no action at all.

Each field company of the Guard Reserve Pioneer Regiment had 200 men organized into three combat platoons. A combat platoon was comprised of five flamethrower detachments of two *Kleif* squads each, one machine-gun detachment on loan from the infantry, and one replacement detachment. Each combat platoon was armed with six to eight *Grof* and 54 *Kleif.*

June 2-5 – During the attack on Fort Vaux, the Germans used both flamethrowers and fire tubes extensively. Even the participants often confused the weapons.[42]

June 2 – Assault troops of Pioneer Battalion No. 20 used fire tubes on long guide poles to force gun crews from the flanking galleries in the northwest and northeast corners of the fort, allowing the Germans to enter the underground tunnels.

June 4 – The 8th Company of the Guard Reserve Pioneer Regiment sent ten *Kleif* squads to Fort Vaux to eliminate stubborn pockets of resistance in the dark, narrow concrete tunnels. Four flamethrowers were destroyed by artillery on the way.

At 12:30 P.M. three *Kleif* squads attacked a barricade in the western tunnel of the fort. Simultaneously a shock troop of men from Pioneer Battalion No. 27, Infantry Regiment No. 39, and three *Kleif* squads attacked through the eastern tunnel and up a flight of concrete stairs, into a shower of French hand grenades. The French reported that they killed flamethrower operators assaulting the southeastern bunker and captured their weapons. However, German accounts indicate that there was no flamethrower attack.

Opposite

Top: Kleif squad of the 3rd Guard Pioneer Battalion at Verdun, early 1916, armed with the Kleif M.1914. The men have recently experienced combat, as shown by the mud and torn clothing. Note the gas-mask containers in the "alert" position and the spent igniter in the holder of the lance. The lance and hose have been disconnected from the flamethrower outflow pipe, an operation that required the use of a wrench. For ease of transport the outflow pipe is held vertically in its clamp, and the 1.5m (5ft.) hose is wrapped around the end of the lance.

Bottom: Men of the 1st Replacement Company, 2nd Guard Pioneer Replacement Batalion (1. Ersatz-Kompagnie, II. Garde-Pionier-Ersatz-Bataillon), the replacement unit of the two flamethrower battalions. It was established on February 25, 1916, and included four replacement companies and a garrison company. These pioneers are all uniformed in the M1915 blouse with unpiped shoulder straps in field gray.

Above: This flamethrower pioneer of the 9th Company, Guard Reserve Pioneer Regiment, wears full parade finery of M1895 service jacket in dark blue, black trousers, light gray overcoat with plain red shoulder straps, and spiked helmet (Pickelhaube) with black horsehair plume. The Guard Reserve Pioneer Regiment was established April 20, 1916.

Left: Six noncommissioned officers (Unteroffiziere) and a Feldwebel (center) of the 6th Company, Guard Reserve Pioneer Regiment, in a postcard sent on June 6, 1916. The many styles of rank insignia on the collars are noteworthy, as are the three types of tunic (M1910 service jacket, simplified service jacket, and M1915 blouse) worn during the war. The physical fitness and strength required to be a flamethrower pioneer are apparent in this photo. These men were likely firefighters in civilian life.

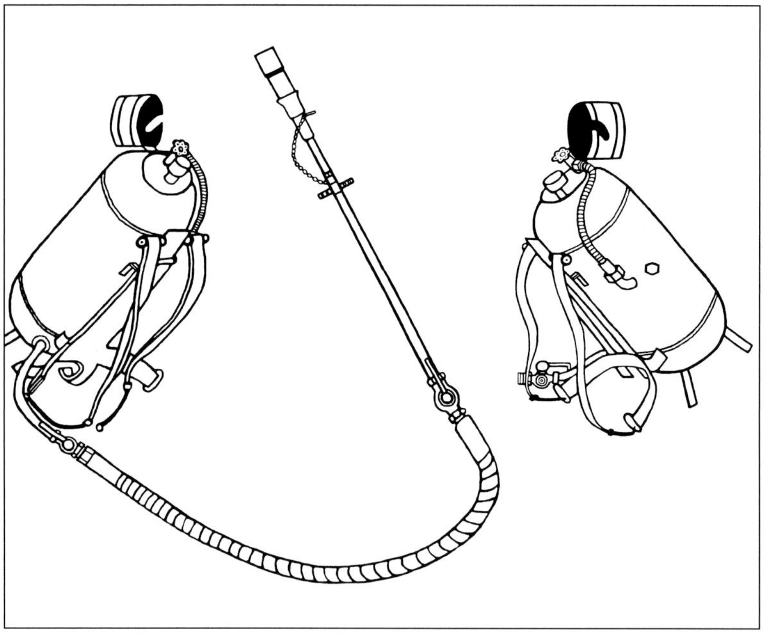

Figure 3.--GERMAN PORTABLE FLAMMENWERFER

(Left view: compressed-gas valve and pressure gage; right view: in carrying position ready for use)

Left: Kleif M.1916, which supplanted the Kleif M.1914. Changes included replacing the swiveling outflow pipe with a shorter, fixed pipe, and the threaded lid with a hinged version. On the left is the later, leather-padded carrying harness, while the earlier is on the right. The two instruments on the top of the oil tank are the pressure gauge and oil-pressurization valve; the propellant hose is connected to the oil-filler tube. Beside this tube is the hexagonal head of the threaded relief plug.

Right: Kleif M.1916, as illustrated in an American intelligence report. Three metal "feet" on the bottom replaced the metal hemispheres of the Kleif M.1912 and M.1914. The caption notwithstanding, a single man could not operate the Kleif M.1916 by himself.

Below: British illustration depicting an assault in July of 1917, led by German flamethrower operators wearing steel body armor. The 35lb. Sappenpanzer or Grabenpanzer would have drastically reduced the men's speed and mobility. It should be noted that the depiction of the flamethrower is hopelessly inaccurate, corresponding to no German weapon.

June 5 – At 5:00 A.M. five shock troops of Pioneer Battalion No. 15 assaulted the tunnel leading to the southwestern bunker of the fort, using concentrated charges and fire tubes. The hole blown by the explosives in the masonry was too small for the smoke and flame from the fire tubes to enter; a draft blew the flames out toward the Germans. The Germans reported that at 9:00 A.M. a shock troop of the 1st Company of Pioneer Battalion No. 15, accompanied by four *Kleif* squads of the 8th Company of the Guard Reserve Pioneer Regiment, assaulted the southwestern bunker and managed to inject smoke through the loopholes, sickening the gun crew. This incident was described by the French as a failed attack by a single man armed with a fire tube. On June 7 Fort Vaux was surrendered.

June – According to one primary source the 3rd Battalion of the Guard Reserve Pioneer Regiment was added this month; other sources gave the regiment three battalions from its inception.[43] Initially the 3rd Battalion had only two companies, the 9th and 10th, formerly the 1st and 2nd Companies of the 4th Guard Pioneer Battalion.

July 1 – At the beginning of the Battle of the Somme the Germans used portable flamethrowers defensively, against the will of *Major* Reddemann. He ordered explosives attached to all such weapons, so that they could be blown up before the men were captured.[44] During the battle, which lasted until February 19, 1917, eight companies of the Guard Reserve Pioneer Regiment fought 44 times.

July 8 – *Jäger* Battalion No. 3 *(Brandenburgerisches Jäger-Bataillon Nr. 3)* was transformed into *Jäger* (Assault) Battalion No. 3 *(Jäger- [Sturm-] Bataillon Nr. 3),* with a flamethrower platoon as a permanent componant.[45] Flamethrower operators were transferred from the 2nd Guard Pioneer Replacement Battalion. The new battalion was composed of four assault companies, one machine-gun company, one trench-mortar company furnished with eight light weapons, one infantry-gun battery equipped with six small field pieces captured from the Russians, and one flamethrower platoon *(Flammenwerferzug)* armed with six *Kleif.* Members of the flamethrower platoon were rotated in from the Guard Reserve Pioneer Regiment.

July 25 – The flamethrower platoon of *Jäger* (Assault) Battalion No. 3 was strengthened with an additional officer and 25 NCOs and men from the 2nd Guard Pioneer Replacement Battalion.[46]

July 28 – The Crown Prince awarded the death's head sleeve badge to the Guard Reserve Pioneer Regiment.[47] Worn on the lower left sleeve, on or directly above the cuff, it gave the regiment its informal name of the Death's Head Pioneers *(Totenkopfpioniere).* The men in the flamethrower platoon of Assault Battalion No. 5 (Rohr) displayed their badges directly below the elbow of the left sleeve. When

Light Grof (Lichtgrof) M.1916, which replaced the Grof M.1912. A five-man squad consisting of lance operator, assistant, two Grof staff, and one squad leader operated the device. The range and duration were the same as the earlier version. Courtesy Thierry Ehret

Spiked helmet authorized for the flamethrower platoon of Assault Battalion Rohr on June 6, 1916. It was an M1897 Guard Pioneer helmet, to which was affixed a small silver death's head in the Brunswick pattern. It is not known if the helmet was widely distributed. Courtesy Daniel Griffin.

Kleif shock troop of Assault Battalion Rohr practicing how to roll up a trench (Aufrollen). The flamethrowers are the Kleif M.1917, which replaced the M1916. The first flamethrower squad leads the way, followed by hand grenade throwers and the shock-troop leader. On the left, the second Kleif squad brings up the rear.

Humorous postcard published by Assault Battalion No. 5 (Rohr), depicting a Kleif squad of the battalion flamethrower platoon. These men were transferred in from the 2nd Guard Pioneer Replacement Battalion and joined the Guard Reserve Pioneer Regiment after an unspecified time in the assault battalion. Note that the Kleif carrier has removed his helmet, most likely in order to hear more clearly over the roar of the flamethrower.

Right: Men of the Guard Reserve Pioneer Regiment displaying their newly awarded death's head sleeve badges. Two of the pioneers wear their badges just below the left elbow, indicating their previous service in Assault Battalion No. 5 (Rohr). As members of the assault battalion, these flamethrower pioneers would also have worn black shoulder straps piped in red, with a red "5." The two men in leather jackets belong to a motor-transport battalion (Kraftfahr-Bataillon).

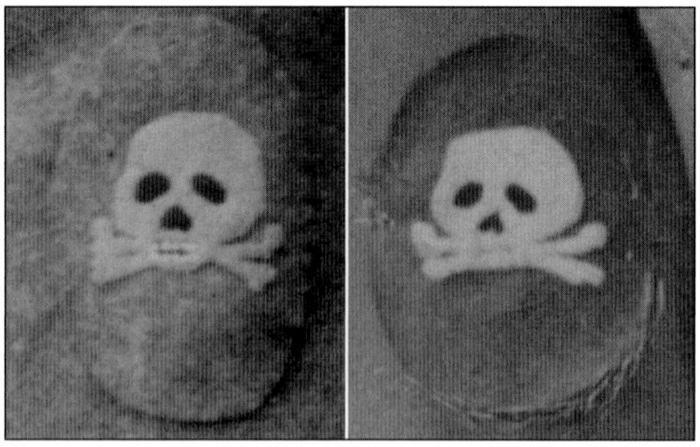

Below: The death's head sleeve badge, awarded to the Guard Reserve Pioneer Regiment by Kaiser Wilhelm II on July 28, 1916. The version on the left – cut from medium gray cloth for enlisted men and embroidered in silver bullion for officers – was the most common. On the right is an official variation. Both had eye and nose holes in black velvet and ten white teeth in white thread separated by black thread. The field-gray oval cloth backing varied greatly in size.

Fusilier of Fusilier Regiment No. 80 (Füsilier-Regiment von Gersdorf [Kurhessisches] Nr. 80), wearing the field-gray M1915 peacetime jacket (Friedensrock). In late 1916 shock troops of this unit developed their own single-shot flamethrower in the form of an iron tube with two handles. It was filled with flammable liquid and ignited with a friction fuse.

CDV of a former member of the flamethrower platoon of Assault Battalion No. 5 (Rohr). An Unteroffizier, he wears the M1915 blouse of a Saxon infantry regiment, with a death's head sleeve badge in the position that identifies men of Rohr's unit. The badge itself is the less-common variation.

Men of a foot-artillery regiment serving a Maxim MG08. Each field company of the Guard Reserve Pioneer Regiment was armed with two water-cooled 7.92mm MG08 machine guns, each of which weighed 126 lbs. Fed by 250-round cloth belts, the weapon had a range of 4800 yards.

they transferred out of the assault battalion into the Guard Reserve Pioneer Regiment, they moved the emblem to the lower position.

September 26 – The 11th and 12th Companies were added to the Guard Reserve Pioneer Regiment, using officers and men from the recruit depot and the 2nd Guard Pioneer Replacement Battalion.[48] In addition the Fifth Army High Command transferred 500 young infantrymen into the regiment.[49]

October 23 – *Generalquartiermeister* Erich Ludendorff ordered that each army on the western front form an infantry assault battalion.[50] Each would include an attached flamethrower platoon from the Guard Reserve Pioneer Regiment.

November – Fusilier Regiment No. 80 *(Füsilier-Regiment von Gersdorf [Kurhessisches] Nr. 80),* Infantry Division No. 21, trained its shock troops in the use of one-shot flamethrowers called by the French *"Flammenwerfer de jet"*:

> These small flamethrowers (between 1 and 1.2 meters *[3.3 to 3.9 feet]* long) are made of iron and equipped with two handles. They contain a flammable liquid and a wick inside, one end of which is ignited with a primer and the other of which leads into the liquid near the mouth of the apparatus. These flamethrowers are held to the openings of bunkers or shelters and are discarded afterward.[51]

November 9 – The Germans launched the largest mass-flamethrower attack in history at Skrobova, Russia. An entire flamethrower battalion of four companies used 24 *Grof* and 216 *Kleif* in the "Knife Tactic" *(Messertaktik)* devised by *Major* Reddemann to cut through extensive Russian defenses of hardened concrete bunkers, blockhouses, and flanking installations. The flamethrower troops were organized into long, snaking formations of *Kleif* squads, hand-grenade throwers, light machine gunners, and automatic riflemen who fired on the run. Infantry shock troops and six battalions of regular infantry followed; intelligence officers in aircraft coordinated the operation with two-way radios, dropping fresh orders to the troops below.

The Germans took an area 1.9 miles wide by over 1000 yards deep, along with over 3500 prisoners.[52] They reported that the use of flamethrowers led directly to victory. According to the Russians, however, the effects of the flamethrowers were negligible. In addition, the Germans allegedly used portable flamethrowers to spray "vitriol" or sulfuric acid,[53] although no German records have yet been found to support this claim. German flamethrowers had rubber hoses, which would have been unable to withstand spraying corrosive substances. (See Appendix 5.)

Two MG08/15 light machine-gun squads of the infantry. Each field company of the Guard Reserve Pioneer Regiment was armed with five MG08/15 7.92mm light machine guns, which weighed 43 lbs. with full water jacket and 100-round drum. In this photo the young machine gunners wear dragging straps and pose with 250-round ammunition boxes and 5.5-pint water cans shaped like ammunition boxes.

Grenade-launcher squad of the 8th Company of Landsturm-Infanterie-Regiment Nr. 10; the Granatenwerfer 16 was operated by the pull of a lanyard (left). Each combat platoon of flamethrower pioneers was armed with a grenade launcher for use in the assault. The launcher and its steel mounting platform together weighed 88 lbs. Flamethrower pioneers discarded the platform and cut lightening holes in the base of the weapon, reducing its weight by half. The finned fragmentation grenade weighed 4.1 lbs. and had a range of 330 yards.

December – The 12 field companies of the Guard Reserve Pioneer Regiment were each reduced to 181-182 men and reorganized into five combat platoons and one replacement platoon *(Ergänzungszug.)* Four combat platoons were each composed of four *Kleif* squads and either a machine-gun or grenade-launcher squad. Two of these platoons also included a squad of hand-grenade throwers. The fifth combat platoon was detached for duty with the emerging assault battalions; it had six *Kleif* squads but lacked hand-grenade throwers and machine-gun or grenade-launcher squads.[54] By this time the regiment had acquired its own MG08 heavy and MG08/15 light machine guns, which flamethrower pioneers operated themselves.[55]

In 1916 the Germans carried out a total of 158 flamethrower attacks, 34 of which were not successful.

1917

April 3 – The 3rd, 4th, and 7th Companies of the Guard Reserve Pioneer Regiment attacked the Toboly bridgehead in Russia. Ten flamethrower shock troops armed with 64 *Kleif* penetrated up to 3300 yards along a front of 4400 yards, taking over 10,000 prisoners. For speed, the flamethrower troops were organized into half-*Kleif* squads *(Halbkleiftrupps)* whose weapons were only half filled with oil. These squads moved very quickly, at the cost of a drastically reduced number of flame bursts from the lightened devices.[56]

During assaults, the Guard Reserve Pioneer Regiment fielded 12-man flamethrower shock troops armed with two portable flamethrowers, carbines, pistols, hand grenades, and sharpened spades. When rolling up trenches, the shock troop advanced single file in the following order, the men two yards apart:

first *Kleif* squad (lance operator, carrier, assistant)
first hand-grenade thrower
second hand-grenade thrower
first shock-troop leader
third hand-grenade thrower
fourth hand-grenade thrower
second *Kleif* squad (lance operator, carrier, assistant)
second shock-troop leader.

Pioneer Otto Jakob of the 11th Company, Guard Reserve Pioneer Regiment. Only 19 years old in this photo, his face shows the strain of combat. He survived the war and served in the Wehrmacht during World War II. His M1915 blouse with black shoulder straps and gray guard lace on the collar exemplifies the seldom-achieved regulation uniform of flamethrower pioneers after September 21, 1915.

Triple Lichtgrof (Dreifachgrof) consisting of three oil and propellant tanks connected to a single lance. Capacity was increased to 78 gallons, duration to two minutes. Courtesy Thierry Ehret

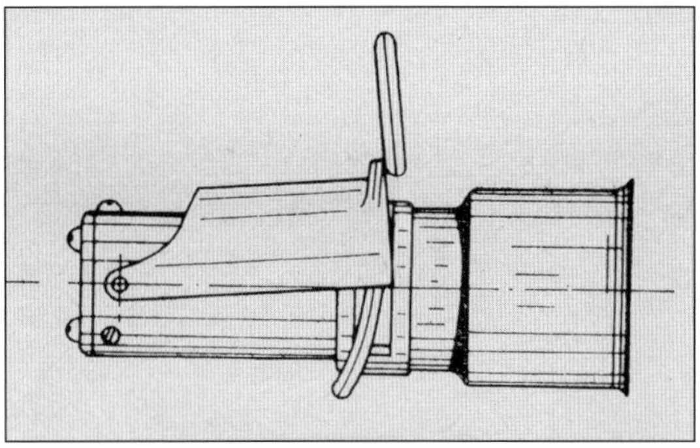

M1917 igniter holder, with fork incorporated into hinged flap. This model holder was used on both large and small lances. Courtesy Thierry Ehret

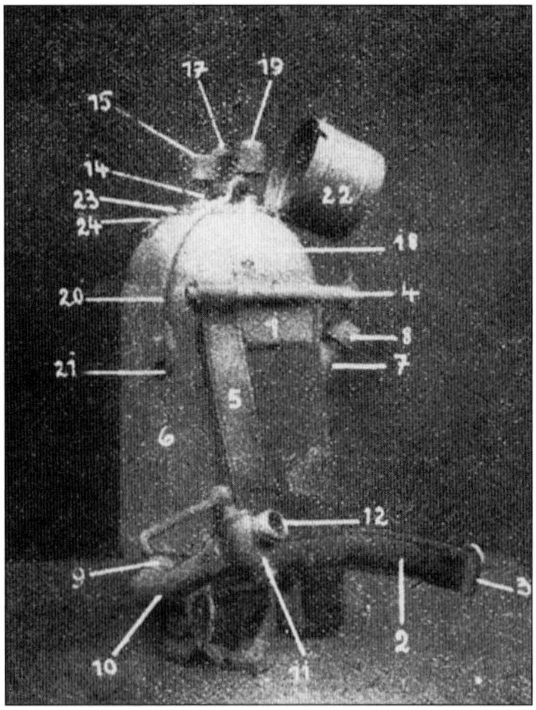

Poor-quality image of the Kleif M.1917, which replaced the M.1916. 1) leather-padded backrest; 2) leather-padded metal waist support; 3) carabiner; 4) shoulder-strap support; 5) shoulder strap; 6) oil tank; 7) oil-filler tube; 8) oil-filler cap; 9) welded joint; 10) oil-outflow pipe; 11) stopcock; 12) threaded connector; 13) [none]; 14) pressure-gauge support; 15) pressure gauge; 16) [none]; 17) propellant-filler tube; 18) oil-pressurization valve support; 19) oil-pressurization valve; 20) propellant feed line; 21) propellant feed-line connection; 22) hinged lid; 23) raised lip for hinged lid; 24) retainer for lid strap. Courtesy Thierry Ehret

June 29 – Assault Battalion No. 5 (Rohr) attacked Hill 304 in Verdun, deploying its entire flamethrower platoon. For three and a half hours 40 men of the French 24th Dragoon Regiment engaged the Germans in trench fighting with grenades, rifles, and a light machine gun. Rohr's men used grenades and flamethrowers to push the French 200 yards down the trench, but eventually the Germans retreated.[57]

July 10 – During Operation Beach Party *(Unternehmen Strandfest),* the German preemptive strike against the Nieuport beachhead, the 400-man Assault Detachment of the *Marinekorps Flandern* organized five shock troops of 25 to 45 men each. Flamethrower squads of the 6th and 12th Companies of the Guard Reserve Pioneer Regiment were assigned to the shock troops and also served as "flame accompanying squads" *(Flammenbegleittrupps)* for Naval Infantry Regiments No. 1 and No. 2.

The 26 small flamethrowers used were probably the new *Wechselapparat (Wex) M.1917,* a ring-shaped device adopted in May. Four *Grof* were also fired in the successful attack, which took place at 7:51 A.M. after much low-level strafing and bombing by aircraft and a sustained artillery barrage that included the first use of mustard gas.[58]

In 1917 the firepower of flame shock troops was increased dramatically. Two more assault formations were developed.

The first was the shock unit in the form of an attacking wedge *(Stosseinheit in Form eines Angriffskeils),* which consisted of two *Wex* or *Kleif* shock troops, three light machine-gun squads, three grenade-launcher squads, two infantry squads, one squad of pioneers with explosives, one infantry half-squad as machine-gun ammunition carriers, one infantry squad as grenade-launcher ammunition carriers, and one infantry half-squad as hand-grenade throwers.

The second was the shock unit for rolling up a trench *(Stosseinheit in Form zum Aufrollen eines Schutzengrabens),* which consisted of two *Wex* or *Kleif* shock troops, two light machine-gun squads, one grenade-launcher squad, and one infantry squad.

August 18 – Canadian accounts of the Battle of Hill 70 at Lens describe in detail the flamethrower attack that took place at 4:45 A.M. *Wex* squads and hand-grenade throwers assaulted the trenches of the 2nd Canadian Battalion, which responded with Lewis guns, rifles, and grenades. One *Wex* operator climbed over the parapet into the Canadian trench and fell into hand-to-hand combat with a Canadian officer, who killed him and sent his flamethrower back to headquarters.[59] Allied accounts indicate heavy casualties among German flamethrower operators, and official photos show the *Wex* that were captured that day, yet there are no German records of any flamethrower pioneers fighting or dying at Lens August 16-18, 1917. The reason for this discrepancy remains a mystery.

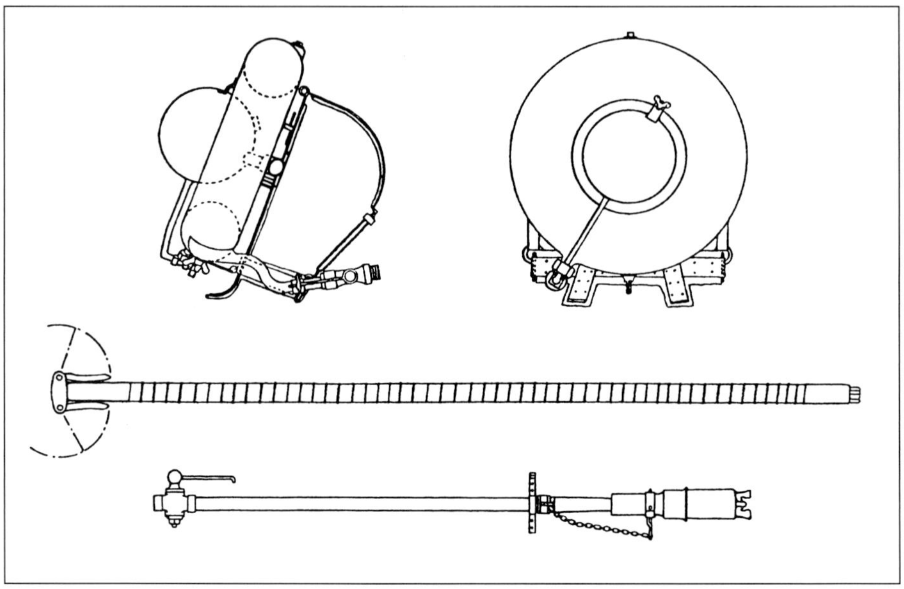

Wechselapparat (Wex) M.1917, designed and built by the Guard Reserve Pioneer Regiment and introduced in May of 1917. Originally three Wex were to be assigned to each lance; the friction coupling attached to the hose made exchanging the empty flamethrower easy and quick. However, this operation could not be carried out in combat. As a result, the Wex was deployed singly, with the same four-man squad as the Kleif. Note the M1916 lance and igniter, the protective cover of which has been removed to expose the zinc blades that hold the firing-pin assembly in place.

Right: Flamethrower squad of Assault Battalion No. 5 (Rohr) at Malancourt, armed with the Kleif M.1917. The men wear Guard Pioneer uniforms, with black shoulder straps that display the number "5" in red. Capacity and duration of the Kleif M.1917 were the same as the M1916, but the propellant feed line was moved to make it less vulnerable.

Below: Double Kleif M.1917. From left: lance operator, assistant, first Kleif carrier, second assistant, and second Kleif carrier. The third assistant and squad leader are not present. This is a postwar image, as shown by the badge of the 15. Reichswehr Brigade on the second assistant's upper left arm. The double Kleif was used in place of the Grof when the latter could not be moved forward. As an igniter is not present in the lance, the operator is spraying the oil on a flame source such as an incendiary grenade. Courtesy Thierry Ehret

Five Leutnants of the Guard Reserve Pioneer Regiment at a training ground. Two hold Kar 98AZ carbines and two display practice hand grenades with drilled heads painted red. The death's-head sleeve badges are the officers' version, embroidered in silver bullion. During the war 23 officers of the flamethrower regiment were killed in action or died of disease or accidents.

October-November – Two detached flamethrower platoons carried out several attacks on the Italian front. On October 17 at Mount Piano Platoon Jahns *(Zug Jahns)* slid with its flamethrowers down a steep, snow-covered mountainside into a ravine, climbed the opposite side undetected until it was ten feet below the Italian trenches, and opened fire. The surprised Italians retreated and the platoon rolled up the trenches.[60]

The Guard Reserve Pioneer Regiment fought 169 times on the western and eastern fronts in 1917. Twenty-four operations were not successful.[61]

1918

January 1 to March 20 – The Germans conducted 49 flamethrower attacks on the Western Front, mostly reconnaissance in force aimed at identifying enemy units in preparation for the spring offensive.[62]

February-March 20 – The Guard Reserve Pioneer Regiment was reorganized into March Companies *(Marsch-Kompagnien)* that would allow the men to remain in the field longer and advance more quickly.[63]

Each March Company contained three March Platoons *(Marsch-Züge)* and one Ordnance Platoon *(Gerät-Zug)*. A March Platoon was comprised of a combat platoon *(Kampfzug)*, a replacement troop *(Ersatztrupp)*, and a maintenance section *(Gefechtstross)*. The combat platoon was made up of four *Wex* squads *(Wextrupps)*, one machine-gun squad, and one grenade-launcher squad. Each *Wex* squad was armed

Side view of Wex, which shows the friction coupler (29) and handles (30), as well as the stopcock in the "open" position. The pressure gauge is visible behind the carrier's upper arm. Courtesy Thierry Ehret

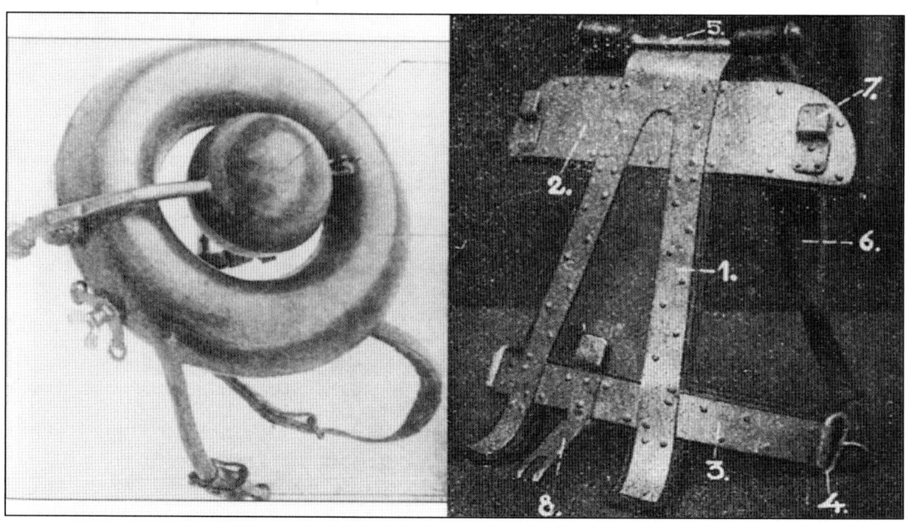

Rear view of oil tank and spherical propellant container of Wex (left) and carrying frame. Note the oil-outflow pipe on the lower right. The flamethrower was removed from the frame when filling the propellant container. To pressurize the oil the assistant opened the valve on the lower left-hand side of the tank: 1) leather-padded back support; 2) leather-padded shoulder support; 3) leather-padded waist support; 4) carabiner; 5) shoulder-strap support bar; 6) leather shoulder straps; 7) and 8) support brackets for oil tank. Courtesy Thierry Ehret

Above: The flamethrower platoon of Bavarian Assault Battalion No. 15, in a photo dated April 24, 1918. The weapons include two Wex, one Kleif M.1917, and two M1917 small lances. Kneeling on the right is a veteran of Assault Battalion No. 5 (Rohr); the pioneer sitting to the right of the beer barrel wears a plain uniform with no Guard insignia or sleeve badge. Flamethrower operators were issued such "work outfits" in order to preserve their more prestigious Death's Head Pioneer uniforms.

Right: Emergency fire tube (Ersatz Brandröhre). It was a pasteboard tube 11.8 inches in length by 2.8 inches in diameter: C) pasteboard cover, P) chlorated powder primer, F) pulverulent powder, N) compressed black powder fuse, B) wooden discs, M) incendiary filling, T) pasteboard cylinder, A) striker coated with phosphorus sulfide. The user removed the pasteboard cover and rubbed the striker on the primer, which ignited the compressed black-powder fuse. The fuse in turn ignited the incendiary filling.

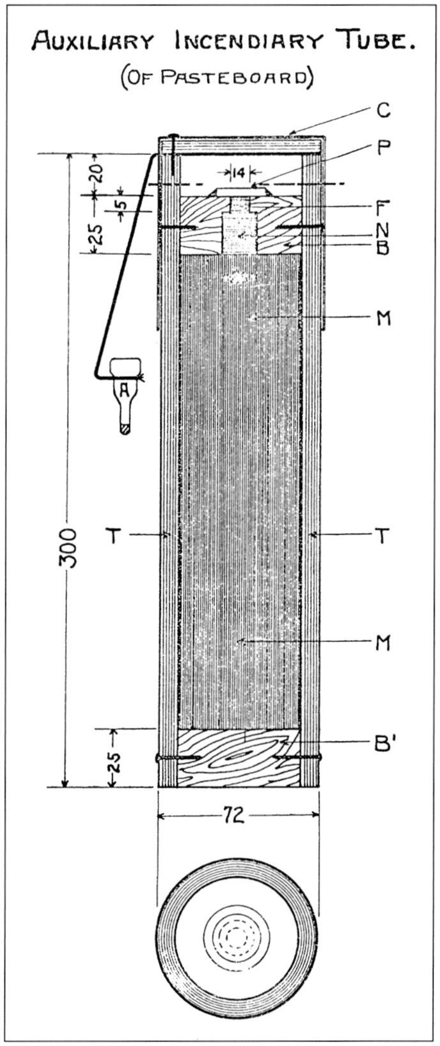

with two flamethrowers and reinforced with additional men. The grenade-launcher squad could be converted to a fifth flamethrower squad by arming it with the two reserve devices, bringing the total number of *Wex* per March Platoon to ten.

Each March Company was equipped with three horse-drawn carts for the flamethrowers and three trucks that carried oil, nitrogen, igniters, and reserve equipment. Trucks of the company Ordnance Platoon carried more supplies and members of the regimental Experimental Company, who repaired weapons.

March 21-July 17 – Ludendorff launched five offensives on the western front, all of which failed. The first, Operation Michael, saw the insertion of the 1st, 6th, 8th, 9th, 10th, 11th, and 12th March Companies. Each was armed with 30 *Wex* flamethrowers, three light machine guns, and three grenade launchers divided among its three March Platoons. The March Companies were attached to attack divisions *(Angriffsdivisionen),* which distributed them by platoon to their infantry regiments. There was a total of 21 flamethrower platoons for the 42 attack divisions of the Second, Seventeenth, and Eighteenth Armies. From May 27 the 3rd, 5th, and 7th March Companies were brought in for single engagements.

The Guard Reserve Pioneer Regiment carried out 105 attacks on the western front during this period, the Death's Head Pioneers serving either as shock troops that spearheaded frontal attacks to break through the enemy line, or as flame accompanying squads that escorted the infantry, mopped up, or were sent against specific points of resistance.

The remaining March Companies and flamethrower platoons attached to infantry assault battalions took part in 49 attacks on other fronts. Nine of these missions were unsuccessful.

March 21 – Assault Tank Detachment No. 1 *(Sturmpanzerkraftwagen-Abteilung Nr. 1),* comprised of five A7V tanks, saw combat at St. Quentin. Conceived in late 1916, the A7V was built in the cannon-armed "male" version and "females" that were to carry machine guns and two flamethrowers. By late November of 1917, however, flamethrowers were abandoned as too dangerous and complicated. Instead, Assault Battalion No. 5 (Rohr) trained A7V crews to fight as assault troops armed with hand grenades and carbines carried in the tanks and flamethrowers provided by pioneers on foot.

German A7V tanks. Nineteen "male" versions were produced, each armed with one 57mm Maxim-Nordenfelt cannon and six MG08 machine guns. Originally the single "female" tank was to be armed with two flamethrowers and six MG08 machine guns; this plan was dropped in favor of having the vehicle merely carry two flamethrowers, an idea eventually abandoned as too dangerous and complicated. Eighteen-man A7V crews, however, were trained to dismount and fight as assault troops, the pioneers among them assigned flamethrowers supplied by foot troops. Courtesy Ronny Pobucky.

At St. Quentin, the dismounted crews of the disabled A7V tanks 505 and 507 used hand grenades and flamethrowers to roll up a British trench, cutting off the heavy machine-gun, mortar, and rifle-grenade fire that held up the German advance.[64]

July 17-August 12 – The March Companies and the flamethrower platoons attached to infantry assault battalions fought 19 times on the western front. After August 12 there were no more large-scale flamethrower attacks.[65]

August 12-31 – The 9th Company of the Guard Reserve Pioneer Regiment engaged the American 77th Division on the Vesle. On August 27 shock troops of Infantry Regiments No. 113 and No. 142 were sent toward Fismette in Operation Baden *(Unternehmen Baden)*. Eight of the 13 assault units included one flamethrower squad each. The Germans took the town the next day, capturing three American officers and 254 men. Additionally, two companies of the American 112th Infantry in Fismette lost 165 of their 206 men.[66]

August(?) – A German aerial flamethrower was used in combat, date and place unknown. An eyewitness account by an American soldier of the 371st Infantry Regiment described low-flying aircraft spraying troops with liquid fire,[67] which comports with German patent No. 325694, filed by Robert and Richard Bunge on February 15, 1918. No further information has yet been found.

September 28 – Pioneer companies on the western front received six portable flamethrowers each.[68] The line pioneers were organized into special units and trained by the Guard Reserve Pioneer Regiment to use the devices in antitank warfare.

A Grof squad igniting a 1.75m large telescoping lance with a makeshift stick fuse or igniter (behelfmässigen Stockzünder). The squad leader carried out this duty. Courtesy Thierry Ehret

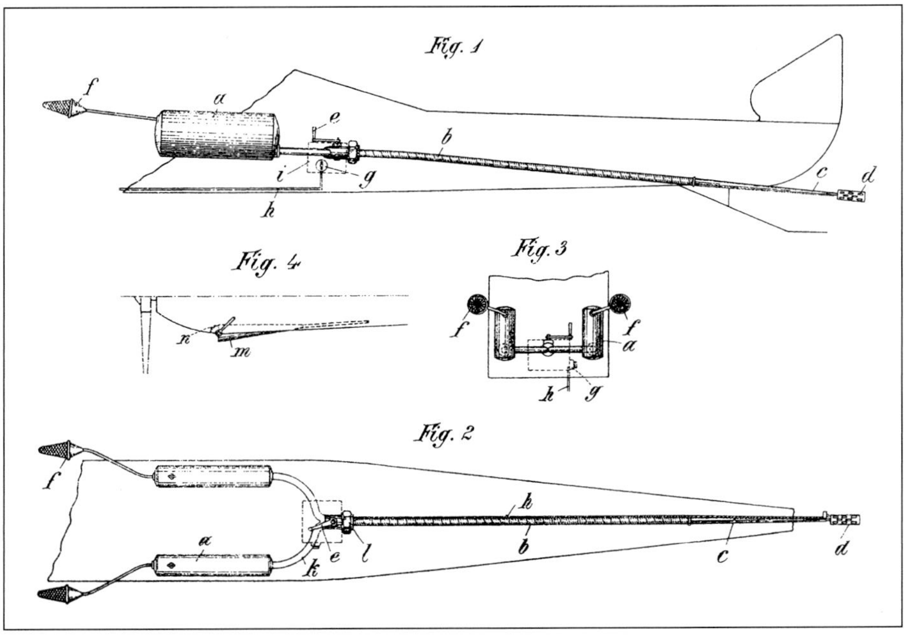

German Patent No. 325694, for the Bunge Aircraft Flamethrower: a) oil container; b) hose; c) lance; d) electric fuse; e) supply cock; f) compressed-air funnel; g) fuse-control switch; h) electrical fuse-control line connected to magneto; i) insulated covering; k) main fuel line; l) hose connector; m) funnel; n) hood. This weapon was apparently used in combat.

Line pioneers training in the use of the Wex, in compliance with a War Ministry order of September 28, 1918. Each pioneer company on the western front received six portable flamethrowers and organized special units, which were trained by the Guard Reserve Pioneer Regiment in antitank warfare. The pioneer in the center left holds a capped igniter in his right hand. Note the painted camouflage patterns on the helmets, mandated July 7, 1918.

October 6-7 – In the Argonne, flamethrower troops attacked the American Lost Battalion – elements of the 77th Division that included companies of the 307th and 308th Infantry Regiments and the 306th Machine Gun Battalion. This mission was carried out by Assault Battalion No. 2, which provided two NCOs, a 16-man shock troop, eight rifle grenadiers, and 15 flamethrower operators armed with five portable devices.[69] The Guard Reserve Pioneer Regiment appears not to have been involved, indicating that by this point in the war some flamethrower troops may have been granted autonomy.

November 11 – Following the Armistice, the Guard Reserve Pioneer Regiment destroyed most of its flamethrowers and retreated to Germany.

During the war Bernhard Reddemann's flamethrower formations carried out 653 attacks, of which 535 were successful.[70] A total of 890 flamethrower pioneers were killed in action or died of wounds, accident, or disease.[71] Fourteen men of the flamethrower platoon of Assault Battalion No. 5 (Rohr) were killed in action or died of wounds, accident, or disease.[72] The total casualties of flamethrower operators serving in line-pioneer formations are unknown.

1919

January – The Guard Reserve Pioneer Regiment was disbanded in Berlin.

March 6 – The National Assembly created the Provisional Army *(Vorläufige Reichsheer),* which maintained a flamethrower battalion that was later reduced to a single company. Most Death's Head Pioneers mustered out of the service and joined either the communist Sparticists or the government-loyal *Freikorps,* using their weapons extensively in the German Civil War of 1918-1923.

June 28 – The Allies and the new Republic of Germany signed the Treaty of Versailles. Article 171 prohibited Germany from using, manufacturing, and importing poison gas and flamethrowers.

1920

January 10 – The terms of the Versailles Treaty came into effect.

June – The *Reichswehr* Flamethrower Company was disarmed by the Allies.[73]

Several *Reichswehr* pioneer battalions retained their flamethrowers and used them in combat, as did dozens of *Freikorps* units, Sparticists, and police formations. The Germans continued to illegally manufacture flamethrowers, claiming that they were needed in order to spray insecticide.

Stürmer
von
Ronvaux. 9.8.18

Opposite
Top: Flamethrower platoon of Assault Battalion No. 14, photographed on May 19, 1918; the sign reads "The happy flamethrowers, Pentecost 1918." Details abound, such as the Bavarian flamethrower pioneer in an M1916 service jacket standing second from the left; the officer in the center, wearing the "small jacket" (kleine Rock) with black collar patches; and older pioneers who are former firefighters. The pioneer sitting in the front center was recently transferred from Assault Battalion No. 5 (Rohr), as shown by the position of his sleeve badge. At least one other man is also a former member of Rohr's battalion.

Bottom: Some of the same men from the previous image, posing with infantrymen of Assault Battalion No. 14 and French prisoners. The sign reads "Assaulters of Ronvaux, August 9, 1918." Kneeling on the right is the former member of Assault Battalion Nr. 5 (Rohr). He has resewn his sleeve badge onto a larger oval cloth backing and moved it into the lower position that was regulation for the Guard Reserve Pioneer Regiment. Assault Battalion No. 5 (Rohr) received its flamethrower replacements directly from the 2nd Guard Pioneer Replacement Battalion. After serving with the assault battalion, many then joined the flamethrower regiment. In this photo the French POWs do not seem particularly upset to have been captured.

Right: Postwar photo of a Wex carrier whose flamethrower and helmet have been fitted with cloth camouflage covers. He also holds a makeshift stick fuse or igniter consisting of kerosene-soaked rags wrapped around the end of a board. Courtesy Thierry Ehret

Poor quality but very interesting photo of a flamethrower platoon comprised of former members of the Guard Reserve Pioneer Regiment (left) attached to a shock troop of Freikorps Paulssen in 1919. The flamethrower pioneers retain their wartime uniforms, complete with black shoulder straps. All of the men are armed with P08 pistols, while rifles are stacked behind the flamethrower pioneers. Freikorps Paulssen was raised in Mountain Machine-gun Detachment 229 (Gebirgs-Maschinengewehr-Abteilung 229) on December 10, 1918. A Silesian unit, it fought the Poles in Poznania.

Postwar photo of a flamethrower pioneer of the Provisional National Army (Vorläufigen Reichsheer), established on May 5, 1919. A Gefreiter, he is a former member of the Guard Reserve Pioneer Regiment. As the Crown Prince authorized flamethrower pioneers to wear the official gray death's head only for the duration of the war, this young veteran has replaced his badge with a white facsimile. He may belong to the Reichswehr flamethrower battalion or later flamethrower company that existed until the summer of 1920.

Tactics

Prior to March of 1915, the Germans had not formulated flamethrower tactics. Two-man flamethrower squads of line-pioneer formations were trained in the technical operation of the weapon, the only tactic being to aim the lance and release the flaming oil. With the formation of the official flamethrower battalions and later regiment, specific tactics were developed and given names:

1) Stationary attack *(stehenden Angriff)* – large flamethrowers were installed in trenches or saps in intervals of 55 yards and fired to "shock" the enemy from his position.

2) Combined stationary and pouncing attack *(vereinten stehenden und springenden Angriff)* – large flamethrowers were fired first, then squads armed with portable flamethrowers attacked to drive the enemy further back from his position.

3) Pouncing attack *(springenden Angriff)* – small-flamethrower squads alone were used to drive the enemy from his position.

Right: Combined Stationary and Pouncing Attack (vereinten stehenden und Springenden Angriff). While Grof and double Kleif lay down smoke and flame from saps and shell holes, Kleif squads advance into the enemy line, followed by infantry. Courtesy Thierry Ehret

Below: Pouncing attack of small flamethrowers. Behind a rolling artillery barrage (right), several Kleif squads (bottom) launch a flanking attack on the enemy trench system to cover the advance of Kleif shock troops and the infantry (left). Courtesy Thierry Ehret

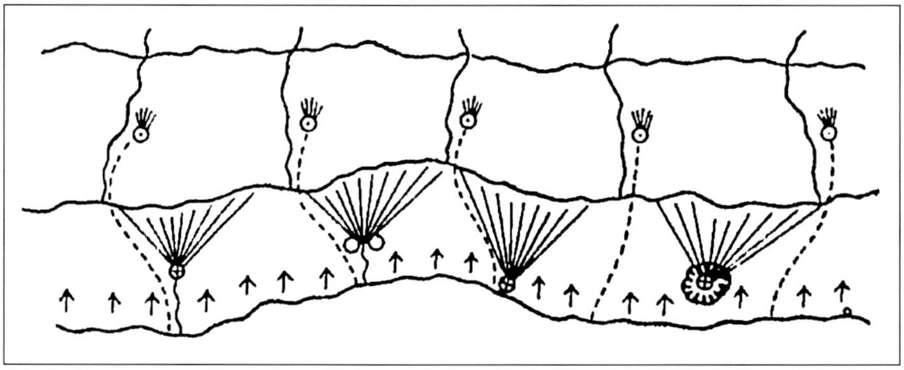

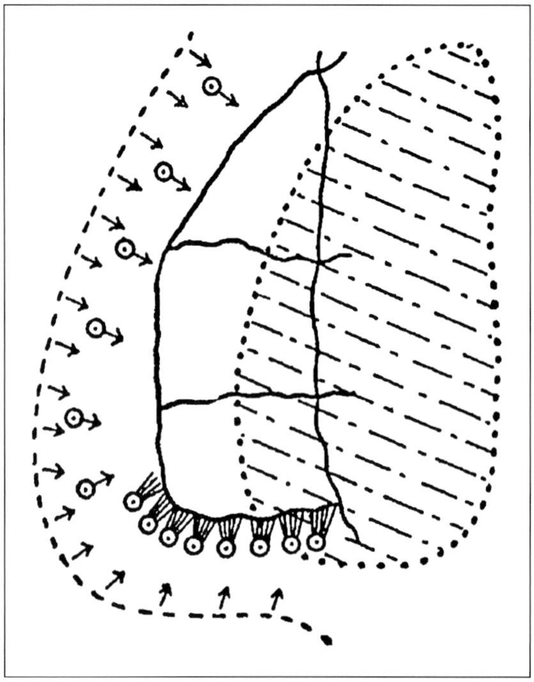

4) Shock troops *(Stosstrupps)* – small units of specially trained assault troops that went in ahead of the regular infantry.

5) Rolling up *(Aufrollen)* – small flamethrowers were introduced into enemy trenches in flanking attacks, generally in conjunction with hand-grenade throwers.

6) Tunneling – long tunnels were dug into No Man's Land, ending in vertical shafts no more than 44 yards from enemy trenches. Large flamethrowers were placed in the shafts; when the attack began, the lance operators emerged from the ground and sprayed the enemy at point-blank range. If the tunnel could not be dug to within 44 yards of the enemy trench, lance operators were trained to leap into the open and fire on the run, while assistants carried the hose behind.

7) Indian-style forward stalking *(indianermässigen Vorpirschen)* – portable-flamethrower squads approached the target indirectly as individuals instead of a unified mass, describing wide arcs and moving forward in leaps and bounds. They stayed within hearing distance of each other, constantly varying their intervals and using the natural cover of the terrain.

Grof in action. The lance is the telescoping model, which extended to 5.7 ft. (1.75 m) in length. The large flamethrower was used in the tactics of tunneling, the stationary attack, the combined stationary attack,

Curved-trajectory firing of a flamethrower. This technique was used in order to kill enemy troops crouched at the bottom of trenches. Flame jets were also bounced off trench walls to fire around corners, or fired vertically into the air as a signal to increase the speed of an infantry assault and temporarily suspend an artillery barrage. Courtesy Thierry Ehret

8) Covering jet *(Deckungsstrahl)* – a jet of flame fired by a large or small flamethrower to cover the advance of assault troops.

9) Pincers tactic *(Zangentaktik)* – machine-gun squads that accompanied flamethrower squads to the target lay down suppressing fire from the flanks, while grenade-launcher squads provided covering fire either from the jumping-off points or No Man's Land as the flamethrowers advanced; the target was thus squeezed between machine guns, grenade launchers, and flamethrowers.

10) Flame-accompanying squads *(Flammenbegleittrupps)* – portable flamethrower squads attached to infantry assault troops to mop up.

11) Knife tactic *(Messertaktik)* – using flame shock troops *(Flammenstosstrupps)* organized as long, single-file formations comprised of six *Kleif* troops, a hand-grenade squad from the Guard Reserve Pioneer Regiment, and several infantry groups that included light machine gunners and automatic riflemen, under the command of flamethrower officers and deputy officers. Each *Kleif* troop contained two *Kleif* squads, for a total of 12 flamethrowers per flame shock troop. The flame shock troop attacked the enemy line perpendicularly at great speed. Once it had punched through, the hand-grenade throwers, machine-gunners, and automatic riflemen turned to the sides to suppress flanking fire and screen infantry assault troops that followed 55 to 110 yards behind the flame shock troops.

12) Antitank warfare *(Tankbekämpfung)* – using portable flamethrowers in frontal attacks against tanks.

13) Flame signals *(Flammensignale)* – using portable flamethrowers to fire short, vertical jets into the air, to call for the suspension of artillery strikes and increase the speed of an assault.

AUSTRIA-HUNGARY

Sappeur Alois Franzeck in a postcard dated December 2, 1915. A housepainter, he writes that he was wounded by a Russian hand grenade but has recovered and will soon be sent back to the battlefield. Flamethrower operators were drawn from the sappers. Franzeck wears the field-gray M1915 cap (Kappe) and greatcoat (Einheitsmantel), the latter with the engineers' cherry-red collar patches (Paroli). His equipment consists of M1888 belt, M1908 cartridge pouches, M1915 rucksack with rolled blanket and tent section, M1888 haversack or breadbag, and M1888 entrenching tool. Weapons are the 8mm M1895 Steyr-Mannlicher rifle and M1895 bayonet.

1914

August(?) – In the Austro-Hungarian Common Army, also called the Imperial and Royal Army (*kaiserlich und königlich* or *k.u.k. Armee*), flamethrowers were assigned to the sappers *(Sappeure)* rather than the pioneers. Although early in the war Germany was involved in the Austrian flame-warfare effort, the full extent of that aid is unclear.

The Germans provided *Kleif* and *Grof M.1912,* as well as instructors from line-pioneer formations. Additionally, the five models of Austrian flamethrower used during the war were derived from a Fiedler patent of 1910. According to Russian and Italian accounts of late 1914 and early 1915, the Austrians also adopted the German tactic of spraying poison gas with *Kleif M.1912*. However, indisputable evidence of this has not yet been found.

Late 1914 – Flamethrower sappers were recruited from the 14 sapper battalions and trained by the Special Sapper Formation *(k.u.k. Sappeur-Spezial-Formation),* a company of the Replacement Battalion for Special Weapons *(Ersatzbataillon für besondere Kampfmittel)*. The Special Sapper Formation was based in Krems, on the Danube River in Northern Austria.[1]

1915

Early 1915 – The first Austrian flamethrower adopted by the army was the semi-portable *50l M. 15 Flammenwerfer,* which held 13 gallons of oil.[2] It appears to have been a Fiedler design that the inventor demonstrated to the Russians in 1909. (See Introduction.) Initially flamethrower squads were assigned piecemeal to the 72-man sapper platoons *(Sappeurzüge)* of infantry regiments. As more sappers were trained, flamethrower detachments *(Flammenwerfer-Abteilungen)* of about 12 men and two flamethrowers each were attached to an unspecified number of infantry regiments, Tyrolean *Kaiserjäger* regiments, *Feldjäger* battalions, and Austrian and Hungarian *Landwehr* regiments at the front. Given the newness and complexity of the weapon, the training was time consuming, leaving flamethrower troops in short supply.

June 23-July 7 – The Austrians first used flamethrowers in combat on the Carso, attacking Italian positions during the First Battle of the Isonzo.[3]

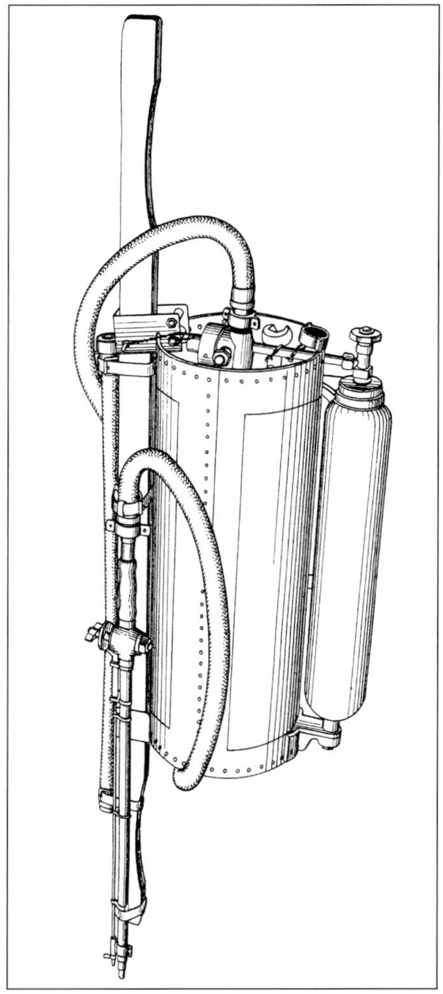

***Left:** Member of the Tyrollean Home Guard (Tiroler Standschützen), 17th Home Defense Command (17. Landesverteidigungskommando), Schöbl, armed with a German Kleif M.1912. The home guardsman is uniformed in the M1915 field-gray service jacket (Waffenrock). Note the protective face mask, abandoned by the Germans early in the war. The telescoping lance is in the retracted position, and the igniter appears to have the protective cover removed, indicating that the weapon is ready to be fired. It is not clear how many flamethrowers the Germans provided the Austrians or when the devices were delivered.*

***Right:** The 50l M. 15 Flammenwerfer, the first flamethrower adopted by the Austrian army in early 1915. It is shown prepared for transportation into battle by the three-man squad of "Flame shooter" (Flammenschütze), assistant, and NCO. Initially used as an offensive weapon without infantry protection, it proved too heavy and cumbersome and was soon reclassified as a static, defensive device.*

Summer – Austrian flamethrower sappers suffered high casualties due to the cumbersome nature of the *50l M. 15 Flammenwerfer* and the fact that the weapon was used offensively, with no infantry support. Flamethrower sappers were therefore reassigned a defensive role, and the *50l M. 15 Flammenwerfer* was reclassified as a static weapon.[4] Instead of carrying their flamethrowers sappers now installed them in trenches, built into sandbagged stations.

Late 1915 – Italian *Bersaglieri* encountered Austrian flamethrower sappers in the mountains south of Plezzo:

> Like hounds scenting their prey the famous *Alpini* tracked the Austrians into snowy caves, which, without a moment's warning, spouted vast sheets of fire, generating intolerable heat. Yet the *Alpini* prevailed. The first ranks emptied their magazines in a last agony, burning alive before their comrades' eyes. But meanwhile the great Italian howitzers plastered the caves with monstrous shells, till the foe was buried by the very rocks he'd rolled up to hide his treacherous lair. Here vast hoards of munitions were found, among them fire-squirts of German make, each weighing 270 lbs. when fully charged.[5]

1916

Early 1916 – The large flamethrower *(grosse 200l M. 15 Flammenwerfer)* and small flamethrower *(kleine 22l M. 15 Flammenwerfer)* were introduced, and the 50-liter model was redesignated a medium flamethrower *(mittlere 50l M. 15 Flammenwerfer)*.[6] Flamethrower platoons *(Flammenwerferzüge)* of 64 men armed with all three sizes of weapon were organized by the Army High Command (*Armeeoberkommando* or *AOK*) and made available to infantry commanders to reinforce vulnerable sections

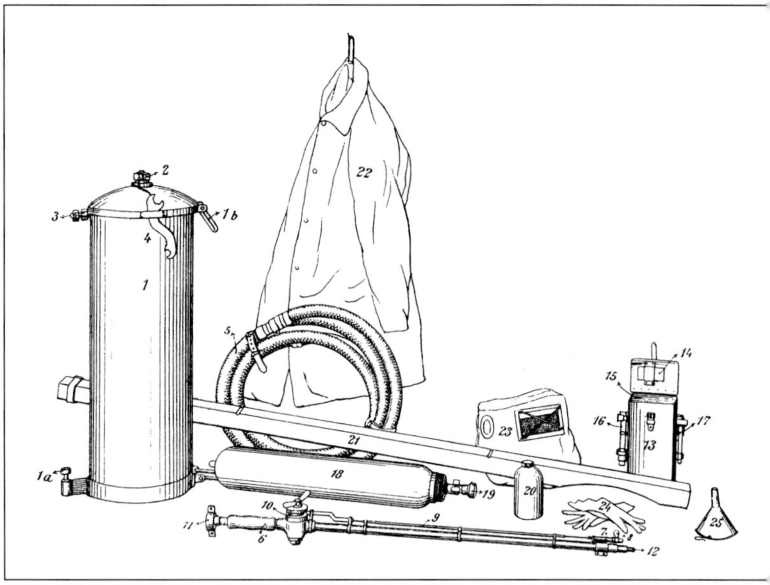

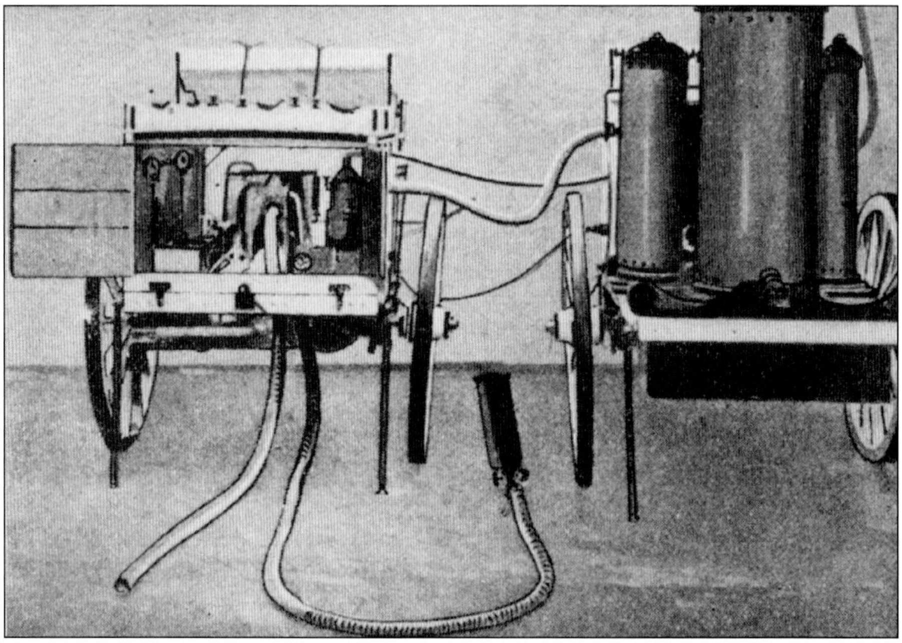

Top
Left: Fortified flamethrower post of a mountain-infantry regiment. The weapon is the mittlere 50l M. 15a Flammenwerfer, an improved version of the first device. Below the oil tank is a sign that reads "Smoking Strictly Prohibited." Austrian flamethrowers had a high incidence of accidental ignition and explosion; simply releasing the pressurized oil by turning the valve on the propellant tank carried a high risk. The operation had to be carried out slowly and deliberately. If the valve were opened too quickly, the rush of oil could cause an explosion.

Right: Mittlere 50l M. 15a Flammenwerfer and related equipment: 1) oil tank with 1a gas-bottle bearing and 1b carrying stirrup; 2) filler and filler cap; 3) gas-connection tube including loose nut; 4) wrench; 5) hoses; 6) lance; 7) igniter holder; 8) clamp; 9) release rod; 10) ball valve; 11) connection sleeve; 12) nozzle; 13) accessory box; 14) ignition cartridges; 15) protective caps for wicks; 16) wick holder; 17) elbow; 18) gas bottle; 19) screw valve; 20) valve cap; 21) carrying cross-beam; 22) asbestos firing coat; 23) asbestos firing mask; 24) gloves; 25) filling funnel.

Right: Illustration of an Austrian mobile flamethrower filling station, dated October 27, 1915. The three tanks on the right hold around 80 gallons of oil. A propellant bottle lies on the ground, connected by hose to the cart on the left, which contains a gasoline-operated pump. The flamethrower to be filled was connected to the pump by the hose in the left foreground.

of the front line.[7] They were also attached to German infantry regiments on the eastern front.

Depending on the assignment, these platoons were armed with either two large, four medium, and eight small flamethrowers, or four large and eight small flamethrowers. One NCO and four sappers served each large device, while one NCO and two sappers served each medium and small device; for certain operations the personnel in each flamethrower squad would be doubled. The number of weapons was adjusted according to the nature of the mission.

Flamethrower platoons were deployed as unified bodies in order to avoid diluting the flame effect. Only in special cases were flamethrower squads assigned individually.

Austro-Hungarian flamethrowers caught fire or exploded at a high rate. The large flamethrower was positioned far from troop shelters and ammunition bunkers. It was inserted deeply into the breastworks of trenches between heavy earthen weirs so that the entire area did not have to be evacuated in the case of an accident. Medium and small flamethrowers were often used lying on their sides, covered in a layer of dirt.

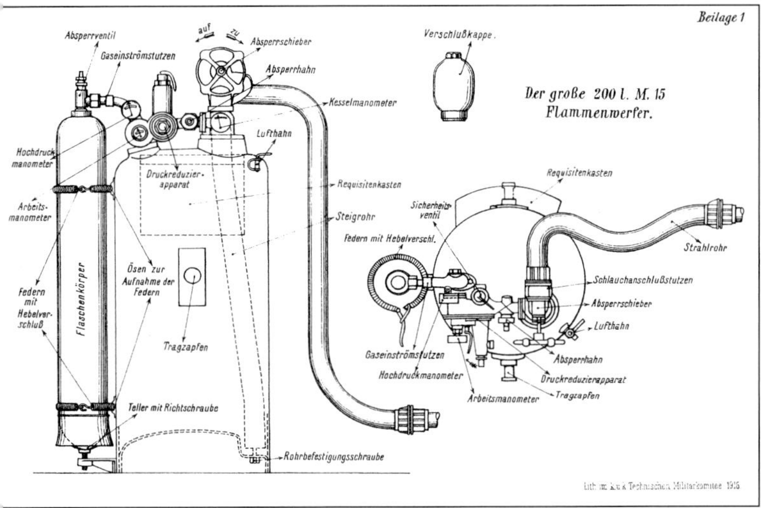

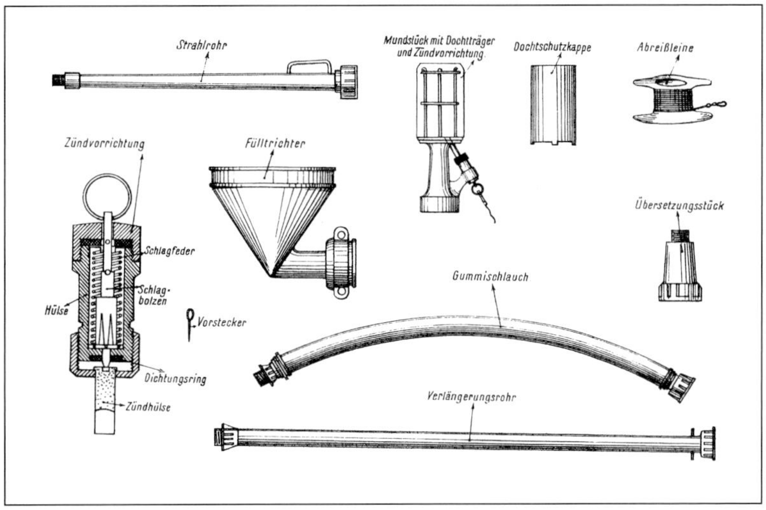

Top

Left: Grosse 200l Flammenwerfer M.15. This model of static flamethrower was so dangerous to its users that it was usually placed in a fortified position far away from the lance operators and other personnel. Hoses several meters long were used to keep the lance operators at a safe distance. A five-man squad served this device.

Right: Equipment for the grosse M. 15 200l Flammenwerfer, including lance, lance extension (bottom), rubber hose, wick holder and protective cap, igniter, and lanyard. Two men held the lance, one of them detonating the igniter by pulling on the lanyard.

Hoses up to 33 feet long were used with all models of flamethrower, so that the "flame shooter" *(Flammenschütze)* could be stationed far from the oil tank. This was to prevent the shooter from spraying the oil tank if he became distracted, which could cause an explosion.

1916 – The pioneer platoon of each infantry battalion was expanded into a "technical company" *(technische Kompagnie)* of three 72-man platoons of pioneers and sappers equipped with searchlights, trench mortars, hand grenades, and portable flamethrowers.

April 22 – East of Selz:

> Italian infantry, supported by artillery, despite obstinate resistance occupied strong trenches 350 meters long. The Austrians receiving reinforcements, violently counterattacked twice during the night, the second time succeeding in retaking part of the lost trenches. After a deadly hand-to-hand struggle in which the Austrians suffered severely, the Italians drove them out, capturing 133, including six officers, two machine guns, 200 rifles, several flame throwers, and numerous cases of ammunition and bombs.[8]

Far left: Italian soldier modeling a captured kleine 22l M. 15 Flammenwerfer, the first Austrian portable flamethrower. One section of the two-piece rubber hose is shown; in action, the longer hose was used. The Austrian three-man portable flamethrower squad consisted of carrier, lance operator, and squad leader. Courtesy Gaetano Nieddu.

Left: Rear view of kleine 22l M. 15 Flammenwerfer, showing the propellant bottle on the side of the oil tank and the pressure-reducing valve on the top. Courtesy Gaetano Nieddu.

Mid 1916 – The *kleine 15l M. 16 Flammenwerfer,* also known as the *Sturmtruppen-Flammenwerfer M. 16,* was adopted. It was specifically designed as an offensive weapon used by assault troops.

June 18 – Attacking Russian troops suffered heavy losses south of Radziviloff, Galicia, due to the extensive use of flamethrowers by Austrian and German defenders.[9]

September 9 – A "technical training ground" *(technisches Übungsfeld)* was established by the Fifth Army at Parje, on the Isonzo front, to train Austrian engineers in close-combat techniques and trench warfare, including flamethrower operations.

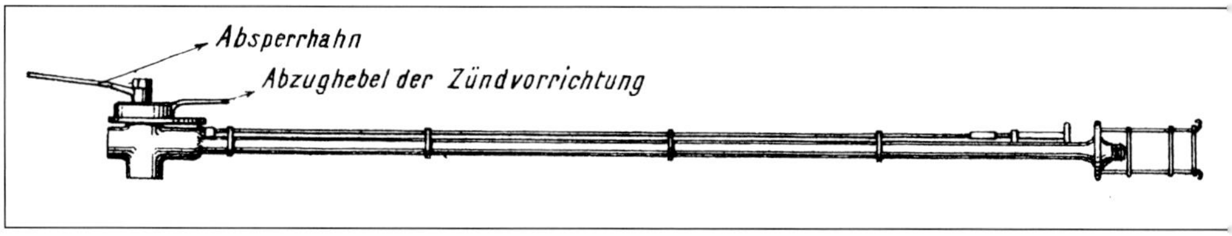

***Above:** The improved flamethrower lance, which featured one lever for setting off the ignition cartridge and one lever for releasing the oil. It was used with both medium and small flamethrowers. The wire enclosure around the lance nozzle is the holder for the paraffin-soaked wick, which burned for several minutes and allowed for multiple emissions.*

***Left:** Sapper Korporal Pusztay, date unknown, uniformed in the field-gray M1915 service jacket and trousers. The two six-pointed white stars on collar indicate his rank. Although Pusztay's unit is not identified, both of his hands are deeply stained with what is likely tar oil, a feature often seen in photos of Austrian flamethrower sappers. Corporals commanded individual flamethrower squads; note the M1895 bayonet with yellow-and-black NCO's knot (Troddel) and the 1906 Sapper and Pioneer Proficiency Badge (Sappeur- und Pionierauszeichnung) on the right breast. He has also been awarded a bravery medal, probably in silver.*

***Below:** Part of the Technical Company (technische Kompagnie) of an infantry battalion. Almost all wear the M1916 field-gray duty blouse (Einheitsbluse), identified by the stand-and-fall collar. In 1916 the pioneer platoons of infantry battalions were expanded into Technical Companies. They were composed of pioneers and sappers equipped with searchlights, trench mortars, hand grenades and portable flamethrowers. The two kleine 15l M. 16 Flammenwerfern in this photo are fitted with lances of greatly differing lengths. It appears that the short lance was used offensively in trenches, while the long lance was a defensive weapon. Courtesy Antonio Rossetto*

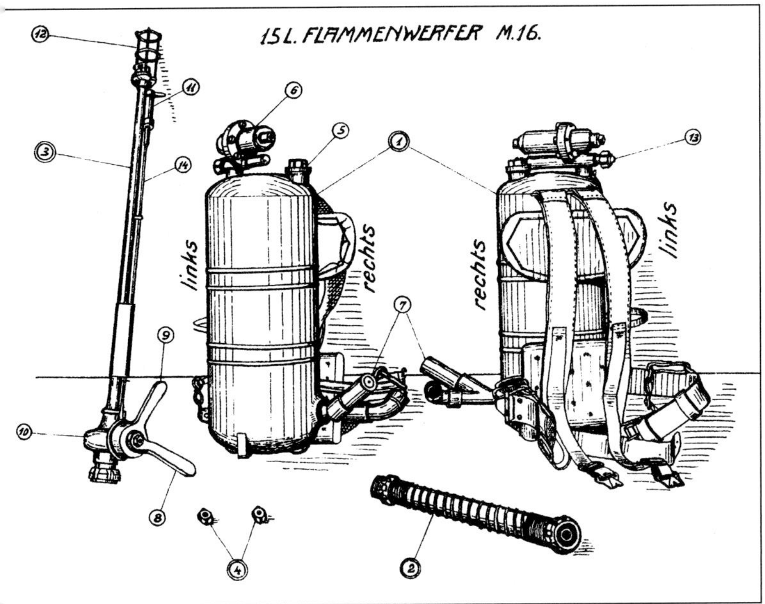

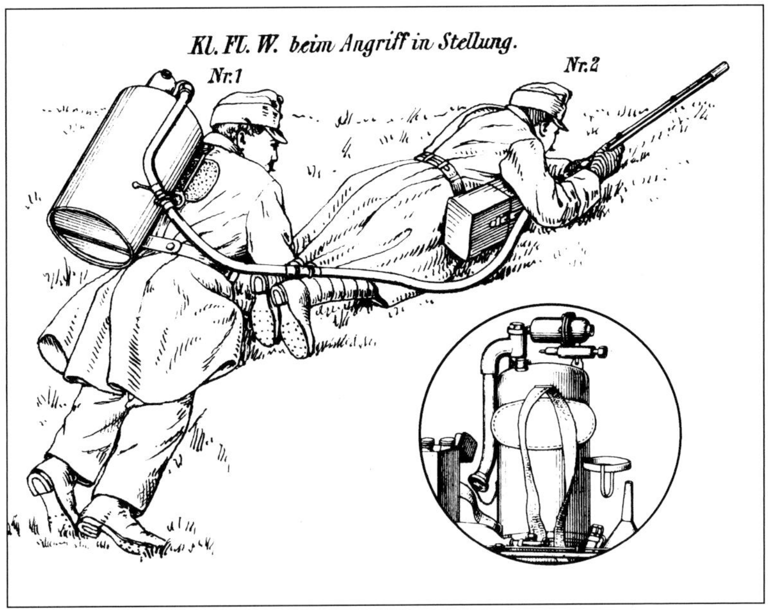

Left: Kleine 15l M. 16 Flammenwerfer, also known as the Sturmtruppen-Flammenwerfer M. 16: 1) oil tank; 2) wire-reinforced rubber hose; 3) lance; 4) 6mm and 8mm nozzles; 5) oil filler tube; 6) reducer valve; 7) oil-release block valve; 8) oil-release lever; 9) ignition lever; 10) ball valve; 11) igniter holder; 12) wick holder; 13) gas-connection nipple with swivel nut.

Right: Kleine 22l M. 15 Flammenwerfer in position during an attack. Nr. 1 is the carrier (Träger), and Nr. 2 the flame shooter, who is equipped with an accessory box that contains ignition cartridges and spare wicks. Portable-flamethrower squads also included an NCO as leader. The improved lance did not create heat blowback, eliminating the need for a protective facemask. Inset: Front view of the flamethrower, including details of the felt-padded back rest, woven hemp shoulder straps reinforced with leather, and rigid oil-outflow pipe.

Pioneers and sappers of other armies and corps were sent to Parje to study the training ground and then return to their own armies to set up similar facilities.[10]

September 10-16 – *Oberst* Theodor Brosch von Aarenau, head of engineers at the *AOK*, observed a German assault course taught by Assault Battalion Rohr at Beuville. The first Austrian to take part in such a demonstration, he apparently requested that other Austrian officers be allowed to attend.[11]

September 26 to October 7 – Two groups of Austrian sapper and pioneer officers were sent to Beuville instead of Parje for training. They wrote up their experiences and submitted them to the *AOK*.

November-December – Three special one-week training courses for 40 Austrian officers and 100 NCOs were conducted by Assault Battalion Rohr at Beuville. The courses included training in flamethrowers.

November 24 – The Austrian army organized its first "Assault Patrols" *(Sturmpatrouillen),* which were raised in all infantry and *Jäger* units. Every infantry company would have one or two Assault Patrols comprising one NCO and eight men. Each infantry and *Jäger* battalion would also have one or two officers trained in assault techniques.[12] Up to three portable-flamethrower squads could be attached to an Assault Patrol.

1917

February – The *AOK* ordered that assault battalions be formed. An Army Assault Battalion *(Armeesturmbataillon)* consisted of four infantry companies, each of which had two nine-man Assault Patrols; one or two machine-gun companies; one mountain-artillery battery with four guns; one infantry-gun battery with four pieces; one trench-mortar platoon with four grenade launchers and four medium trench mortars; one flamethrower platoon with six portable devices; and one construction company.[13] The flamethrower used by assault troops until the end of the war was the *kleine 15l M. 16 Flammenwerfer.*

Spring – The Austro-Hungarian Army was reorganized. Most engineering duties were shifted to the sappers, while pioneers were relegated to bridging activities.[14]

May – All flamethrower sappers not attached to assault battalions were integrated into four companies *(Flammenwerferkompagnien),* numbered 1 to 4. Each flamethrower company consisted of four 64-man platoons. Two flamethrower companies were assigned to the Special Sapper Formation in Krems; one was sent to the technical training ground at Parje to train flamethrower troops for the southwestern front; and the last was ordered to a camp at Huszt to supply flamethrower sappers for the northeastern front.[15]

Sappeur Joseph Dengg of the Flamethrower Detachment, 1st Tirolean Kaiserjäger Regiment (Flammenwerfer Abteilung, 1. Tiroler-Kaiserjäger-Regiment). He was killed in action on July 16, 1916, at the age of 25. Due to poor tactics and faulty equipment, Austrian flamethrower sappers suffered heavy casualties during the war. In this photo from his death card (Sterbebild), he wears the M1909 service jacket in pike gray (hechtgrau) with cherry-red collar patches.

Sappers emplacing a grosse M. 15 200l Flammenwerfer with an extended lance. Note the two-wheeled cart on the right used to transport the weapon. Each large flamethrower was served by a four- or five-man squad. They wear the M1915 and M1916 uniforms in different shades of field gray and field green, (Feldgrün), also called "nettle green" (Nesselgrün).

Three flamethrower squads armed with kleine 15l M. 16 Flammenwerfern, attached to an Assault Patrol (Sturmpatrouille) of an Army Assault Battalion. The assistant of each two-man squad poses as if ready to release gas from the propellant bottle, the first step in preparing the weapon for firing. However, since no wicks are present on the wire holders, the flamethrowers are likely empty. The men wear M1915 and M1916 uniforms in field gray and green. M1916 Berndorfer and German-style M1917 steel helmets are painted khaki brown. Portable-flamethrower squads were issued 9mm Steyr M12 automatic pistols and 8mm Mannlicher M95 "Stutzen" carbines as personal arms, as shown here. Courtesy Antonio Rossetto.

June-September – The two flamethrower companies at Parje and Huszt expanded into two companies each.[16]

June 25 – At 2:30 A.M. seven battalions of Austrian *Kaiserschützen* and regular infantry counterattacked at Monte Ortigara. Flamethrowers in the second and third waves illuminated the vicious hand-to-hand combat between Italian *Alpini* and Austrians, who fought each other with firearms, grenades, trench clubs, pick-axes, knives, and even stones. The Austrians took the peak by daybreak, the Italians losing nearly 2000 dead, wounded, and captured.[17]

June 30 – The *AOK* ordered a reorganization of the assault battalions. Army Assault Battalions were transformed into Divisional Assault Battalions *(Divisionsturmbataillone)*. Every infantry division would now have an assault battalion consisting of one assault company from each regiment in the division; one machine-gun company; one infantry-gun battery; one sapper platoon; one ordnance platoon; one flamethrower platoon armed with six portable devices; and one telephone detachment.[18]

September – For logistical and administration reasons, the six flamethrower companies were amalgamated into Special Sapper Battalion No. 61 *(Spezial-Sappeurbataillon Nr. 61)*. The two flamethrower companies at Parje and the two at Huszt were merged into one company at each facility, giving the new battalion a total of four companies.[19] Each company contained one machine-gun and one grenade-launcher platoon as well as maintenance sections; the battalion may therefore have had about 1500 effectives. The Special Sapper Formation in Krems provided replacements. Following the German example of the Guard Reserve Pioneer Regiment and the *OHL*, Special Sapper Battalion No. 61 was directly subordinate to the *AOK*.

October 4 – The Austrians launched multiple counterattacks on Mount San Gabriele:

> They first came forward always with bombs and bayonets, followed by parties with flame throwers and men for consolidation of positions which they did not take. Every attack failed. Machine guns and double barreled Fiat machine pistols, which are the most rapid firing firearms in the world, held them up every time.[20]

October 12-November 24 – The Battle of Caporetto, also called the 12th Battle of the Isonzo. Special Sapper Battalion No. 61 took part in a major breakthrough *(Durchbruch)* battle, the four companies dispersed by platoon to infantry regiments or battalions. For the duration of the battle the flamethrower platoons were put under the temporary command of infantry officers.

November 20 – *Kaiserjäger* Regiment No. 3 lent its assault company and a mountain platoon to the 1st Battalion of Infantry Regiment No. 14 for an attack on fortifications in the Brenta Valley, particularly the Termine Tunnel. A flamethrower platoon and a pioneer section provided support. The attack failed because it lacked the element of surprise. However, a second attack on the 23rd succeeded, surprise having been achieved through firepower and the actions of Assault Patrols, which blew a passage through the barbed wire.[21]

It was soon clear that infantry commanders did not know what to do with flamethrower platoons. Since flamethrower troops were sappers, they were often put to work in construction or improving trenches instead of engaging in combat, or they were marched to their assembly points with field tools, ordered to leave their flamethrowers in the rear. The few times that flamethrower platoons were used correctly, as at Rombon, the Brenta Dam, and Bonatto Ridge, they were most effective when paired with Assault Patrols of divisional assault battalions.

After the battle the *AOK* put the Eleventh Army Headquarters in administrative charge of Special Sapper Battalion No. 61, having realized that infantry commanders continued to use flamethrower sappers in construction instead of allowing them to train.

Unit badge (Truppenabzeichen) of Special Sapper Battalion No. 61 (Spezial-Sappeurbataillon Nr. 61), the flamethrower battalion. In 1917 five such gray, waxed-cloth badges were issued to each soldier in a unit. They were sewn on the left side of the cap and on the shoulder straps of the tunic and greatcoat so that they could be read from the front. For sappers the lettering on the badge was blue. This system of identification was not widely adopted.

Sapper Markiewicz, whose unit badges on his cap and shoulder strap have been retouched by the photographer to obscure the number. This, coupled with the dark staining of his hands, indicates that he is likely a member of Special Sapper Battalion No. 61, information about which was carefully guarded during the war. Although he wears the M1909 pike-gray service jacket with cherry-red collar patches, his cap, trousers, and puttees are field gray. He is armed with the M1895 bayonet.

Opposite
Top: Unauthorized private photo of Austrian machine gunners and men of German Landwehr-Infanterie-Regiment Nr. 99 attending an assault course at a "model garden" (Modelgarten) or mock trench system in Hucisco-Olesci, Galicia, June of 1917. They are armed with grenade bags and 8mm Schwarzlose M.7/12 heavy machine guns on tripods. Each company of Special Sapper Battalion No. 61 contained one machine-gun platoon of four weapons each, served by flamethrower sappers also extensively trained as hand-grenade throwers.

Bottom: A line of 15 mittlere 50l M. 15a Flammenwerfern connected in parallel in a fixed, defensive position and fired simultaneously to create a vertical flame barrier. One sapper controlled a single oil-release valve that operated all the lances together. It is not clear if this tactic was used very often or if it was successful.

Above: Flamethrower squad training with a kleine 15l M. 16 Flammenwerfer adapted for use by a five-man squad. The short hose has been replaced with the two-piece version used with the kleine 22l M. 15 Flammenwerfer; on the left, a sapper removes the protective cover from a drum that houses a detonator cap at the mouth of the lance nozzle. This experimental ignition system was not adopted. Courtesy Antonio Rossetto.

Right: The same five-man squad as in the previous photo. One sapper opens the block valve on the flamethrower, while a second squad member and the NCO in the soft cap support the hose for the flame shooter. This photo was likely taken at the flamethrower training ground at Parje. Courtesy Antonio Rossetto.

Cap badge of the 2nd Company, Special Sapper Battalion No. 61. Made of white metal with a glaze of red enamel on the oval, it measured 1.8 in. by 1.5 in. The skull motif used by Austrian assault troops was inspired by the death's head sleeve badge worn by the flamethrower pioneers of Assault Battalion No. 5 (Rohr).

1918

Early 1918 – The *AOK* determined that flamethrowers were useful only when deployed with assault troops. It therefore directed the Eleventh Army Headquarters to order the four companies of Special Sapper Battalion No. 61 to the following Divisional Assault Battalions:

> 1st Flamethrower Company to Assault Battalion No. 55, I Corps;
> 2nd Flamethrower Company to Assault Battalion No. 27, XXVI Corps;
> 3rd Flamethrower Company to Assault Battalion No. 6, III Corps;
> 4th Flamethrower Company to Assault Battalion No. 18, VI Corps.

The companies were not to be split up without authorization from the *AOK*. They would be under the control of the corps commander, who could transfer them to different assault battalions within the corps at his discretion. This order did not affect flamethrower platoons attached to divisional assault battalions.

The four flamethrower companies took part in large-scale assaults and individual attacks, instructed new recruits and officers in flame warfare, carried out demonstrations, tested new equipment, trained the flamethrower platoons assigned to assault battalions, and maintained and repaired their weapons.

Spring – Special Sapper Battalion No. 61 was reorganized by the *AOK* to better reflect its duties as an offensive flamethrower battalion. The number of flamethrowers was set at 48 *kleine 15l M. 16 Flammenwerfer* and 20 *mittlere 50l M. 15 Flammenwerfer* to be placed in fixed positions for defense. Auxiliary weapons were reduced to one machine-gun platoon of four weapons per company, to ensure that flamethrower companies would not be deployed without infantry cover.

May 18 – The Italians foiled a large-scale Austrian attack with flamethrowers:

> During the early hours yesterday the enemy attempted in vain for the third time to reconquer Monte Corno, which we occupied in the night of May 9-10. Two columns provided with machine guns and flame projectors and strongly supported by artillery, attacked our positions. They were caught under our very effective artillery barrage, and kept under violent bursts of machine gun and rifle fire until compelled to retire in confusion. Two flame projectors remained in our hands.[22]

Mid 1918 – Special Sapper Battalion No. 61 was renamed Special Assault Battalion No. 61 *(Spezial-Sturmbataillon Nr. 61)* due to its offensive role.

By this time there were also 75 flamethrower platoons attached to the divisional assault battalions. A flamethrower platoon had six *kleine 15l M. 16 Flammenwerfern* operated by three squads armed with two devices each. A portable-flamethrower squad consisted of eight sappers and an NCO.

June 15-23 – The Battle of the Piave River, the final Austrian offensive of the war.

June 18 – Austrian assault troops captured Capo Sile using flamethrowers and poison gas.[23] Under the cover of a smoke screen, Assault Patrols accompanied by flamethrower sappers overran the gassed Italian trenches and managed to occupy half of the Montello, a low, flat-topped hill that ran along the west side of the middle Piave. However, fierce Italian resistance stopped them, leaving the Montello "a very shambles, thickly strewn with Austrian dead."[24]

July-November 3 – Following the failure of the June offensive, the Austrians adopted a defensive posture. Assault units, including flamethrower troops, were removed from the fronts and sent back to their training camps. They took part only in reconnaissance and local assaults until Austria requested an armistice on October 30, which was signed on November 3.

Machine gunner of Special Sapper Battalion No. 61, wearing the M1916 duty blouse in nettle green. The flamethrower badge is barely visible in the shadow on the right side of his cap. On his collar he displays the single six-pointed white stars of a Gefreiter, machine-gun badges, and cherry-red facing stripes (Paroli) of the sappers. He has been awarded a silver or gold bravery medal and is armed with an M1895 bayonet.

Assault troops using a kleine 15l M. 16 Flammenwerfer with a very long hose consisting of several sections connected together. Such hoses were generally used on large flamethrowers, which had a high danger of explosion. It is unclear why the hose is in use with the safer portable weapon; one reason would be to allow the flamethrower carrier to remain under cover while only the flame shooter exposed himself to enemy fire. Courtesy Antonio Rossetto.

Steel-helmeted sappers firing an unknown model of flamethrower in the Dolomites, May of 1917. Note the burning wick wrapped around the holder over the nozzle of the lance.

Below: Mittlere 50l M. 15a Flammenwerfer; the caption reads "From the eastern theater of war: Austro-Hungarian flamethrower." This squad likely belongs to a flamethrower platoon. The men wear the M1909 pike-gray uniform replaced by field gray in 1915. Note that the flame jet is being blown violently to the left by the wind, indicating very low propellant pressure. This deficiency frequently caused explosions when the flame raced up the hose and into the oil tank.

Opposite: Squad preparing to fire a mittlere 50l M. 15a Flammenwerfer from a defensive post. Both wear the asbestos facemask with reinforced glass windows, while the flame shooter has also donned gloves and the asbestos firing coat. Austrian lances were made in several lengths. The flame shooter wears the M1915 field-gray uniform, while the assistant is outfitted in the M1916 nettle-green duty blouse. Courtesy Antonio Rossetto.

1919

September 9 – The Allies and the new Republic of Austria signed the Treaty of Saint-Germain. Article 135 prohibited Austria from using, manufacturing, and importing poison gas and flamethrowers.

1920

June 4 – The Allies and the new Republic of Hungary signed the Treaty of Trianon. Article 119 prohibited Hungary from using, manufacturing, and importing poison gas and flamethrowers.

Tactics

Initially the flamethrower was considered an offensive weapon, which was deployed in combat without infantry support. High casualties among flamethrower sappers led the War Ministry to decree that the apparatus was a "close-combat weapon for small-scale attacks or defense, and will mainly be used to defend fortified positions."[25]

Flamethrower Platoons

With the advent of Flamethrower Platoons in 1916, tactics expanded to include the attack with stationary flamethrowers, carried out to drive the enemy from his trenches, and the attack with stationary and portable flamethrowers, in which flamethrower shock troops left the Austrian trenches and entered the enemy line.[26] Flamethrower platoons were generally not divided up when deployed. Only rarely were individual squads assigned single attacks.

Above: Sappers of Sapper Battalion No. 61 or Special Assault Battalion No. 61 pose with M1915 gas masks (Gummimasken), M1916 Berndorfer steel helmets, and 8mm Mannlicher M95 rifles. All wear the M1916 duty blouse, some with unit badges on the shoulder straps. As in many photos of Austrian flamethrower sappers they wear no puttees, most likely so that they can quickly remove their trousers if they are accidentally doused in flaming oil.

When flamethrower platoons were sent to frontline trenches, large and medium devices were emplaced at distances that corresponded approximately to the weapons' range. For engaging live targets, the oil was ignited at the nozzle of the lance; for burning inanimate objects such as barricades, barbed-wire posts, bridges, and shelters, the target was first sprayed with oil and the jet was then ignited.

Flamethrowers were used offensively only when the opposing trenches were about 60 yards apart. If the distance was greater than the range of the flamethrowers, saps or tunnels were dug, and the devices were situated at the heads.

The thick, black smoke from flamethrowers was used to conceal infantry during attacks.

Flamethrower companies and flamethrower platoons attached to assault battalions

Flamethrower companies carried out large-scale attacks during breakthroughs. Individual squads were occasionally assigned single attacks.

Portable flamethrowers attached to assault battalions were assigned to the second and third wave of the assault force and were used mainly for mopping up. Frontal assaults against machine-gun nests or other strong points were avoided.

Static flamethrowers were used defensively, often by connecting them in parallel and aiming the lances skyward to create a vertical wall of flame. They were activated when a single operator released a valve.

Opposite

Top: Sappers of Flamethrower Platoon 3 (Flammenwerferzug 3), attached to German Reserve Infantry Regiment No. 233, date and place unknown. The Austrians are armed with a mittlere 50l M. 15a Flammenwerfer, and two wear M1917 steel helmets. Being sappers, they have built a wooden shelter for the flamethrower. Note that the flame shooter is armed with a trench dagger (Nahkampfmesser) on his hip. The two German officers – one wearing a spiked helmet – are identified as Laucht and Fahning, while the two Austrian officers in the foreground are Minksch and Münchausen, the latter displaying unusual dark shoulder straps.

Bottom: Austrian flamethrower sapper firing a very thin, unidentified model of lance. He wears the M1915 field-gray overcoat and khaki-brown M1917 steel helmet. The burning wick appears as a dark blob over the nozzle. Courtesy Antonio Rossetto.

BULGARIA

1916

September 23 – Germany sent a training command of two officers, four NCOs and 25 men of Assault Battalion No. 5 (Rohr) to Bulgaria to create a pioneer *(pioner)* assault battalion *(Shturmova Druzhina)* in the Bulgarian First Army. This formation would provide troops for operations and would train Bulgarian officers, NCOs, and men of the First and Second Armies, as well as Turkish officers, NCOs, and men.[1] The instruction included the use of the flamethrower, *ognepryskachka* or *ognehvyrgachka* in Bulgarian.

November – Army Group Below intended to form an assault detachment in each of its armies. These units would be independent of the assault battalion in Sofia and would each consist of one German and one Bulgarian company, under the command of German officers. The plan was not carried out.[2] During the same month the Bulgarian Headquarters of the Standing Army issued a formal order that an assault battalion be established.[3]

November 13 – Enclosure No. 14. Document: War Diary of Assault Battalion No. 5 (Rohr).

Enclosures. Training Plan for the Bulgarian Assault Battalion.[4]

German Pioneers from Assault Battalion Rohr (right) training Bulgarian pioneers in the use of hand grenades. Rohr's men also created the Assault Battalion (Shturmova Druzhina) of the Bulgarian First Army, which included a flamethrower detachment of one officer, four NCOs, and 34 pioneers. In this photo, the Bulgarians wear the M1899/1906 uniform in tobacco brown.

Pioneers of the First Army Assault Battalion. Their youth and obvious fitness is noteworthy. They wear the M1915 field-gray service jacket with dark shoulder straps, breeches, low jackboots, M1908 ammunition pouches in black leather, and German M1916 steel helmets. Weapons are Austrian M95 carbines and Bulgarian M1895 bayonets. Following the German example, the flamethrower pioneers of the Assault Battalion were trained in the use of carbines, pistols, and hand grenades.

Pioneer lieutenant (poruchik) of the First Army Assault Battalion. He wears a Russian-style shirt-tunic in white cotton and is armed with an M1889 saber. His field-gray M1915 service cap features the black band of the engineers. A lieutenant commanded the flamethrower detachment of the battalion.

1st Week: 13-18 November
(Morning 8-11:00 Practical Training. Afternoon 3-4:00 Instruction.) For all: Assault companies, trench mortars, flamethrowers!
a) Explanation of the German B.Z. stick hand grenade and the B.Z. training hand grenade. *[Note: B. Z. =* Brennzünder *(igniting fuse).]*
b) Throwing from a standing position: 1. as far as possible in a straight line, 2. toward targets at different distances, 3. from the trench toward targets at different distances, 4. from sapheads into other sapheads.
c) Rapid breaking out of a trench and sapheads.
d) Obstacle course.
e) Instruction on equipment, composition, and establishing of assault troops, then the task, positioning, and procedures of assault troops.

2nd Week: 20-25 November. For all:
a) Repetition of the first week. Obstacle course.
b) Throwing of wooden dummy [grenades] various distances while lying.
c) Throwing of wooden dummy [grenades] various distances while running.
d) Explanation and throwing of egg grenades various distances.
e) Overcoming of obstacles of all kinds.
f) Rapid manufacturing of obstacles.
g) From sapheads, the throwing back of and practicing with half-armed training hand grenades. Practicing from under cover.
h) Rapid reaching of and penetration into the enemy position.
i) Throwing of half-armed training hand grenades from traverse to traverse.
k) Instruction on protection from hand grenades (lattice, etc.).
l) Instruction on investment of own assault positions and investment of enemy defense positions.

3rd Week: 27 November to 2 December.
a) Repetition of first and second weeks. Obstacle course.
b) Advance of an assault troop against enemy trench.
1. Vacant with destroyed obstacle.

***Right:** Privates (Redniki) of the First Army Assault Battalion. As in the previous image, they are very young and extremely fit. Two pose with the assault-troop accouterments of slung Austrian M95 carbines and single M1908 ammunition pouches, which left room on the belt for German stick grenades. All wear the breeches and riding boots of elite units; the men in the center and on the left are outfitted in privately purchased M1915 field-gray officers' style service jackets, while the trooper on the right is uniformed in the M1908 gray-green tunic with black collar patches of the engineers. This man also displays a metal dragon badge on the flap of his right breast pocket, which may identify him as a flamethrower pioneer.*

***Below:** Metal badge worn on the breast pocket by the pioneer in the previous image. A winged, fire-breathing dragon measuring about 1 in. by 1.25 in., it may be a flamethrower-qualification badge, although whether official or unofficial is not known.*

2. Occupied with intact obstacles at various distances.
c) Throwing with live hand grenades from [various] thrower's attitudes.
d) Digging a secure assault position.
e) Rolling up trench with half-armed hand grenades and dummy grenades (also approach trench, defended traverse).
f) Clearing and occupying of the assault position. Fixing of the bayonets.
g) Advance of assault troops according to the clock.
h) Conduct during gas attacks. Running with gas masks on.
i) Instruction on use of hand grenades for the production of concentrated and elongated charges. [Instruction] on reconnaissance of our own and the enemy position.
k) Preparation of reconnaissance sketches and messages of all kinds.

In Addition for Trench Mortars and Flamethrowers:
a) Explanation of trench mortars and/or flamethrowers.
b) Composition of trench-mortar squads and/or flamethrower squads.
c) Operation of trench mortars and/or flamethrowers.

4th Week: 4-9 December.
a) Repetition of 1st to 3rd weeks. Obstacle course.
b) Changing and shoring up of won positions.
c) Use of steel shields.
d) Conduct during counterattacks.
e) Activity of labor and carrying squads.

f) Use of telephones during attacks.
g) Setting up of messenger routes.
h) Assaulting of blockhouses with hand grenades.
i) Breaking out of infantry in three waves, led by shock troops.
k) Instruction on production and use of attack sketches.
l) Instruction on preparation and execution of an attack.
m) Instruction on grenade launcher 16 and its use.

For Trench Mortars and Flamethrowers:
a) Practice with the trench mortar in positions prepared for this.
Practice with the flamethrower in rolling up trenches.
b) Practice with the trench mortar in changing positions and shooting training ammunition.
Practice with the empty flamethrower in blockhouse fighting.
Afternoon. 3-4:00 Live firing the trench mortar.
4-4:30 Practice with the filled flamethrower.

5th Week: 11-16 December
a) Repetition of 1st-4th weeks. Obstacle course.
b) Instruction on the use of the machine gun.
c) Explanation of the infantry-gun company and instruction on its use.
d) Execution of an attack with assault troops and flamethrowers.
Afternoon. 1:30-2:00 Practice with filled flamethrowers.
3-4:00 Live firing of the trench mortar.
4-5:00 Live firing of the grenade launcher
6th Week: 16-23 December
a) Repetition of the 1st through 5th weeks. Obstacle course.
b) Execution of an attack with all weapons.
c) Instruction on fighting and training activities of the battalion.
Afternoon. Training of assault companies in machine guns.
Signed, *Oberleutnant* Fitz.

Pioneer private first class (Efrietor) wearing the black M1899 peaked cap and the field-gray M1915 tunic, which was identical to that worn by the infantry. Note the red piping on the collar and shoulder straps. The cap cockade displays the national colors of white, green, and red. A private first class or corporal (mladshi podofitser) commanded each squad in the flamethrower detachment.

Below: Assault pioneers of an unidentified unit, uniformed in gray-green M1908 tunics and several styles of M1915 field-gray jackets. The First Army Assault Battalion was identically equipped with Austrian M95 carbines and gas masks, and German 9mm P08 pistols and M.1916 steel helmets. Two of the men wear opanci, traditional Bulgarian footwear. The Germans also supplied the assault battalion with its flame-throwers, including the Lichtgrof M.1916, Kleif M.1917, and likely the Wex M.1917.

December 29 – Order No. 653 of the Headquarters of the Standing Army officially established a trench-mortar battalion and an assault battalion[5] of around 650 men. Order No. 654 of the same day decreed that the assault battalion would consist of two pioneer assault companies, one trench-mortar detachment, one howitzer battery, and one flamethrower detachment *(ogneprvskachno otdelenie, ognehvyrgachno otdelenie)*.

The flamethrower detachment was comprised of one first lieutenant *(Poruchik)* as commanding officer, four sergeants and corporals *(Podofitseri)*, and 34 privates first class *(Efreitori)* and privates *(Rednitsi)* assigned as 22 combatants, three reserves, six porters, one security guard, one orderly, and one bicycle courier. Eleven horses (eight draught, one saddle, one transport, one water transport) and four wagons (two horses each) provided local transportation.

During the war, the Germans gave the Bulgarians a total of 3127 heavy machine guns, 284 light mortars, 162 medium mortars, 1932 grenade launchers, 528 artillery pieces, and eight flamethrowers.[6] The flamethrower detachment was thus armed with six small flamethrowers (*Kleif* and possibly *Wex*) and two *Lichtgrof M.1916*.

The First Army Assault Battalion never fought as a unified whole but instead sent detachments to divisions or brigades for particular operations. It was formed mainly for training purposes, as the Bulgarian army followed the early German practice of creating ad hoc assault units from regular infantry. The assault battalion, as a coherent unit, was under the command of the Engineer Corps *(Inzherni Voinski)*.

1917

March 3 – In preparation for the Second Battle of Doiran, General Vladimir Vasov strengthened the defensive positions and fortifications of the 9th Pleven Division and amassed over 200 guns, 440 trench mortars, 550 heavy machine guns, and portable-flamethrower squads provided by the First Army Assault Battalion, attached to the 33rd Svishtov Infantry Regiment. The battle began on April 22 and continued fitfully until May 9. Although ready for action, the flamethrowers were not used.[7]

May 2 – The German military plenipotentiary in Sofia asked the *OHL* on behalf of the Bulgarian War Ministry that the training command of Assault Battalion No. 5 (Rohr) be allowed to remain in Sofia to continue its mission. Due to the heavy fighting on the western front that required the assistance of all German assault-troop instructors, the *OHL* rejected the request.[8]

May 18 – The Bulgarians used flamethrowers in combat for the first time against the French at the Red Wall, a heavily fortified defensive position at Baba Planina in Macedonia.

From March 14 the Red Wall changed hands several times. By May the Bulgarian 6th Bdin Division had prepared a decisive counterattack. First a massive artillery bombardment shattered the trenches occupied by two French infantry regiments, which were clearly visible in the rocky terrain. Under cover of the barrage, pioneers of the First Army Assault Battalion approached undetected. They attacked with hand grenades and flamethrowers, setting fire to a warehouse filled with food and drink sent by French cognac producers. The flames set off stacked ammunition, completing the devastation. When the explosions ceased, a Bulgarian infantry regiment calmly marched to the peak with fixed bayonets and took prisoner two officers and 259 men, the only survivors of the two regiments.[9]

December 16 – Order No. 1182 of the Headquarters of the Standing Army, for the supplement and reform of the material state of the Engineer Corps, stated:

> The flamethrower detachment will consist of one first lieutenant as commander, one sergeant major *(Feldfebel)*, one sergeant *(Starshi Podofitser)*, two corporals *(Mladshi Podofitseri)*, and 44 privates first class and privates.

1918

August 11 – Order No. 1578 of the Headquarters of the Standing Army, for the supplement and reform of the material state of the First Army Assault Battalion, transformed the detachments into separate companies.

Opposite
Top: Painting titled Storm Assault (1916), by Mihail Lyutov, war artist attached to the 9th Pleven Division. An assault trooper of the 14th Macedonian Infantry Regiment is equipped in the German style with steel helmet, slung M95 Austrian carbine, shovel, and grenade bags. In the background, a Kleif squad of the First Army Assault Battalion fires its weapon. The Germans gave the Bulgarians a total of six small flamethrowers during the war. Collection of National Museum of Military History, Sofia.

Bottom: Bulgarian assault pioneers training at Buczacz, Galicia, November of 1917. On the right side of the photo, a four-man Kleif squad takes the lead. Note the shell explosions in the background. The German Assault Battalion No. 8, with an attached flamethrower platoon from the Guard Reserve Pioneer Regiment, also took part in this exercise.

Poor-quality image of a Bulgarian small-flamethrower squad, armed with a Kleif M.1917 or a Wex M.1917. Note the German steel helmets.

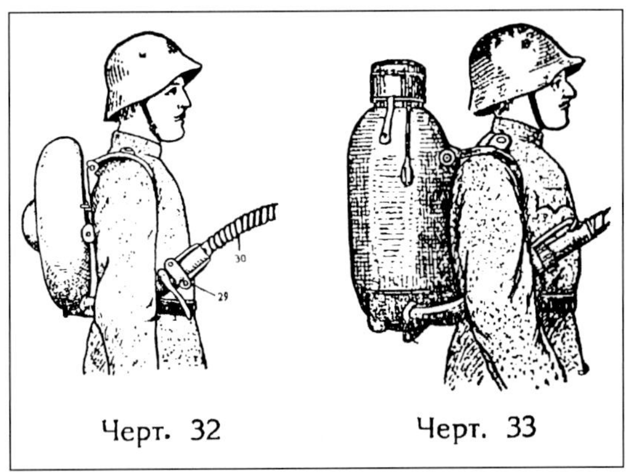

Image taken from a 1937 Bulgarian army manual, illustrating the types of flamethrowers the Bulgarians used during World War I. The Germans gave the Bulgarians two Lichtgrof M.1916 and six unidentified small flamethrowers that included the Kleif M.1917. This drawing – copied from the German postwar manual Sturmtruppen und Flammenwerfer – would seem to indicate that the Bulgarians were equipped with the Wex M.1917 as well. Courtesy Ventzislav Gramatsky.

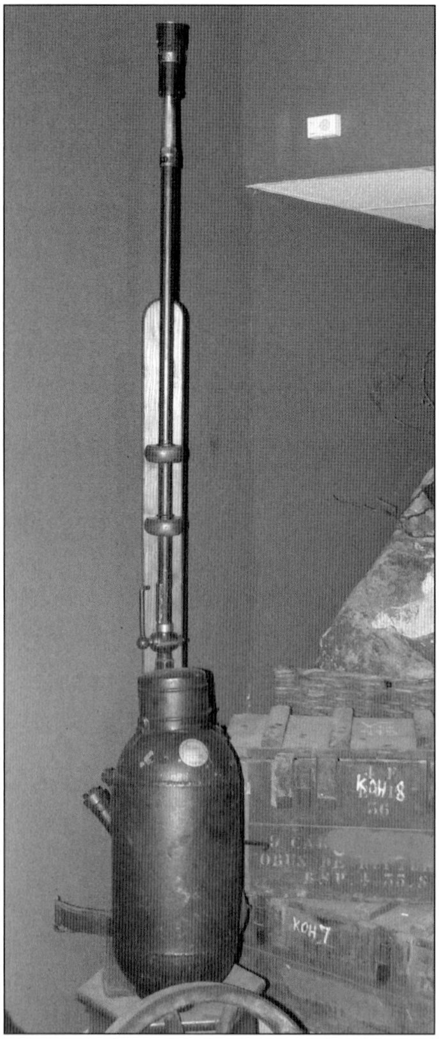

Opposite
Top left: Kleif M.1917 of the Flamethrower Company (Ognepryskachna Rota or Ognehvyrgachna Rota), First Army Assault Battalion, in the collection of the National Museum of Military History, Sofia. The M1914 1.2m lance has been mounted on a wooden support for display. Courtesy Ventzislav Gramatsky.

Top right: In this second view of the Bulgarian Kleif M.1917, note the lance stopcock handle, the rubber hose wrapped in linen and steel wire, the leather-padded carrying harness, and the prominent weld seams of the oil tank. The round orientation plaque identifies the weapon as product No. 1442, manufactured by the Fiedler-Flammenapparate-Gesellschaft m. b. H. and pressure tested on February 2, 1917. Courtesy Ventzislav Gramatsky.

Bottom: Bulgarian assault pioneers photographed at Salonica. They display a German MG08 7.92mm heavy machine gun on an improvised trench mount (left) and a Danish Madsen M1904 8mm light machine gun. Their arsenal also includes Austrian "Stutzen" carbines, German M1917 stick grenades, and a saber. The Flamethrower Company was armed with heavy and light machine guns as auxiliary weapons.

Above: Bulgarian pioneers armed with a German Granatenwerfer 16. The Bulgarian Flamethrower Company contained at least three grenade-launcher squads, one for each Light Flamethrower Detachment. In this photo, the major (mayor) kneeling on the left wears the metal winged-dragon badge on his right breast pocket, possibly identifying him as a qualified flamethrower pioneer.

The resultant Flamethrower Company *(Ognepryskachna Rota, Ognehvyrgachna Rota)* had a strength of about 120 men in four flamethrower detachments and an unknown number of machine-gun and grenade-launcher squads, likely three or four each. Armed with two flamethrowers each, the three Light Flamethrower Detachments *(Leki Ognepryskachni Otdeleniya, Leki Ognehvyrgachni Otdeleniya)* and one Heavy Flamethrower Detachment *(Tezhko Ognepryskachno Otdelenie, Tezhko Ognehvyrgachno Otdelenie)* were essentially reinforced flamethrower shock troops based on the German model. Order No. 1578 also established the 2nd Assault Battalion.

September 17-19 – The Battle of Doiran. In preparation, the area of responsibility of the 9th Pleven Division was divided into two sub-sectors of one brigade each:

The 3rd Brigade occupied the sub-sector of the right side, called *Dubski*. It was 4.7 miles wide and lay between the heights of Varovita and Dub. The 3rd Brigade was composed of the 57th Regiment, the 33rd Svishtov Regiment, and a battalion of the 34th Regiment, a total of seven battalions armed with 80 machine guns, 18 trench mortars, 56 grenade launchers, five searchlights, 18 heliographs, two howitzers, and one flamethrower of undetermined size operated by a squad from the Flamethrower Company of the First Army Assault Battalion. One company of pioneers was attached to the brigade as well.

The 1st Brigade was assigned the sub-sector of the left side, called *Doiranski*, an area 4 miles wide between the height of Dub and Lake Doiran. The 1st Brigade was made up of the 17th Dorostol Regiment and the 58th Regiment, a total of six battalions armed with 80 machine guns, 16 trench mortars, 56 grenade launchers, five searchlights, 21 heliographs and one flamethrower of undetermined size operated by a squad from the Flamethrower Company. Two companies of pioneers and three platoons of cavalry were also attached to the brigade for the mission.[10]

September 18 – At 6.30 A.M. the British attacked a Bulgarian strong point on the height of "Cerberus," where the flamethrower of the 3rd Brigade was located. The flamethrower squad was attached to the 33rd Regiment, which positioned it in a hardened shelter. Eight machine guns and 320 men of the 2nd, 11th, and 12th Companies of the 33rd Regiment defended the post. As the flamethrower squad readied its weapon to fire, British troops suddenly appeared. In the vicious hand-to-hand fighting, a Bulgarian officer was killed trying to prevent a British officer of the 12th Cheshires from throwing a hand grenade at the flamethrower. The British troops attacked the shelter, killing the garrison and destroying the flamethrower with hand grenades.[11]

Poor-quality image of pioneers of the First Army Assault Battalion training in full assault order at Doiran, September of 1918. They are equipped with German steel helmets, stick grenades, grenade bags, and slung carbines. The figure in the rear echelon, second from the right, carries a Kleif. He is part of a "Flamethrower Accompanying Squad," the duty of which was to follow behind the assault troops and mop up points of resistance.

Battered wooden mockup of a British Mark IV tank used to train Bulgarian troops in antitank tactics, including the use of flamethrowers. For such exercises, flamethrowers were often filled with water, which made them useless for combat even after they had been emptied and dried out. Given that the Bulgarians had only eight flamethrowers in total, it does not seem likely that they would have sacrificed any for water-training.

Officers and men of the 33rd Svishtov Infantry Regiment at Doiran in September of 1918. Note the German M1916 steel helmets, M1917 stick grenades, and M1915 respirators. A Lichtgrof, Kleif, or Wex squad of the Flamethrower Company, First Army Assault Battalion, was attached to this regiment for the battle. The flamethrower, placed in a hardened bunker similar to the one behind these troops, was destroyed by British hand grenades and its squad killed before it could be used. The Flamethrower Company suffered significant casualties during the battle and lost two of its eight devices.

Wex shock troop of a postwar German Freikorps, consisting of two flamethrower squads, four hand-grenade throwers, and one shock-troop leader. Note the white smoke rising from the igniter in the lance. The Flamethrower Company of the Bulgarian First Army Assault Battalion formed three Kleif and/or Wex shock troops, one for each Light Flamethrower Detachment (Leki Ognepryskachni Otdelenie or Leki Ognehvyrgachni Otdelenie).

German flamethrower pioneer transporting an empty Lichtgrof M.1916, from which the propellant tank has been removed. The Bulgarian Flamethrower Company had two such devices, which it may have carried far up into the mountainous terrain around Lake Doiran, Macedonia. Courtesy Thierry Ehret

Beyond "Cerberus" lay the ridge called "P. 4" by the British. Their advance delayed by the stiff Bulgarian opposition, the three remaining companies of the 12th Cheshires continued the assault led by a colonel. An explosion from either a mine or a hand-grenade dump caused many casualties among the British and threw them into confusion. Simultaneously they came under very heavy fire from machine-guns, trench mortars, and a flamethrower at the western end of P. 4. When the British emerged from the barrage and reached P. 4, they found the Bulgarians ready for them in the trench. As the close-quarter combat began, a bullet struck the oil tank of the flamethrower and it exploded.[12]

At Belasitsa, British and Greek troops attempted a flanking maneuver, climbing the near-vertical slopes as the men of the Bulgarian 1st Brigade, 11th Macedonian Division, watched in disbelief. When the attackers had struggled to within 70 feet of the Macedonians, "Belasitsa erupted like a volcano," the Bulgarians responding with hand grenades and heavy fire from rifles, machine guns, and a flamethrower that set the dry grass and brush ablaze.[13] The flamethrower squad was half of a Light Flamethrower Detachment of the Flamethrower Company. It was attached to either the 1st or 6th Infantry Regiment.

During the Battle of Doiran the Flamethrower and Trench-mortar Companies of the First Army Assault Battalion suffered 68 casualties: 10 other ranks killed, three officers and 25 other ranks wounded, 30 other ranks missing.[14]

September 24 – Bulgaria asked the Allies for a ceasefire.

September 29 – The kingdom signed an armistice that removed it from the war.

1919

November 27 – The Allies and the kingdom of Bulgaria signed the Treaty of Neuilly. Article 82 prohibited Bulgaria from using, manufacturing, and importing poison gas and flamethrowers.

Tactics

Assault Battalion No. 5 (Rohr) trained Bulgarian flamethrower pioneers in German tactics. (See Germany.)

OTTOMAN EMPIRE

1914

August 2 – When the Ottoman Empire mobilized, the German Military Mission in Constantinople had been reorganizing and improving the Turkish military since July of 1913. Pioneers assigned to the Mission before the war likely took with them a small number of *Kleif* and *Grof M.1912* flamethrowers and trained Turkish sappers *(Istikiam alai)* in their use, although records of this have yet to be found.

The Turks referred to the flamethrower as either "flame machine" *(alev makinası)* or "hellfire machine" *(cehennemi ateş makinası).*

***Below:** Members of the German Military Mission commanded by General-Major Otto Liman von Sanders, photographed in Turkey prior to the war. Their assignment was to train, improve, and reorganize the Ottoman military. The officer standing on the left appears to be a member of the pioneers; it is almost certain that pioneers of the Military Mission trained Turkish sappers in the use of the Kleif M.1912 and possibly the Grof M.1912, which the Turks were said to have in their arsenal at the beginning of the Battle of Gallipoli in April 1915.*

***Right:** Turkish soldier of an unidentified branch of service. Sappers wore the same M1909 khaki uniform as the infantry and artillery, occasionally with rectangular collar patches in blue. The Engineer Corps was responsible for the 30 flamethrowers that the Germans gave the Ottoman army during the war. Note the "Enver Pasha helmet" (enverieh) consisting of a strip of cloth wound around a straw frame.*

***Above:* Turkish troops mustering at Gallipoli. The Ottoman Army was equipped with flamethrowers during the Battle of Gallipoli but did not use them. It is not clear if Turkish commanders disapproved of the weapons or if they simply felt their sappers were not properly trained. The Germans were in the process of creating flame tactics when the battle began.**

***Below:* Drawing of a German pioneer armed with a *Kleif M.1912* used as a poison-gas sprayer. In 1915 the Germans trained a Turkish gas company of 200 men and armed them with *Kleif M.1912*. Some 50 of these "Gas Men" (Gazcilar) were sent to Iraq, but they never saw combat.**

1915

April 25 – Allied troops landed at Gallipoli. According to General Sir Ian Hamilton, Commander-in-Chief of the Mediterranean Expeditionary Force, the Turks were armed with flamethrowers but chose not to use them.[1] As a result members of the East Lancashire Regiment spoke highly of the chivalrous, "clean-fighting Turk."[2]

The German 3rd Guard Pioneer Battalion was established March 15 but had not yet developed effective flame tactics and would not have been ready to send instructors to Turkey. The flamethrowers the Turks had at Gallipoli would have been obsolete *Kleif M.1912* and *Grof M.1912,* the latter used by the Germans until late 1916. Training would have consisted of nothing more than instruction on how to fill the weapons with oil and propellant gas, install an igniter, open valves, and aim the lance.

As far as the East Lancashire Regiment knew, the Turks refused German offers of poison gas. However, this was not the case.

In 1915 German officers selected 200 Turkish sappers and sent them to a camp outside Istanbul, where they were trained in gas warfare.[3] Issued special German-made uniforms, masks, and tanks carried on their backs, the personnel of this company were known as the "Gas Men" *(Gazcilar)*. They were "ordered to throw gas at the enemy instead of bullets," a description which together with the details of the equipment indicates that the Turks adopted the German procedure of spraying poison gas with *Kleif M.1912* flamethrowers.

The Gas Men were warned to keep their mouths shut about their training. Fifty of them were sent to Baghdad by train in a special car segregated from the rest of the troops. At their destination, they were kept in tents in the desert, where they waited nearly a month for their six to eight flamethrowers, prohibited from interacting with other soldiers. After six months word came from Istanbul that gas would not be used in combat. The company was disbanded and the Gas Men transferred into other units.

1916

January 9 – The Turkish 19th and 20th Infantry Divisions were combined to form the XV Corps, which was sent to the eastern front in July. When it arrived in Galicia in August, the corps was assigned to the German Army South and given a 17-mile sector on the west bank of the Zlotalipa River, where it endured several months of extremely heavy fighting.[4]

August – Army South gave two *Kleif* to the XV Army Corps at Galicia.[5] Sappers of the 19th Infantry Division – likely from the 3rd Company of the 3rd Engineer Battalion – began experimenting with them.

October – Turkish officers, NCOs, and men from the XV Army Corps and the VI Army Corps (15th and 25th Infantry Divisions) at the Romanian front were sent to assault courses in Bulgaria taught by the assault battalion of the Bulgarian First Army. The course included training in flamethrowers.[6]

Sappers of the Turkish 25th Engineer Company, VI Army Corps (left), pose at Braila, Romania, with German, Austrian, and Bulgarian pioneers and sappers. The VI Army Corps sent selected officers, NCOs, and men of the 15th and 25th Engineer Companies to Bulgaria to take part in assault courses that included training in flamethrowers.

Men of the Guard Reserve Pioneer Regiment, at least two of whom are former members of Assault Battalion No. 5 (Rohr), as indicated by the higher position of their death's head sleeve badge. Assault Battalion No. 5 (Rohr) trained Turkish flamethrower sappers in Bulgaria and possibly in Galicia. The pioneer third from the left wears an Austrian M1888 haversack over his right shoulder and holds a cable drum (Kabeltrommel) for telephone wire under his left arm.

Below: Turkish Kleif shock troop (Kleifstosstrupp) of the XV Army Corps training at Rohatyn, Galicia, in late spring or early summer of 1917. Composed of two Kleif squads, four hand-grenade throwers, and two shock-troop leaders, this unit is equipped with Kleif M.1917, slung carbines, shortened shovels, rolled assault packs, and German steel helmets with cut-down brims. They are probably members of the 3rd Company, 3rd Engineer Battalion.

Opposite
Top: The lead Kleif squad. Note that the Kleif carrier wears a helmet camouflaged in vertical bands of color. It appears that all three sappers wear fire-brigade balaclavas to protect their faces from the heat. Unusually, the lance operator is equipped with a rolled assault pack and a shovel.

Bottom: The second Kleif squad and the hand-grenade throwers. More camouflaged helmets are in evidence. The man behind the Kleif carrier wears a boxlike pack seen in other photos of flamethrower shock troops, which may contain spare igniters and tools.

The sappers dispatched to Bulgaria to train in flame warfare were from the 3rd Engineer Battalion (19th Infantry Division), the 20th Engineer Battalion (20th Infantry Division), the 15th Engineer Company (15th Infantry Division), and the 25th Engineer Company (25th Infantry Division). Some of these men also attended Austrian-German assault courses in Galicia, particularly during the winter months.

1917

January – The XV Corps formed two divisional assault companies.[7] The assault company of the 19th Infantry Division included a *Kleif* shock troop of two flamethrower squads, the personnel of which were probably sappers of the 3rd Company, 3rd Engineer Battalion.

Spring or summer – The Turkish *Kleif* shock troop trained at an Austro-German camp at Rohatyn, Galicia.

June 29-July 7 – The XV Corps took part in the Battle of Brczany in Sector Rohatyn, aided by the German 4th Ersatz Division, the 15th and 75th Reserve Divisions, elements of the 241st Infantry Division, Assault Battalion No. 8, the Austro-Hungarian XXV Corps, and the 4th Company of the Guard Reserve Pioneer Regiment. It is not known if the Turkish *Kleif* shock troop of the 19th Infantry Division assault company saw combat, as it may have been only a demonstration and training contingent.

August – The XV Corps returned to Turkey, taking with it the *Kleif* shock troop. No further information has been discovered about this apparently unique unit.

In 1917 the Turkish Engineer Corps received a total of four flamethrowers from the Germans.[8]

Above: Flamethrower squad training at Rohatyn; most are Germans, but the man furthest to the left is a Turk in a cut-down helmet. This is likely a Kleif squad being observed by a Turkish officer of the 3rd Engineer Battalion.

Below: German pioneer modeling a Kleif M.1917. It is not known how many models of flamethrower the Turks had besides the Kleif M.1912 and M.1917. The Germans shipped 30 flamethrowers to Turkey during the war, a number that may have included at least ten different large and small devices. Courtesy Thierry Ehret

1918

Spring – The Turkish 48th Infantry Division conducted training in the employment of machine guns, hand grenades, and flamethrowers at facilities on the Jordan River on the Palestine front.[9] It is likely that the flamethrower sappers who attended the course belonged to the 4th Engineer Battalion. However, the Turks did not use flamethrowers in combat in the Middle Eastern theater.

October 30 – The Ottoman Empire and the Allies signed the Armistice of Mudros, which terminated hostilities.

During the war the Germans gave the Turks a total of 30 flamethrowers.[10] The only models which can be identified from descriptions and photos are the *Kleif M.1912* and *Kleif M.1917*.

Right: Turkish assault sappers dictating letters home to a professional writer, probably in Jerusalem. The light-colored patches on their collars are blue, and the knees of their trousers have been reinforced. In the spring of 1918 the Turkish 48th Division, assigned to the Jordan Valley, conducted courses in assault tactics, during which sappers trained with flamethrowers. The weapons were not used in combat.

***Above:* German Kleif shock troop rolling up a mock trench. The single Turkish Kleif shock troop was organized and equipped identically, except that the flamethrower in this image (far right) is the late-model Kleif M.1915. Note that the second Kleif squad is not visible, since it would be following the assault trooper in the center foreground.**

***Right:* British soldier demonstrating how a single man could operate the Wex if the three other members of the squad were put out of action. The Kleif, however, was too unwieldy for one man. In 1918 the Turkish 48th Division may have trained with Wex in the Jordan Valley. File #T70628, Record Group 175, U.S. National Archives.**

1920

August 10 – The Allies and the Ottoman Empire signed the Treaty of Sèvres. Article 176 prohibited Turkey from using, manufacturing, and importing poison gas and flamethrowers. The treaty was rejected by the Grand National Assembly of Turkey (GNA), led by Mustafa Kemal Atatürk, former general of the Ottoman army, who commanded Turkish forces in the war of independence against the occupying Allies.

1923

July 24 – The Allies and the GNA signed the Treaty of Lausanne. It contained no articles restricting Turkey's acquisition or development of flamethrowers.

Tactics

The Turkish *Kleif* shock troop would have been used mainly to roll up trenches, as shown in the only known photo of the unit. (See Germany.)

In the Jordan Valley in 1918 the sappers would likely have trained as both shock troops for spearheading attacks and flame-accompanying squads for mopping up. They may also have practiced using flamethrowers in an antitank role.

PART TWO:
THE ALLIED POWERS

French P_4 flamethrower squad (left) at Cantigny on May 28, 1918, during the first major American offensive of the war. A German soldier emerges from an underground shelter in the center, smoked out by the flamethrower, while an American doughboy watches from the right. U.S. National Archives 111-SC-95832.

FRANCE

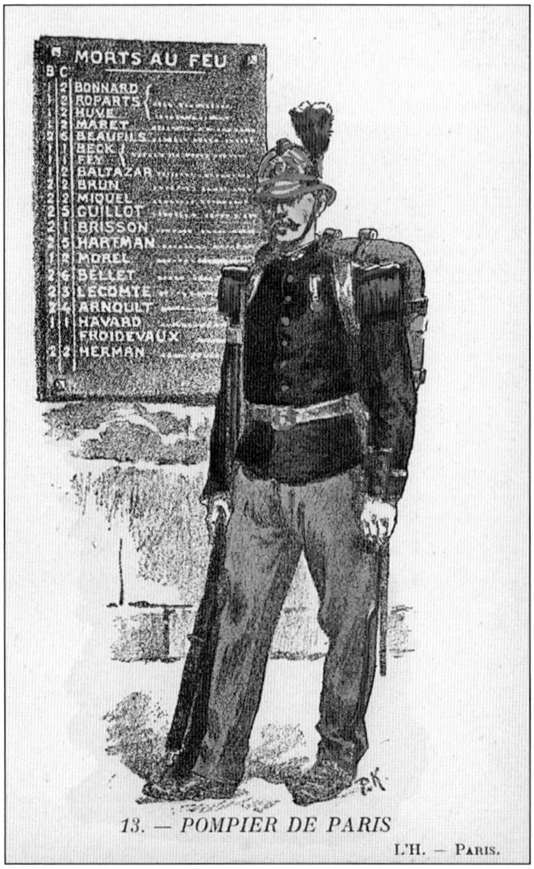

Member of the Paris Firefighting Sapper Regiment (Régiment des Sapeurs-Pompiers de Paris), in dark-blue M1897 service tunic, blue-gray trousers, and brass helmet. The Paris firefighting sappers formed the first flamethrower company, Compagnie Schilt 22/7, in the 22nd Battalion of the 1st Engineer Regiment (1er Régiment du Génie) on May 1, 1915.

1915

March 27 – Jean and George Hersent and Julien Thirion patented a large wheeled flamethrower *(lance-flammes)* that was not adopted by the French army. It may have influenced a Russian design. (See Russia, "General Ershov System.")

May 1 – *Compagnie Schilt 22/7,* the first flamethrower company, was formed in the 1st Engineer Regiment *(1er Régiment du Génie).* It was established in the 22nd Battalion of the regiment and named after Captain Victor Alexandre Joseph Schilt of the Paris Firefighting Sapper Regiment *(Régiment des Sapeurs Pompiers de Paris),* inventor of the first French flamethrowers and originator of flame tactics.[1] The total number of companies per engineer battalion was not fixed and fluctuated depending on the requirements of the Engineer Corps. Schilt Companies were also called "Special Companies" *(Compagnies Speciale).*

In the same month the French army adopted its first flamethrowers, the Schilt No. 1 static device and the Schilt No. 2 semi-portable, initially called a portable weapon. Flamethrower sappers trained at Camp de Satory, near Versailles.

May 19 – Jean and Georges Hersent and Julien Thirion offered a second model of large, wheeled flamethrower to the French Minister of War, who accepted it. This weapon was adopted in modified form by the Italians and served as the basis for both of the large British flamethrowers that saw action from 1916.

May 20 – Schilt Company 22/6 was established in the 1st Engineer Regiment.

June 1 – Schilt Company 22/5 was established in the 1st Engineer Regiment. Schilt Companies 22/8 and 22/9 were established at unknown dates in 1915.

June 6 – The French carried out their first flamethrower attack. Fifty firefighters of the Paris Firefighting Sapper Regiment used 18 Schilt No. 1 flamethrowers against German positions at Vauquois. The assault failed when the wind blew the flames back into the French positions, exploding ammunition and flamethrowers. Losses were substantial: 18 wounded and one killed among the firefighters; 24 dead, 109 wounded, and six missing among the troops.[2]

June 7 – According to American newspapers:

> Reports received from the Flanders front today state that the French have resorted to the use of liquid fire in their efforts to check the German advance. Hundreds of Germans are reported to have been burned to death in the trenches before they could escape from the flaming wave of oil which rolled in upon them.[3]

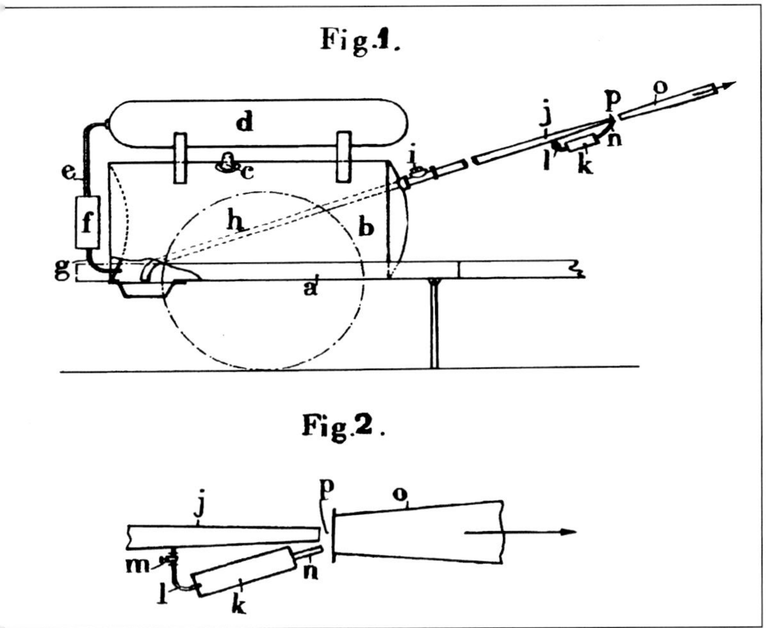

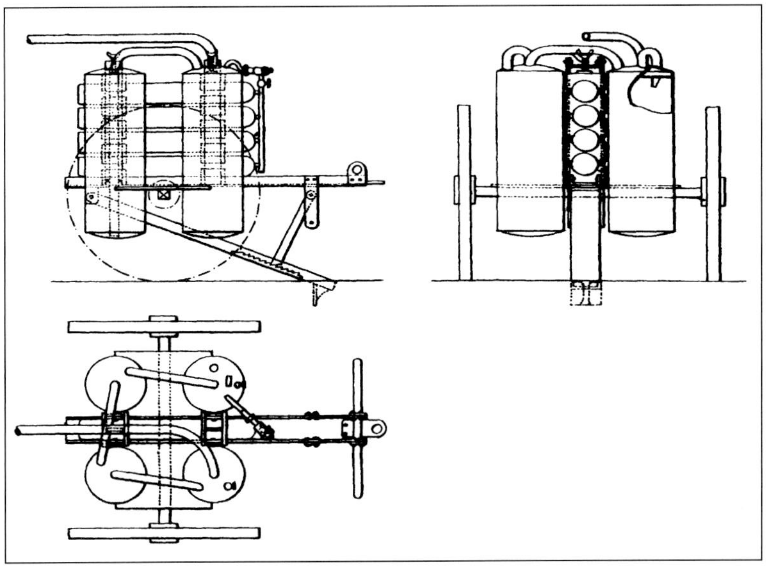

Left: Flamethrower patented by Jean and Georges Hersent and Julien Thirion on March 27, 1915. Although not adopted by the French, it may have influenced a Russian design (See Russia.): a) trolley; b) oil reservoir; c) safety valve; d) propellant bottle; e) propellant feed line; f) propellant release valve; g) propellant feed line; h) pipe for filling oil reservoir and ejecting oil; i) oil-filler stopcock; j) nozzle; k) reservoir for ignition fluid to inject into oil stream; l) pipe; m) valve; n) ignition-fluid injecting pipe; o) conical tube; p) gap for admitting air to be mixed with oil and ignition fluid. From British patent No. 7524.

Right: Hersent-Thirion flamethrower, adopted by the French army in May of 1915. Served by a six-man squad, it was also used by the Italians and was the basis for two large British flamethrower designs. From British patent No. 15,581.

June – The organization of the Schilt Companies was formalized:[4]

The strength of a company was three officers; two adjutants; 95 sergeants, corporals, and sappers; and 18 motor-transport troops.

Each company was comprised of three 27-man "firing" or combat sections *(sections de feu)* and one noncombatant section *(section hors rang);* flamethrower sappers were nicknamed *petroleurs*.

A combat section was armed with 12 flamethrowers and divided into three squads, each under the command of a sergeant and equipped with enough weapons for two combat posts. Each combat post, commanded by an NCO or corporal, had two flamethrowers, giving each Schilt Company a total of 18 Schilt No. 1 static devices and 18 Schilt No. 2 semi-portable devices. Each section covered a front 330 ft. wide.

The noncombatant section was composed of two squads: one engineer squad that carried out general duties and served as replacements for the flamethrower sappers, and one motor-transport squad:

1st Section – 1st, 2nd, and 3rd Squads.
2nd Section – 4th, 5th, and 6th Squads.
3rd Section – 7th, 8th, and 9th Squads.
Noncombatant Section – 10th and 11th Squads.

Each Schilt Company was equipped with two touring cars and seven trucks.

As personal arms sappers were issued the M1892 carbine with 78 rounds each; NCOs were given 36 rounds. The company sergeant major was armed with the M1884 NCO's saber and M1892 revolver with 18 rounds.

Late 1915 – The mission and scope of duties of flamethrower companies were formalized:[5]

1. Assignments of the Schilt Companies:

The flamethrower companies are attached to the engineer troops. They do not become a part of larger units. They are forces assigned to the army groups and placed with care, temporarily and according to their needs, at the disposal of the armies, army corps, and divisions.

For the execution of operations, the flamethrower companies are ultimately put at the disposal of infantry divisions.

Right: Lance operator of the Paris Firefighting Sapper Regiment. French flamethrower sappers wore firefighters' leather jackets and occasionally their dark-blue uniforms. Note the crested brass helmet, which served as the basis for the Adrian steel helmet adopted by the French armed forces in 1915.

Far right: Sapeur Bertrand of the 1st Engineer Regiment, wearing the light blue (bleu clair) adopted in late 1914 and popularly called "horizon blue." His single-breasted M1915 greatcoat (capote) features non-regulation breast pockets, and he has used pieces of dark cloth to cover the numbers on his collar patches (pattes de collet de troupe) and on the front of his cap (képi). This very unusual precaution indicates that he is likely a flamethrower sapper of the 22nd Battalion, as the French army kept its Schilt Companies shrouded in secrecy throughout the war.

Below: Metal engineer helmet badge (top) and collar patches of the 1st Engineer Regiment. The cloth patches – black with scarlet braids (soutaches) and numerals – were mandated on December 9, 1914, and sewn to the collars of both the tunic (vareuse) and greatcoat. Sappers also wore trousers with black piping on the outer seams.

Above: Schilt No. 1, the first flamethrower of the French army, adopted in May of 1915; this photo dates from the spring of that year. A static weapon, it was served by a three-man squad: one sapper lance-operator (sapeur porte-lance) who aimed the triggerless lance; one sapper-mechanic (sapeur-mécanicien) who filled the oil tank and fired the weapon by opening the propellant valve; and one sapper-grenadier (sapeur-grenadier) who either tied fuses to the lance and lit them, or threw incendiary grenades at the target. The captain in the foreground of this image appears to wear the experimental tunic in blue gray (bleu cendré) and the pre-war red trousers and cap. In the background is a sapper in a dark-blue M1877 greatcoat and red cap, while the lance operator is outfitted in white cotton fatigues.

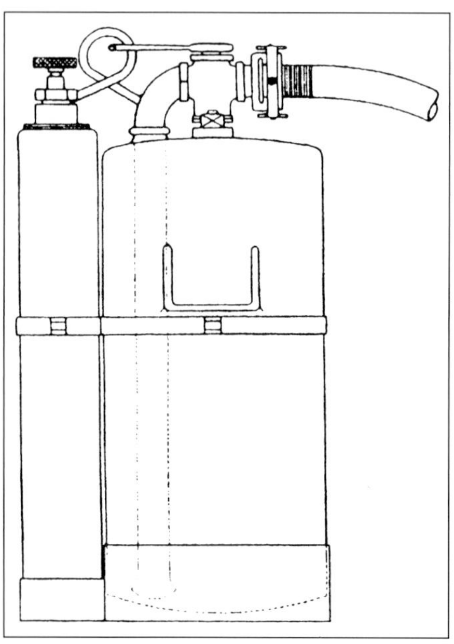

Left: Schilt No. 1 bis, a smaller, lighter version of the Schilt No. 1 introduced because the original weapon was too heavy and unwieldy. As part of the modification, the propellant tank was attached to the flamethrower with a metal band. The capacity was reduced from 21 gallons to 14.5, the laden weight from 276 lbs. to 187. Each of the three combat sections of a flamethrower company consisted of three squads, each with enough weapons for two combat posts. There were two flamethrowers for each post, giving each Schilt Company a total of 18 Schilt No. 1 heavy devices and 18 Schilt No. 2 semi-portable devices. Each section covered a front 330 ft. wide.

Sappers of a Schilt Company training with Schilt No. 1 flamethrowers. They wear tunics in both dark blue and horizon blue. The M1914 cap was horizon blue, while the red pre-war version was issued with a dark-blue cover. This photo is often misidentified as French soldiers testing captured German flamethrowers.

Any flamethrower company available to an infantry division is considered to be in operation. As soon as the operations in that division are finished, when the infantry division is located, the company receives from the army corps an assignment to the new army corps or is made available to the army.

In particular, if because of loss of personnel or material or for any other reason the company is not immediately usable, it is returned to the disposal of the army, which will decide its next destination and determine under which conditions it will be used.

Apart from the periods of operations, the company improves its instruction, takes part in the instruction of infantry units that can be exceptionally employed in this work. In this last case, it must left for two days per week at the disposal of its chief in order to perform the exercises that will maintain its training for combat.

2. General administration of the flamethrower companies; reports; supplies.

A. Administration. The flamethrower companies assigned to an army depend, from the point of view of material and personnel, on the Commander of Engineers of the army, who has with respect to them the rights and prerogatives of a chief of corps. The commander of engineers of the army does not intervene in the preparation and the execution of the operations, which are entirely the responsibility of the infantry units at which disposal the flamethrower companies are put.

During operations with an infantry division, the commander of engineers of the division receives but does not act on the requests of material and personnel; he forwards them through the army corps to the Commander of Engineers of the army, who issues the orders that fulfill the requests.

The officers of the companies or the fractions of a company available to an infantry unit obligatorily receive from the chief of that unit the notes of appreciation of the conduct of special operations which they carried out under its orders: these notes are transmitted through the hierarchy to the Commander of Engineers of the army with the propositions of awards for the officers and the troops, at the time of the detachments of the flamethrower company leave the units with which they operated.

Because of the special recruitment of the flamethrower companies and the provisional nature of their attachment to an Army, the changes of corps concerning the personnel of these units are made by the General-in-Chief.

Flamethrower sapper of the 1st Engineer Regiment and girlfriend. He wears the M1915 tunic and semi-breeches in horizon blue, the latter with black piping on the outer seams. The black M1914 collar patches with scarlet numbers and braids are seen to good advantage. This "petroleur" has also been awarded the Croix de Guerre with two stars.

Complete Hersent-Thirion flamethrower consisting of wheeled carriage that supported four oil tanks, four propellant tanks, and fixed lance. Behind it are the hose sections that connected the flamethrower to the eight extra oil tanks in the foreground. Although the weapon had an impressive range, it was cumbersome and not cost effective, leading the French to withdraw it from service in late 1916.

These sappers of an unidentified engineer unit wear white cotton fatigues and display the personal arms and accouterments issued to flamethrower operators, including 8mm M1892 Berthier carbine and bayonet, M1914 Lebel rifle equipment in leather, and M1915 Adrian steel helmet with engineer badge on the front.

B. Reports. After each operation, the commander of the flamethrower company gives to the infantry division with which it operated a report that is transmitted through official channels to the Army General Staff *[Gran Quartier-Général],* 3rd Office.

Moreover, the first of each month, the commander of the company establishes a summary record on the use of the company during the previous month; this report is transmitted through official channels to the Army General Staff. (3rd Office).

Reports on operations and periodic reports are communicated through the Army to the Commander of Engineers of the army.

C. Supply. Requests for personnel and material made by the commander of the flamethrower company are made to the Commander of Engineers of the army, who forwards them to:

1. The Army General Staff 1st Office, through the Army 4th Office, for that which relates to technical material:

2. The Army 1st Office for personnel and the 4th Office for material other than technical.

Requests for resupply of personnel received by the army are transmitted through official channels to the army to which the Training Company is attached, as this company constitutes the replacement depot of these special units. The deteriorated technical material is sent to the Chief of the Central Establishment for Chemical War Material *(Établissement Central du Matèriel Chimique de Guerre)* in Paris; it is accompanied with a detailed statement.

Above: Sapuer Louis Ceillon of the 1st Engineer Regiment, battalion unknown. Although he wears the M1915 greatcoat, his tunic is the dark-blue M1877. His collar patches are of the lozenge shape mandated in January of 1917. Like the M1914 patches they were black for the engineers, with scarlet braids and numerals. Note the brass number "1" on the cap.

Below: Schilt No. 2, captured by the Germans on March 3, 1916, and displayed by men of Pioneer Battalion No. 29. The three-man squad consisted of a sapper lance-operator who aimed the triggerless lance at the end of the 5m (16ft.) hose; a sapper-mechanic who filled the fuel tank and fired the weapon by opening the propellant valve; and a sapper-grenadier who attached and lit the fuses or threw incendiary grenades at the target. As in the case of the Schilt No. 1, the Schilt No. 2 was deployed in combat posts each armed with two weapons and under the command of an NCO or corporal. Each of the three combat sections of a flamethrower company consisted of three squads that were each equipped with enough weapons for two combat posts. A section covered a front 330ft. wide.

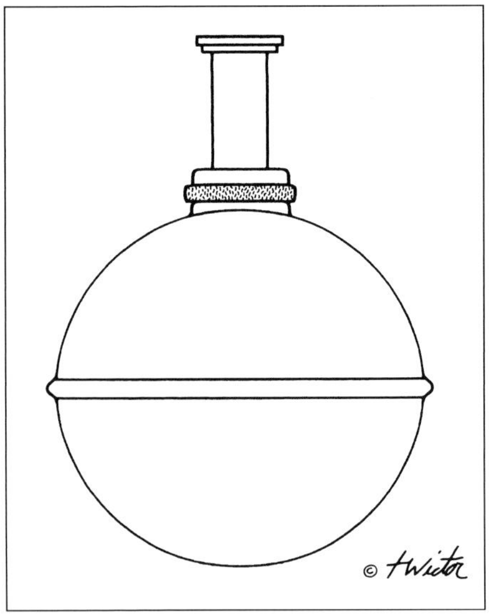

Left: French Model 1916 AB incendiary and smoke grenade (Grenade Incendiaire Et Fumigene AB Modele 1916), used with flamethrowers. The sapper-grenadier of a flamethrower squad was armed with five or six incendiary grenades, which he threw to about 50 ft. in front of the flamethrower sapper.

Men of the 6th Company, 1st Engineer Regiment, photographed in the postwar period. The sign reads "It's Room 40," a reference to quarters in a barracks. Most wear wartime outfits of white cotton fatigues over M1915 tunics and the horizon-blue M1915 side cap (Bonnet de police). The two corporals (caporaux) on either end wear the M1915 greatcoat and dark-blue cap (left) and M1921 tunic and black cap. Although the last of the flamethrower companies was disbanded in April of 1919, men of the 1st Engineer Regiment became flamethrower instructors for the infantry.

A mass French flamethrower attack, likely with Schilt No. 2 devices. The streams of oil appear to be unlit, indicating that incendiary grenades are being used for ignition.

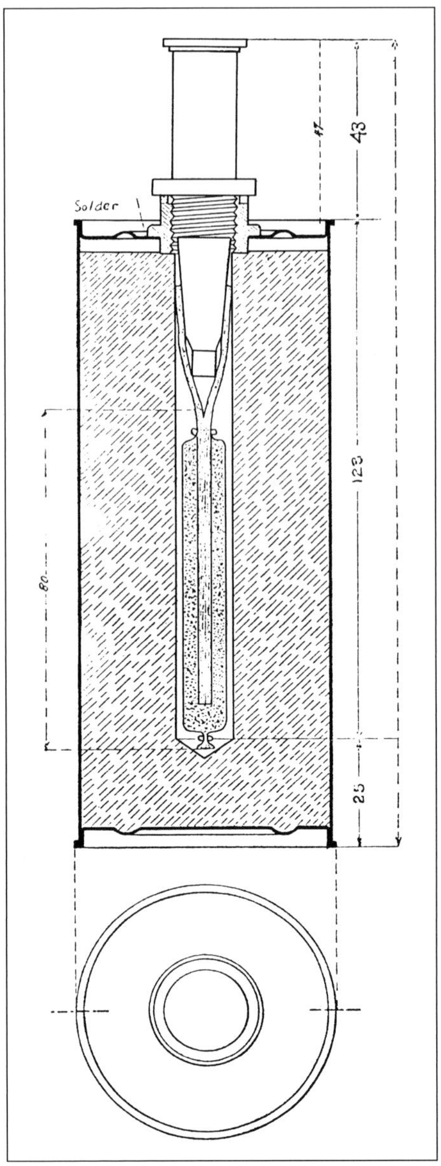

Left: French thermite grenade (Grenade Incendiaire Modele 1916), which was sometimes filled with "Calorite" or thermite bound with water glass. Like the Model 1916 AB grenade, it was fitted with the Bouchon percussion detonator.

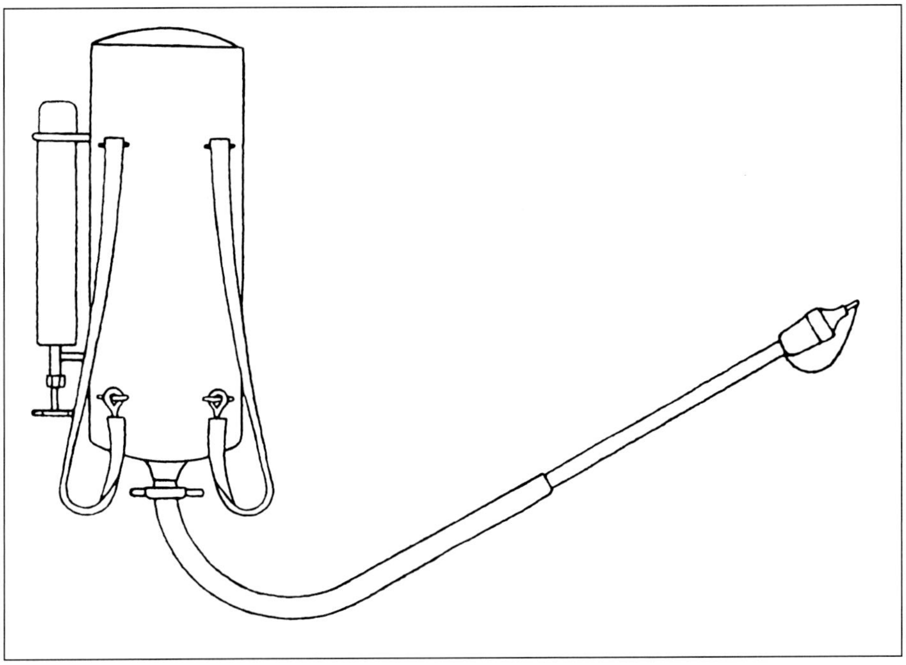

Schilt No. 3, the first portable flamethrower of the French army, adopted in August of 1915. It was served by a three-man squad: a sapper-carrier (sapeur-porteur) who aimed the lance with his left hand; a sapper-mechanic who opened the propellant valve, which simultaneously pressurized and sprayed the gasoline-oil mix; and a sapper-grenadier, who attached fuses to the nozzle or threw incendiary grenades. The Schilt No. 3 had many shortcomings, the most severe of which was its inability to fire intermittent bursts. When the propellant valve was opened, all of the oil was sprayed in a single rush.

August – The French army adopted its first portable flamethrower, the Schilt No. 3, served by a three-man squad of sapper-carrier *(sapeur-porteur),* sapper-mechanic *(sapeur-mécanicien)* and sapper-grenadier *(sapeur-grenadier).* It was not a successful model. Each combat section of a Schilt Company was armed with 12 Schilt No. 3, for a total of 36 per company. Squads were deployed in pairs.

September 25 – Schilt Company 22/5 used the Schilt No. 3 for the first time in combat, accompanying the 22nd Infantry Regiment in an assault on a sector called "The Pocket" *("La Poche"),* west of Perthe-les-Hurlus. The flamethrower sappers went in with the first wave to take the German front-line trenches and then cleaned out shelters while the infantry moved on to the second line of trenches. A total of 180 prisoners were captured, of which 13 were badly burned.

October 18 – Schilt Company 22/10 was established in the 1st Engineer Regiment.

December 23 – Schilt Company 22/11, the seventh and final flamethrower company, was established in the 1st Engineer Regiment.

December 25 – The Flamethrower Training Company *(Compagnie d'Instruction des Lance-flammes)* was established in the 1st Engineer Regiment. It also supplied replacements for Schilt Companies 22/5 to 22/11.

Schilt No. 3 captured by the Germans. Note the stiffness of the rubber hose, another of the weapon's many drawbacks. The flamethrower is in the upside-down traveling position; its top has been painted a dark camouflage color, necessary for when the operator inadvertently exposed the weapon in a trench or shell hole.

1916

April – The Schilt No. 3 bis portable flamethrower replaced the Schilt No. 3. A three-man squad consisting of sapper-carrier, sapper-mechanic, and sapper-grenadier served the new weapon, which had a longer range than its predecessor and the ability to fire intermittent bursts.

April 10 – An unidentified Schilt Company attacked a salient in the German line, which was protected by multiple firing posts. French assault troops followed by flamethrower sappers rushed the salient behind an artillery barrage. All but 15 of the Germans were killed, and the survivors were taken prisoner. As the flamethrowers laid down a "curtain of fire," the infantry retreated without incurring losses.[6]

April 29 – At 3:00 P.M. Schilt Company 22/8 raided a German trench at Four de Paris after an artillery barrage. The flamethrower sappers assaulted the enemy line with the infantry and used their Schilt No. 3 bis and incendiary grenades on three shelters. All of the Germans inside were killed, either burned or asphyxiated. At a signal, the flamethrower sappers fired their weapons and threw incendiary grenades to cover the French retreat.[7]

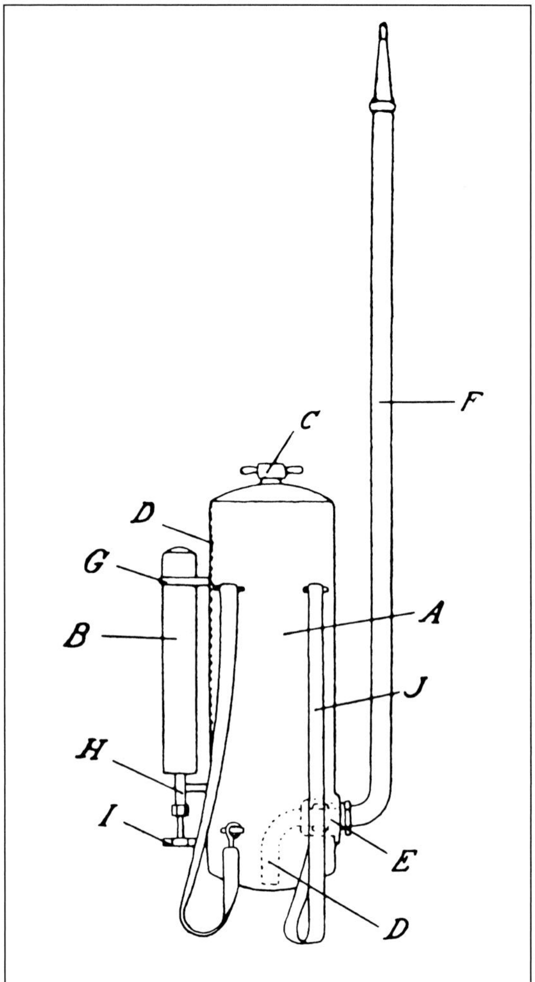

Late-model Schilt No. 3, which essentially consisted of the early model turned upside down, the hose and lance replaced with a rigid, swiveling lance: A) oil tank; B) propellant bottle; C) oil filler cap; D) outflow pipe; E) rotating joint; F) lance; G) retaining ring; H) tap; I) handle; J) shoulder straps.

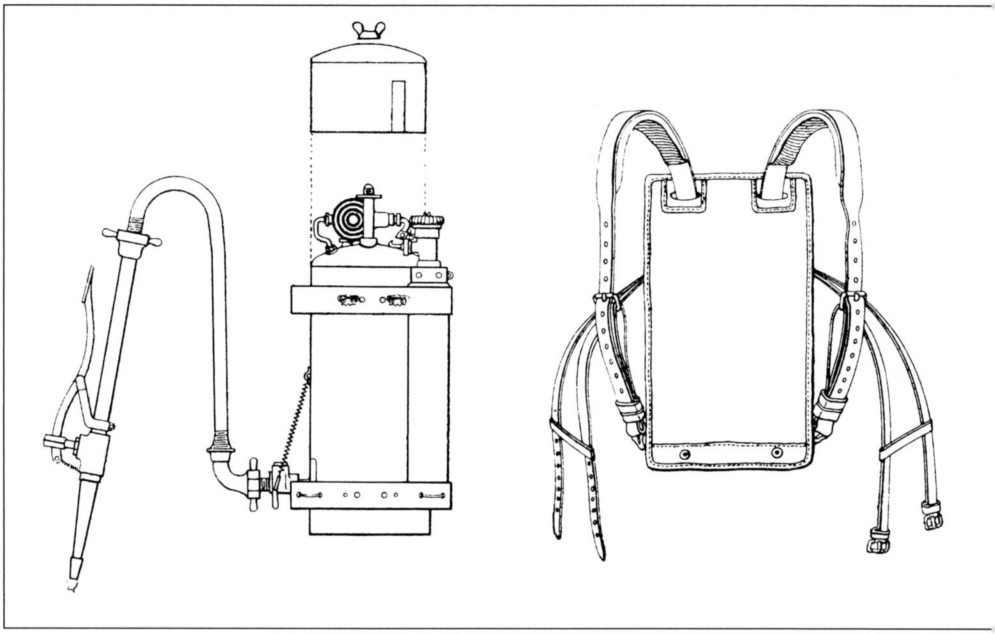

Schilt No. 3 bis portable flamethrower, adopted in October of 1916. It replaced an earlier, experimental twin-tank Schilt No. 3 bis, which itself replaced the unsuccessful Schilt No. 3. The lance – operated with the right hand only – was capable of firing multiple bursts and incorporated a self-closing valve that prevented the sapper from spraying his comrades if he were wounded or killed. This valve was so successful that the Germans copied it. The protective cover for the pressure gauge and oil-filler cap was often eliminated in combat. A three-man squad of sapper-carrier, sapper-mechanic, and sapper-grenadier served each Schilt No. 3 bis.

July 1916 – Captain Schilt introduced the one-handed lance for the Schilt No. 3 bis, which freed up the operator's left hand. The lance incorporated a safety valve that shut off the flow of oil if the operator were wounded or killed.

September 12 – Schilt Company 22/10 was attached to the 15th Colonial Infantry Division to carry out an operation between Barleux and Berny-en-Santerre, using Schilt No. 3 bis. Section L advanced with the infantry and threw hand grenades but was repulsed three times in succession by obstinate enemy resistance. The French sappers were finally victorious when they used a flamethrower against a shelter in the Poivre trench, capturing 40 prisoners.[8]

September 15 – Schilt Company 22/8, armed with Schilt No. 3 bis, was attached to the *21e Bataillon de Chasseurs à Pied.* After a thorough artillery barrage, the attack began at 3:45. The sappers divided into two groups and breached the German barricades with incendiary grenades and flamethrowers. By taking the assigned objective, the sappers facilitated the approach of the 21st *Chasseurs,* who advanced over open ground. When threatened with flamethrowers, the Germans remaining in the shelters surrendered, and about 250 prisoners were taken.[9]

September 25 – General Joseph Joffre, Commander-in-Chief of the French army, requested a portable incendiary device for clearing dugouts. This became the J_1 incendiary can *(Bidon incendiaire* J_1*).*

October – The modified Schilt No. 3 bis with the one-handed lance had replaced all portable flamethrowers in French service.

Late 1916 – Experiments were done on equipping St. Chamond tanks with flamethrowers. One flamethrower consisting of a lance, hose, and a 24-gal. reservoir was mounted on each side of the tank. The devices were operated by means of a stopcock on the lance, which featured an oxyacetylene blowpipe as the ignition system. Although 70 to 80 flame jets with a range of 66-82 ft. were achieved, the ignition system was not reliable, and the flamethrower tank never went into production.

November 7 – The large Hersent-Thirion flamethrower was withdrawn from the front due to its excessive use of oil and the large number of men and vehicles needed to transport it.

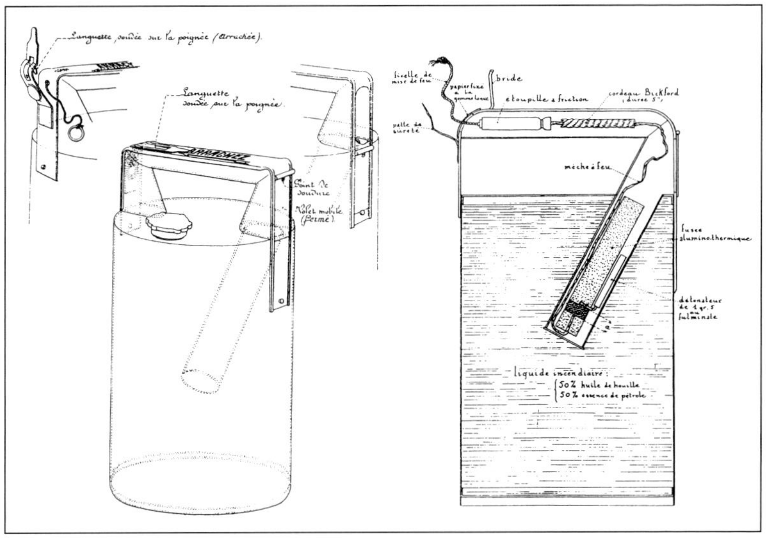

Top

Left: Schilt No. 3 bis fitted with the nine-minute F_9 fuse, attached beneath the lance. As the fuse was consumed, a spring pushed the remainder forward in a metal tube, ensuring that the burning section remained at the mouth of the lance nozzle. The protective top has been removed from the flamethrower; note, too, that the knapsack harness lacks a waist belt, utilizing chest straps instead as a method of evenly distributing the weight of the device.

Right: J_1 incendiary can (Bidon incendiaire J_1), used by flamethrower sappers and flamethrower-trained mortar crews to clear out underground shelters. This three-quart can contained a mixture of 50 percent oil and 50 percent gasoline; inside the handle was a friction primer that ignited a six-second Bickford fuse, which in turn set off a cord fuse and alumino-thermic fuse that activated the fulminate detonator. The detonator burst the can and spread the burning liquid. Special metal handles with hooks were issued, allowing one man to carry up to four 7lb. incendiary cans.

Left: Early St. Chamond tank. In 1916 the French experimented with mounting two flamethrowers in one of these armored vehicles. The flamethrowers each had a 24-gal. reservoir and featured oxyacetylene blowpipes to ignite the oil jets. A range of 66 to 82 ft. was achieved, but the flamethrower tank was abandoned because the ignition system could not be made to work reliably.

December – Sergeant Léon Chapal of the 1st Engineer Regiment produced a twin-tank flamethrower. Although the French rejected the device, Lieutenant Colonel Amos A. Fries of the American 30th Engineers accepted 25 of them as a gift of Chapal's father. Later American designs may have been influenced by Chapal's weapon.

1917

April – The 1st Engineer Regiment had become so large and unwieldy that several of its battalions were split off and designated the 21st Engineer Regiment, a temporary formation. Due to revisions, modifications, and bureaucratic interference, at least one Schilt Company – 22/5 – was listed as belonging to both regiments simultaneously. The issue was never adequately resolved, leaving army records in a state of confusion.

May 5 – Minister of War Paul Painlevé wrote to the Ministry of Armaments that he wanted to send one Schilt Company to the Army of the East, but the unit needed a flamethrower smaller and lighter than the Schilt No. 3 bis.

June 25 – French flamethrower sappers were used to clear the Dragon's Cave, a series of fortified grottos under the German trenches at Hurtebise. The position was too close to French lines for artillery preparation. Flamethrower sappers assaulted the machine-gun nests guarding the main shaft of the cave while the northern exit was sealed with howitzer fire directed by aircraft. Infantry advanced behind the flamethrower sappers and captured the machine-gun positions before they could fire.[10]

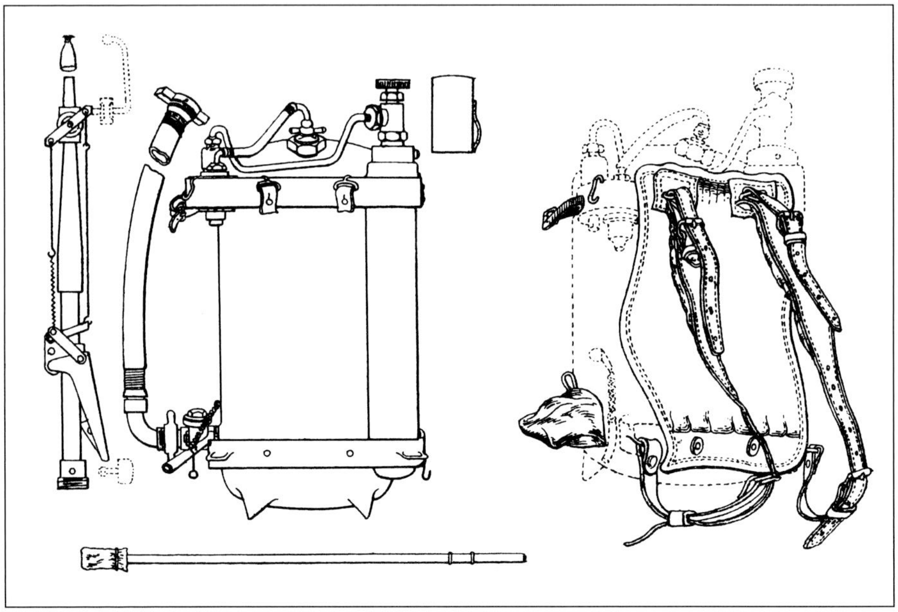

Above: Sappers of a Schilt Company unloading Schilt No. 3 bis flamethrowers at a demonstration for American infantry officers. They wear the horizon-blue tunic and M1915 Adrian helmet and carry M1892 Berthier carbines. The officer on the left is armed with a holstered M1892 Lebel 8mm "Revolver d' ordonnance." U.S. National Archives 111-SC-3275.

Left: French P_3 portable flamethrower, a smaller and lighter version of the Schilt No. 3 bis created in response to an order of June 30, 1917. A two-man squad of sapper-carrier and sapper-mechanic served the device. The small lance had a spring-loaded self-closing valve and could be fitted either with the eight-second F_2 fuse or the nine-minute F_9 fuse, illustrated at the bottom of the drawing. Held in position by the clamps shown in dotted outline, the F_9 contained an internal spring that pushed the burning section forward so that it remained beneath the nozzle to ignite the oil jet.

June 30 – Echoing the desire of the Minister of War, Commander-in-Chief General Robert Nivellle requested a smaller, lighter portable flamethrower from the Ministry of Armaments, to replace the Schilt No. 3 bis. The Inspectorate of Chemical Research and Experiments *(Inspection des Etudes et Expériences Chimiques)* eventually produced the P_3 flamethrower. This was followed soon afterward by a smaller version called the P_4.

August – The Inspectorate for Chemical Research and Experiments introduced the J_1 incendiary can.

Late 1917 – Organization of a Schilt Company:

One staff, three combat sections, one material park. A combat section was divided into two half-sections, each under the command of a sergeant.

Effectives were three officers, 137 NCOs and men.

The material park contained one mobile kitchen, one touring car, six trucks of 2 1/2 or 3 tons, one light truck, and one motorcycle.

Weapons included one L_1 static flamethrower, three L_2 static flamethrowers, and 70 P_3 portable flamethrowers.

A flamethrower company could put into operation 40 P_3 flamethrowers (six half-sections armed with six or seven flamethrowers each), leaving a permanent reserve of 30 flamethrowers in the park at all times.

Mortar squads of infantry regiments were often instructed in the use of portable flamethrowers and J_1 incendiary cans. However, only flamethrower sappers were allowed to operate the L_1 and L_2 apparatuses.

French flamethrower sapper using a P_4 at Cantigny, May 28, 1918. He wears the horizon-blue greatcoat with two dark-blue sleeve chevrons that indicate 18 months' service. The lance is fitted with the nine-minute F_9 fuse. This sapper has two water bottles, and he would have been armed with an automatic pistol as well. He wears leather gloves to protect his hands from the heat given off by the lance. A two-man squad of sapper-carrier and sapper-mechanic served the P_4.

Left: French infantry mortar squad. From 1917, French doctrine called for mortar crews to be trained in the use of portable flamethrowers and J_1 incendiary cans when there were not enough sappers available for a particular operation.

October 3 – The 39th Army Corps wrote "Plan for the Employment of Z Units," which stated that caves would be cleared by flamethrower squads working in conjunction with Cleaner Detachments "Z" *(Détachements de Nettoyeur "Z"),* poison-gas sappers of the "Z" Companies *(Compagnies "Z").* Like the Schilt Companies, the 12 "Z" Companies were part of the 1st Engineer Regiment. Numbered 31/1 to 31/4, 32/1 to 32/3, 33/1 to 33/3, 34/1 and 34/2, they used gas cylinders and explosives when clearing caves with flamethrower sappers.[11]

November – The Inspectorate of Chemical Research and Experiments produced the F_9 fuse, which burned for nine minutes and allowed the P_3 and P_4 flamethrowers to fire multiple shots. To activate it, the sapper pulled a cord that set off a friction primer.

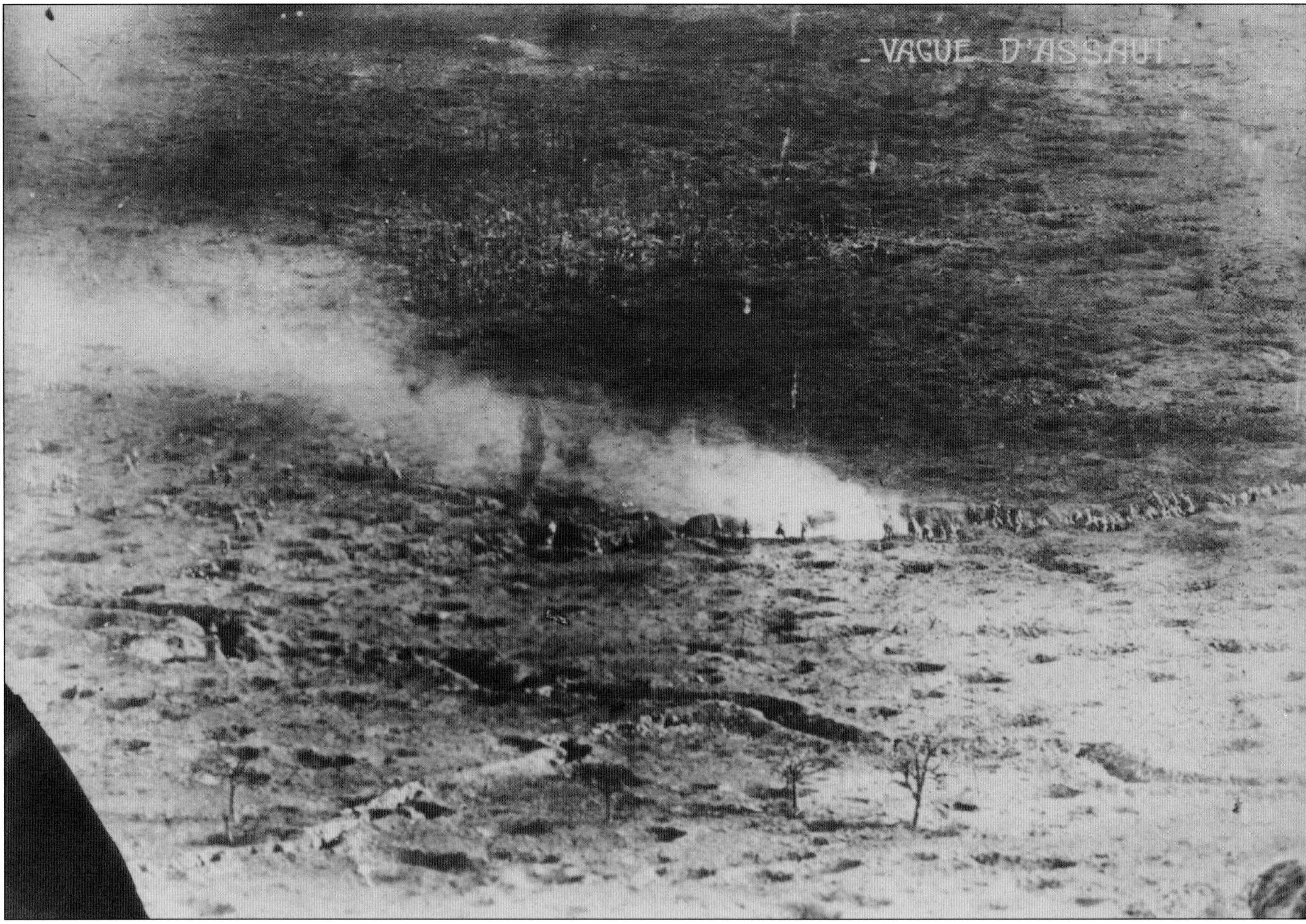

French assault with cloud gas and portable flamethrowers. One of the flamethrower sappers is visible against the light-colored plume of gas in the center of the photo. The Compagnies Schilt often operated in conjunction with the 12 Compagnies "Z" of the 1st Engineer Regiment, the French poison-gas companies. In such attacks French doctrine called for flamethrowers to be used strictly as weapons for mopping up, in the second and third waves and under the command of infantry officers.

1918

January 1 – The 40th Battalion was established in the 1st Engineer Regiment as the flamethrower parent unit, into which the Schilt Companies were gradually transferred. Schilt Company 22/6 became 40/2; Schilt Company 22/7 became 40/3; and Schilt Company 22/9 became 40/5.

April 1 – Schilt Company 22/5 became 40/1; Schilt Company 22/8 became 40/4; Schilt Company 22/10 became 40/6; Schilt Company 22/11 became 40/7; and the Flamethrower Training Company became Schilt Company 40/101.

May – The French tested the feasibility of mounting flamethrowers on aircraft. A P_3 portable was fired from a French fighter on the ground with the propeller spinning, but the experiments were not successful.

May 28 – A platoon of French flamethrower sappers accompanied the American 28th Infantry Regiment into Cantigny, in order to capture prisoners for interrogation. The Americans used every weapon at their disposal except for rifle grenades, because "a French flamethrower in a German's face" made them unnecessary.[12]

September 15 – After the largest artillery bombardment seen in the Balkan theater, French colonial troops were sent against fortified Bulgarian positions at Dobropolje. The German-engineered concrete emplacements and the natural cover of the rock face resisted all but direct hits, forcing the French to use a Schilt Company to reduce machine-gun nests and light-artillery positions manned by fiercely resisting Bulgarians.[13]

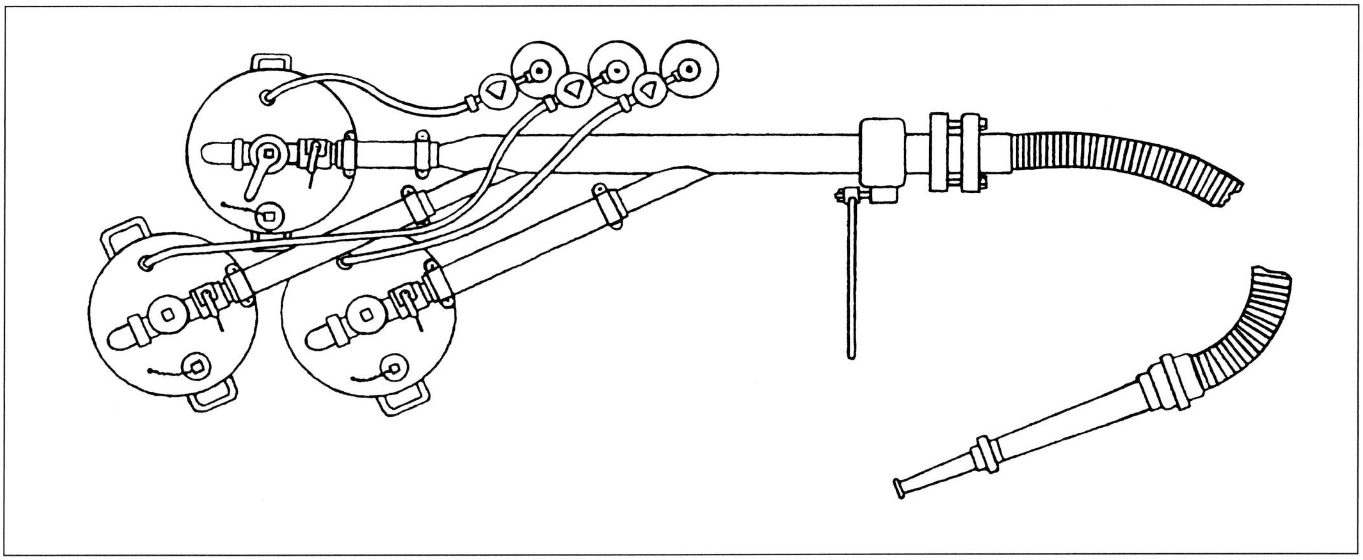

L_1 static flamethrower, consisting of three oil tanks connected by a branched pipe to a single lance. It required 45 minutes to assemble by its three-man squad of one NCO, one sapper-lance operator and one sapper mechanic-grenadier. To fire the weapon, the squad attached a four-minute fuse to the nozzle and opened the valve on the branched pipe behind the hose connection. A defensive weapon, it appears not to have been used in combat.

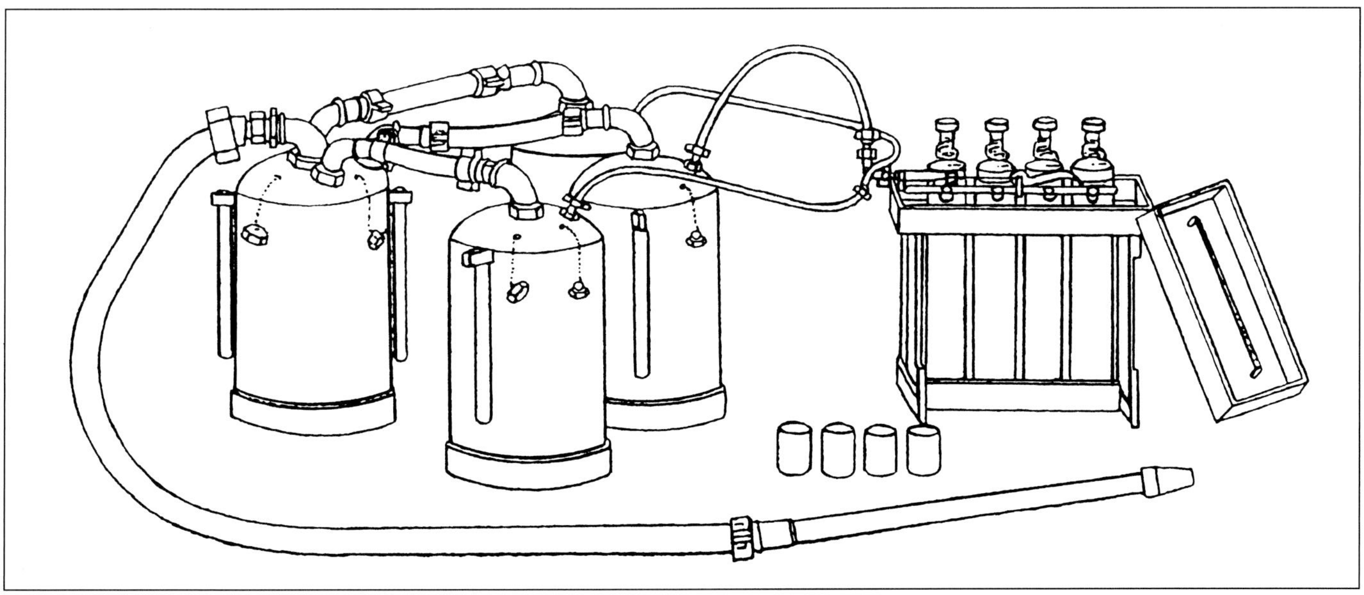

L_2 static flamethrower, which like the L_1 required 45 minutes for its three-man squad to assemble; it consisted of four oil tanks connected in sequence to a single lance. To fire the weapon, the three-man squad of one NCO, one sapper-lance operator, and one sapper mechanic-grenadier attached a four-minute fuse to the nozzle and opened a single valve that simultaneously released carbon dioxide from all four propellant tanks. It, too, was a defensive weapon that appears not to have been used in combat.

During the war the French manufactured 200 Schilt No. 1 static devices; 363 Schilt No. 1 bis static devices; 362 Schilt No. 2 semi-portable devices; 258 Schilt No. 3 portable devices; 896 Schilt No. 3 bis portable devices; 1430 P_3 portable devices; 320 P_4 portable devices; 51 L_1 static devices; and 50 L_2 static devices, a total of 3930 flamethrowers. The number of Hersent-Thirion flamethrowers manufactured is not available.

Approximately 200 flamethrower sappers were killed in action, died of wounds or accident, or went missing from 1915 to 1918.

French P_3 flamethrower squad in action at Cantigny, May 28, 1918, in support of the first major American offensive of the war. They wear the horizon-blue greatcoat, issued in both single- and double-breasted cuts. At Cantigny the French flamethrower sappers were used to smoke the Germans out of underground shelters and cellars; it appears that in this photo, the P_3 squad is helping a wounded prisoner emerge from the rubble.

1919

January 5 – Supreme Headquarters ordered that all Schilt Companies except 40/101 – the Training Company – be disbanded. Over the next month the flamethrower sappers were either demobilized or transferred into other units.

April – Schilt Company 40/101 was disbanded. However, flamethrower instructors were retained by the army and sent to various military schools.

In the postwar French army the flamethrower was assigned to the infantry instead of the engineers. All infantry officers were trained in the use of flamethrowers; once a year the Center for the Improvement of Infantry Specialties *(Centre de Perfectionnement des Spécialités de l'Infanterie)* taught a ten-day flamethrower course for enlisted men.[14]

Each infantry regiment sent one sergeant, one corporal, and eight men, while each battalion of regiments forming an army corps sent one sergeant, one corporal, and four men. Though infantrymen, these flamethrower troops were designated pioneers *(pionniers)*.

Tactics

Portable flamethrowers were used mainly for cleaning out shelters, isolated strong points, villages, houses, cellars, undergrounds structures, etc. They were deployed in pairs with infantry units assigned mopping-up duties. Since they advanced more slowly than regular infantry, they were sent out in the wave of infantry preceding the mopping-up units.

Below

Left: Rear view of P_4 portable flamethrower. Developed concurrently with the P_3, it was essentially a smaller, lighter version of the same weapon. The object protruding from the top right side is the protective cap for the propellant-bottle valve. It was removed in combat and attached to the flamethrower with a leather loop.

Right: Front view of P_4 portable flamethrower. To fire the lance, the operator squeezed the lever at the base; the springs attached to the lever automatically closed the valve when the operator slackened his grip. The pull ring visible under the hose coupler on the side of the flamethrower was another safety feature; when the full flamethrower was transported, the service-valve lever was kept in the "closed" position by a spring. Immediately prior to combat, the operator pulled the ring, releasing one end of the spring and allowing the assistant to move the service-valve lever into the "open" position.

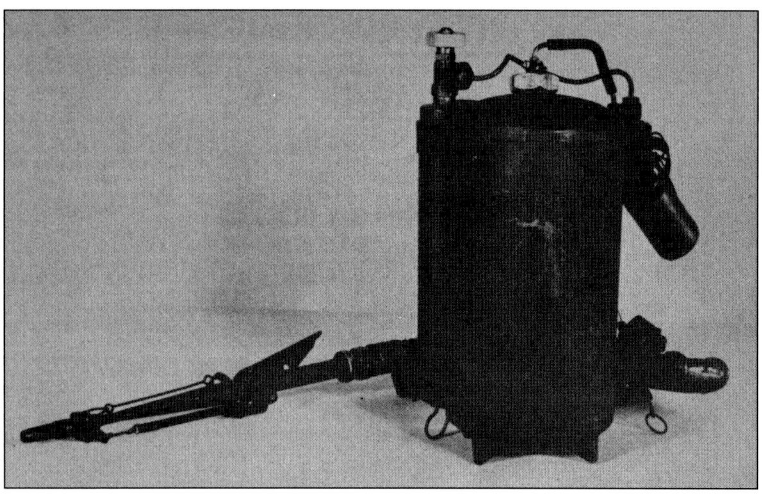

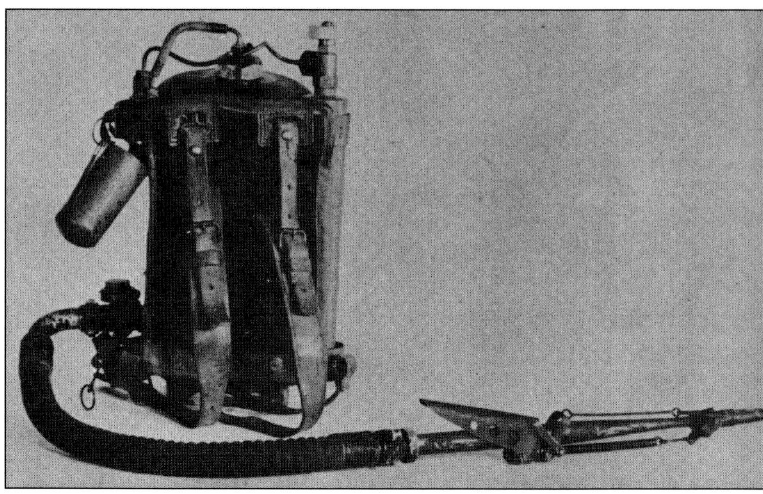

Training exercise for the defensive use of large flamethrowers. The sappers all wear leather jackets and steel helmets, and the hoses of the lances are seen on the lower right, leading to the flamethrowers positioned in a separate trench. Note that the oil stream fired by the foremost sapper has not ignited, due to the failure of the fuse attached to the lance nozzle. The French rarely deployed large flamethrowers in combat.

Secondly, portable flamethrowers were used on the flanks of an attack to carry out a barrage against shallow trenches. Medium and heavy flamethrowers were also used for this duty, in combination with portable devices.

Thirdly, portable flamethrowers were used on captured fronts against enemy communications trenches, in order to prevent the enemy from counterattacking with hand grenades.

Fourthly, portable flamethrowers were used in raids to prevent the enemy from achieving his objective, to spread terror, to capture prisoners, to provide cover for the flanks, and to facilitate counterattacks.

Fifthly, portable flamethrowers were used at the end of a mission to destroy points deemed easily recaptured by the enemy.[15]

Large flamethrowers were used only in exceptional circumstances, either defensively or to break especially stubborn resistance.

Flamethrower companies were deployed judiciously and carefully in order to prevent unnecessary casualties, due to the difficulty of recruiting the personnel. The infantry commander, in consultation with the commander of the flamethrower company, determined the mission of flamethrower troops. Flamethrower and trench-mortar squads were often deployed together in a mopping-up role.

Flamethrower sappers were auxiliaries of the infantry, protected by hand-grenade throwers. When executing their mission they took the initiative only from a technical point of view. Tactically they were under orders of the commanding officer of the infantry unit to which they were attached.

ITALY

Above: Engineer Nicola, a driver, wearing the M1909 gray-green (grigio-verde) uniform adopted by his branch of service in September of 1915. The engineer tunic (giubba) had shoulder straps rather than the padded rolls of the infantry garment. Engineer collar patches (mostrine) were single-tailed "flames" (fiamme) in black with crimson piping. Cavalry riding breeches completed the outfit. Flamethrower sappers (zappatori-lanciafiamme) were identically uniformed.

1915

June 23-July 7 – The Austrians first used flamethrowers against the Italians on the Carso, during the First Battle of the Isonzo.[1]

Autumn – The Italians acquired 24 Schilt No. 1 and No. 2 flamethrowers from the French.

October 16 – The Italian Supreme Army Command *(Comando Supremo)* ordered engineers with previous experience as firemen to Udine to experiment with flamethrowers under the command of engineer Captain Tassinari, fire chief of Turin. Captain Schilt of the Paris Firefighting Sapper Regiment trained these first flamethrower operators.

October 31 – The Independent Flamethrower Unit *(reparto lanciafiamme autonomo)* was organized at Cervignano, under the command of the engineers of the Third Army. It was made up of firefighters and sappers *(zappatori)* of the 1st Engineer Regiment *(1° Reggimento Genio),* a total of one officer and 40 men dubbed *flammieri.*

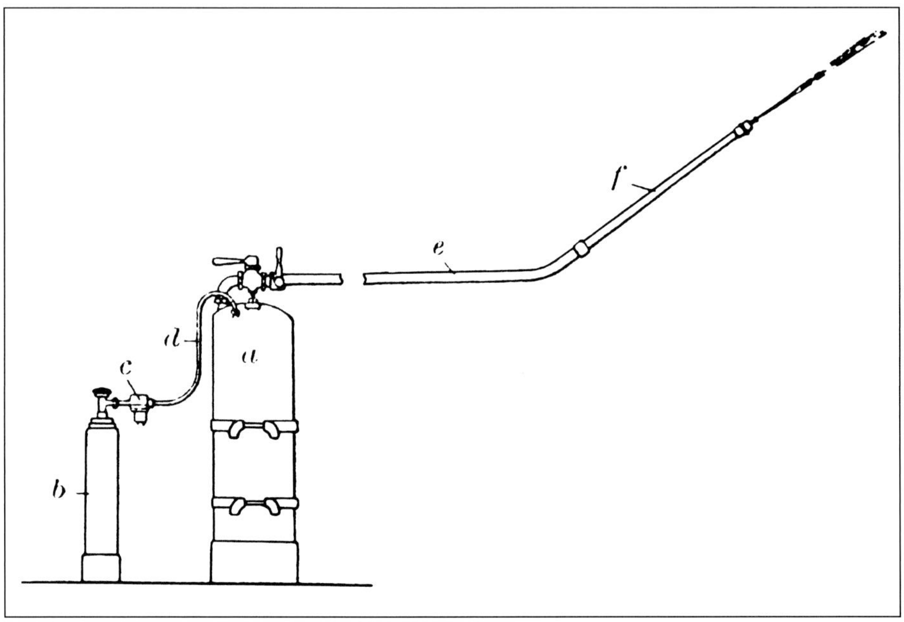

Right: Schilt No. 1, the first flamethrower adopted by the Italian army: a) oil container; b) compressed-gas bottle; c) manometer or gas pressure gauge; d) flexible tubing; e) emission hose; f) lance. The three-man squad consisted of one sapper lance-operator (zappatore porta-lancia), one sapper-mechanic (zappatore-meccanico) who opened the valves, and one sapper-igniter (zappatore-accenditore) who also threw incendiary grenades. A combat post of a flamethrower company was armed with two devices and was under the command of an NCO or corporal (sottufficiale, caporale). Each of the four sections of a flamethrower company consisted of three squads that could each establish two combat posts. A section covered a front 330 ft. wide.

Left: Although this heavily retouched photo is identified as an Italian "poisoned-flame" attack against Austrian positions on the Isonzo, January of 1916, official records state that the Independent Flamethrower Unit did not see its first action until April. To carry out these operations, liquefied poison gases such as phosgene were mixed with flame oil and sprayed with Hersent-Thirion flamethrowers. Such attacks were ineffectual due to the limited range of the weapons and the heat of the flames, which caused the toxic smoke to rise out of the trenches.

Below: Schilt No. 2 semi-portable flamethrower, adopted by the Italians in the fall of 1915. The first Italian flamethrower sappers were firefighters trained personally by Captain Victor Schilt, the driving force behind the French flamethrower effort. Like the French, the Italians tried to use the Schilt No. 2 as a portable weapon, but reclassified it as a static weapon in October of 1916. The three-man squad consisted of one sapper lance-operator, one sapper-mechanic, and one sapper-igniter, who also threw incendiary grenades. It was deployed the same way as the Schilt No. 1, in combat posts of two weapons each.

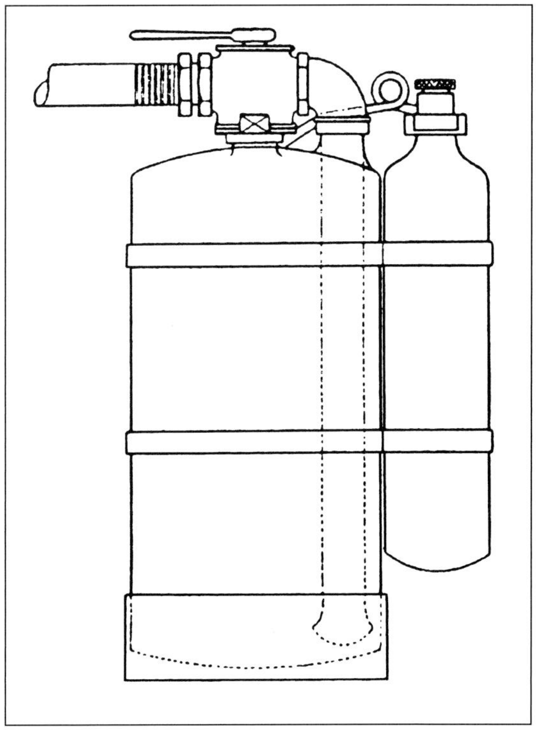

1916

April 20 – The Independent Flamethrower Unit first saw action at Selz.

May 15 – By order of the 14th Division nine soldiers from the 14th Infantry Regiment and six from the 13th were sent to Ronchi to serve with the Independent Flamethrower Unit. At midnight the Austrians attacked with flamethrowers, setting fire to the trench without causing any casualties to the Italians. An hour later they attacked again, but this time Squad Bosani of the flamethrower unit responded with its own device, forcing the Austrians to retreat. The Italian flamethrower was damaged in the fighting and taken out of action.

June – The Independent Flamethrower Unit had amassed an arsenal of 22 large and medium Schilt apparatuses, two Hersent-Thirion, and three captured Austrian flamethrowers.

July – The 2nd Engineer Regiment *(2° Reggimento Genio)* of the First Army formed the Independent Flamethrower Platoon *(plotone lanciafiamme autonomo)* of 70 men, 10 of whom were transferred in from the Independent Flamethrower Unit.

August 10 – The Supreme Command ordered the Third Army to establish two flamethrower companies *(compagnie lanciafiamme),* the first built around the Independent Flamethrower Unit and the second created from scratch. This order also authorized the First Army to retain the Independent Flamethrower Platoon.

September – The Third Army organized two flamethrower companies in the 1st Engineer Regiment, based on the French model. Each company was composed of four 53-man sections *(sezioni lanciafiamme):*

> two medium Schilt No. 2 (initially called "portable") sections,
> one static Schilt No. 1 section,
> one mixed static Schilt and Hersent-Thirion section.

Two Italian flamethrower sappers (flammieri), an enlisted man and a lieutenant (tenente) on the right. They display (from left) a Lagunari static device, a late-model Schilt No. 3 portable, and a Schilt No. 2 medium. The flamethrower lances are fitted with flash hiders to protect the engineers' eyes from the glare of the magnesium fuses used to ignite the oil jets. Courtesy Antonio Rossetto.

Each section, armed with 12 flamethrowers, was divided into three squads that were each commanded by a sergeant and equipped with four devices. These three squads each established two combat posts; a combat post was armed with two flamethrowers and commanded by an NCO or corporal.

October – The Third Army increased its medium-flamethrower sections to eight and added one flamethrower command; the First Army expanded the Independent Flamethrower Platoon into four flamethrower sections and one flamethrower command.

During this month the Schilt No. 2 medium flamethrower was reclassified as a static weapon, since it was too heavy to be carried into action behind assault troops. As a result, the 1st Engineer Regiment began investigating small portable flamethrowers.

At around this time a general flamethrower depot was established at Porpetto, consisting of a group command and four flamethrower sections for the training of personnel. Each of the eight medium-flamethrower sections of the Third Army was

assigned to a different infantry division, their administration and discipline the responsibility of the commander of the divisional engineer battalions.

November 20 – The Supreme Command established the Flamethrower Direction *(Direzione dei Lanciafiamme)* at Porpetto to more efficiently administrate the two flamethrower companies and the flamethrower depot. The Flamethrower Direction consisted of a captain, a lieutenant, one corporal, and four enlisted men.

A third flamethrower company was also established with this order, along with a flamethrower-personnel depot and a depot for flamethrower material, all located at Porpetto.

The 1st Flamethrower Company was comprised of four sections (31st - 34th) based in Verona and assigned to the First Army.

The 2nd Flamethrower Company contained eight sections (1st - 8th) based in Turriaco.

The 3rd Flamethrower Company was composed of four sections (9th, 10th, 35th, 36th) based at the depot at Porpetto.

At around this time the Schilt No. 3 portable flamethrower arrived in Italy. Its many shortcomings were immediately recognized. Although it was issued to the flamethrower companies, the Flamethrower Direction planned to replace it as soon as possible.

With the adoption of the Schilt No. 3, four types of sections were organized in the flamethrower companies:

Type A – armed with 12 Schilt No. 1 heavy static apparatuses;
Type B – armed with 12 Schilt No. 2 medium semi-portable apparatuses;
Type C – armed with 12 Schilt No. 3 small portable devices;
Mixed Type – armed with 12 Schilt No. 1 static and 2 Hersent-Thirion apparatuses.

Types A, B, and C were composed of one subaltern, one sergeant, three corporals, and 48 men. The Mixed Type had four extra flamethrower carriers, for a total of 57 personnel.

The center of mobilization for all flamethrower personnel was the depot of the 1st Engineer Regiment at Pavia.

Cap and arm badge (left) of the Engineer Pioneers and Sappers (Genio Pionieri Zappatori) and shoulder-strap patch worn by sappers of flamethrower companies, formed in September of 1916. The cap and arm badge was embroidered in silver or gray thread for officers and black for enlisted men; the company number and letters "LF" (Lanciafiamme) of the shoulder-strap patch were in white, while the cloth backing was black piped in crimson.

Lagunari static flamethrower, a modified Italian copy of the Schilt No. 1 bis. To operate the weapon, the sapper-mechanic first opened the propellant-release valve on the top of the propellant bottle, pressurizing the oil. He then opened the oil-release valve on the top of the oil tank by pushing on the horizontal handle. At least 30 Lagunari flamethrowers were supplied to the 2nd and 6th Flamethrower Companies.

Italian flamethrower sappers using a French Hersent-Thirion static flamethrower. Note the eight extra oil containers on the left, as well as the additional propellant tank lying on the ground. The Italians also used this flamethrower as a poison-gas sprayer and to dissipate enemy gas attacks. A six-man squad served each Hersent-Thirion. Courtesy Gaetano Niedu.

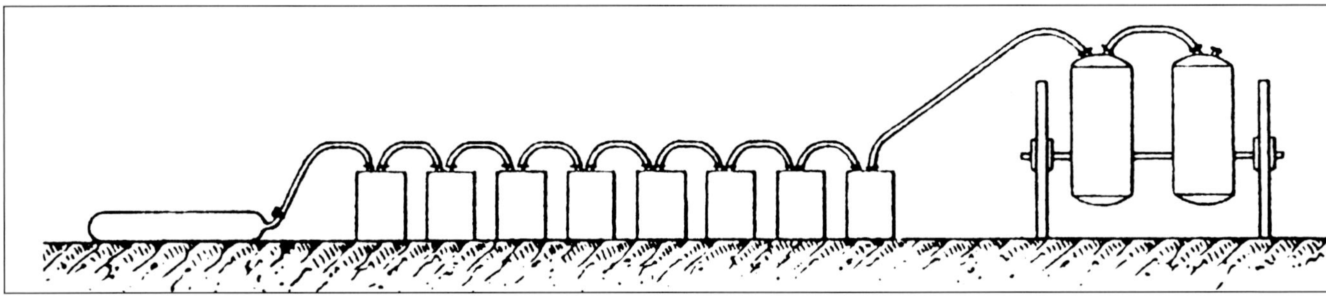

Schematic drawing of the eight extra oil tanks and single propellant tank used to extend the duration of the Hersent-Thirion flamethrower.

Officer and sappers training with a Schilt No. 1 bis. In September of 1916, the Third Army organized two flamethrower companies that contained four sections (sezioni lanciafiamme): two medium Schilt No. 2 sections, one static Schilt No. 1 section, one mixed static Schilt and Hersent-Thirion section. Courtesy Gaetano Niedu.

The same men as in the previous image. The Schilt No. 2 on the left has been fitted with two curved brackets on the sides, into which carrying poles were slipped. This was an Italian innovation not seen on the French version of the weapon. None of the men display flamethrower-company shoulder patches. Courtesy Gaetano Niedu.

1917

January – The Flamethrower Direction expanded into a flamethrower school, in order to meet the increasing demand for flamethrower sappers.

February – A park laboratory was established in the Flamethrower Direction at Porpetto; the staff of the depot took over the responsibility of administering and training the personnel. In order to allow longer rest periods for flamethrower sappers, the number of commanders of forward combat posts of each flamethrower section was increased to 12, and each was assigned an officer aspirant as a relief for the commander during his period at the front.

March – Two more flamethrower companies were added in the 1st Engineer Regiment, increasing the number to five. To provide the two new units, the 2nd Company was divided into the 2nd and 4th Companies, and the 5th Company was built from scratch.

April – The Bergomi Society of Milan supplied the first Schilt No. 3 bis portable flamethrowers produced under license. These intermittent-jet weapons replaced the defective Schilt No. 3, which provided only a single, continuous jet.

April 18 – The 6th Flamethrower Company was established in the 1st Engineer Regiment.

May 18 – The Austrians attacked Casa Diruta at 10:30 P.M. after an artillery barrage that destroyed the Italian machine guns in their blockhouses. As the wave of infantry reached the Italian line, two posts of the 3rd Flamethrower Company opened fire, the first with a Hersent-Thirion and the second a Schilt No. 1. The flames stopped the assault in its tracks, reducing the Austrians to complete disorder. In full retreat, they left smoldering corpses in the slit and communications trenches.

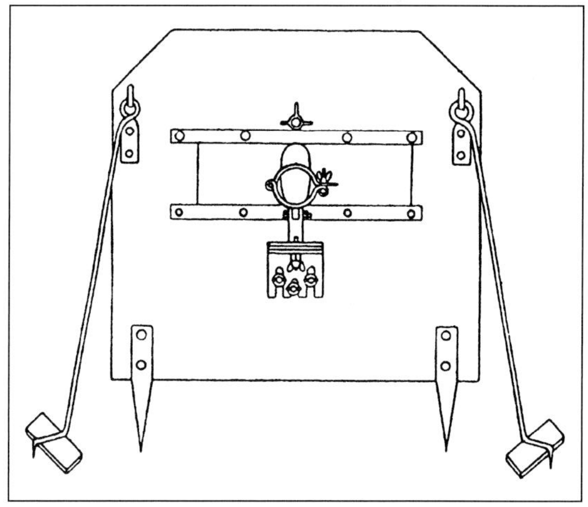

Steel shield used by Italian flamethrower sappers with the Schilt No. 1 bis to protect against both heat and enemy projectiles. The lance nozzle was clamped in the circular aperture in the center of the shield, which was supported upright by metal legs.

Italian flamethrower qualification badge, a black dragon wrapped around a silver staff above a Savoy knot, spouting red flames. Adopted in 1917, it was mounted on a patch of gray-green uniform cloth and worn on the upper left arm by any fighting man – sapper, infantryman, cavalryman, sailor – trained as a flamethrower operator.

This flamethrower sapper, photographed in Napoli, wears the M1909 tunic with unusual colored cuffs and shoulder straps. His dragon badge can be discerned above his left elbow. Note the reinforced riding breeches. Since the engineer tunic lacked pockets, troops often added them in the field.

Flamethrower sapper using a Schilt No. 3 bis, adopted by the Italian army in April of 1917. Portable-flamethrower squads were comprised of a sapper-carrier (zappatore-portatore), a sapper-mechanic, and a sapper-igniter. The Schilt No. 3 bis replaced the unsuccessful Schilt No. 3, which could fire only one continuous burst. This deficiency was wasteful and highly inefficient. Courtesy Gaetano Niedu.

May 30 – The first two portable sections armed with the Schilt No. 3 bis were formed. Initially the sections were each comprised of one officer, one corporal, and 25 men armed with 12 weapons. Twelve of the men were flamethrower carriers *(zappatori-portatori),* 12 were assistants or mechanics *(meccanici),* and one was the section leader.

June 26 – The Italians established battalion-sized assault units *(Reparti d'Assalto).*[2]

June 22 – The revolvers used as personal arms by flamethrower sappers of forward combat posts were replaced with Model 70/87/16 rifles or Moschetto TS carbines and a dagger.

July – One flamethrower section of 27 men armed with 15 portable weapons was assigned to each assault unit; assault troops were known as "Bold Ones" *(Arditi).*

July 20 – The Supreme Command took control of the Flamethrower Direction. Flamethrower schools were ordered opened for all infantry regiments. As an experiment, four portable flamethrowers were distributed to each infantry company.

September 4 – The *I Reparto* of the Second Army became the first *Arditi* to use flamethrowers in combat, during the capture of Mount San Gabriele. The Schilt No. 3 bis flamethrower was considered too heavy and too slow in operation; it was therefore withdrawn from service in assault battalions.[3] By the end of the year, the Schilt No. 3 bis of assault troops had been replaced with the DLF and the Italian twin-tank apparatus.

September 21 – One flamethrower section of 16 men armed with six devices was allocated to each assault company, for a total of three sections per battalion (48 officers and men, 18 weapons). About 26 assault units existed at this time.

Italian flamethrower lance, capable of intermittent firing and fitted with a self-closing valve copied from the French: T) flexible hose; A) lance coupling; L) lever; S) gate valve; M) spring; B) nozzle; C) funnel; P) nozzle fuses.

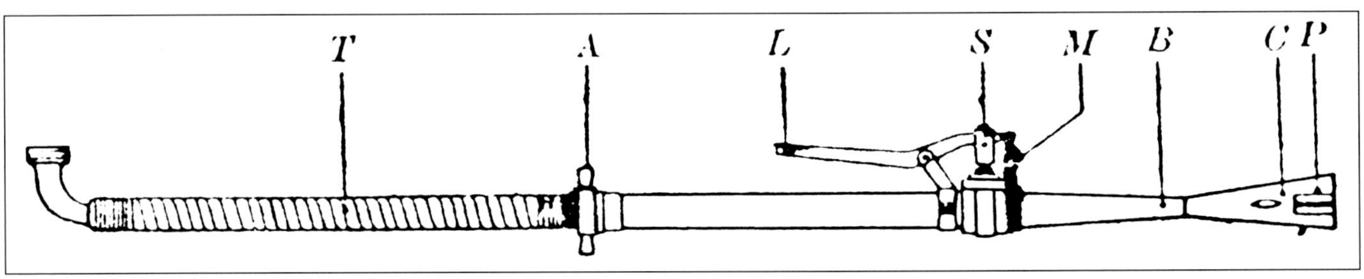

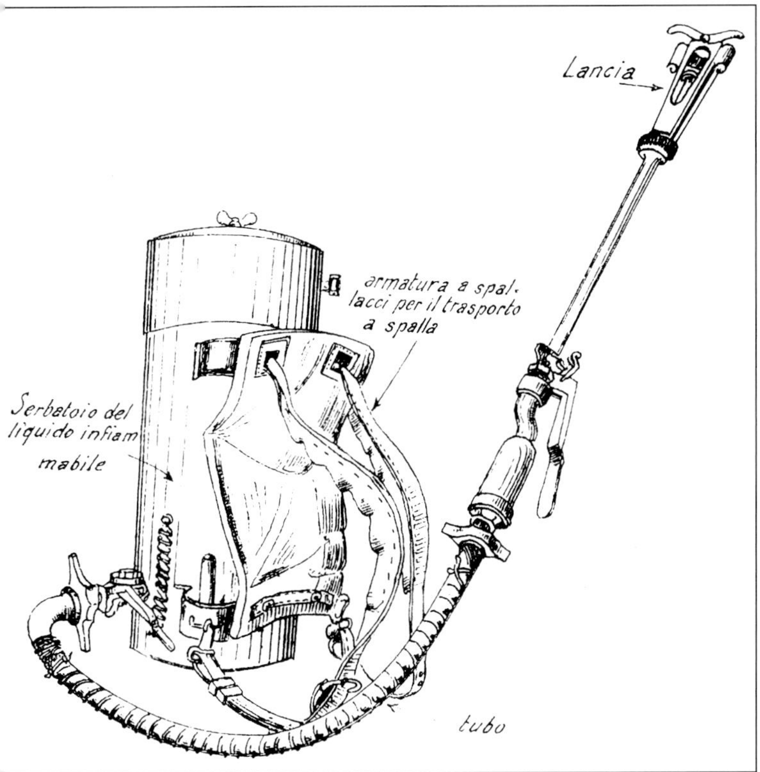

Italian Schilt No. 3 bis with automatic-ignition lance. The ignition system consisted of a ball of spun platinum packed into a holder in front of the nozzle. A hydrogen jet from a container in the lance was ignited with a striker when the firing lever was squeezed; this burning jet heated the platinum ball until it was red-hot, touching off the stream of oil.

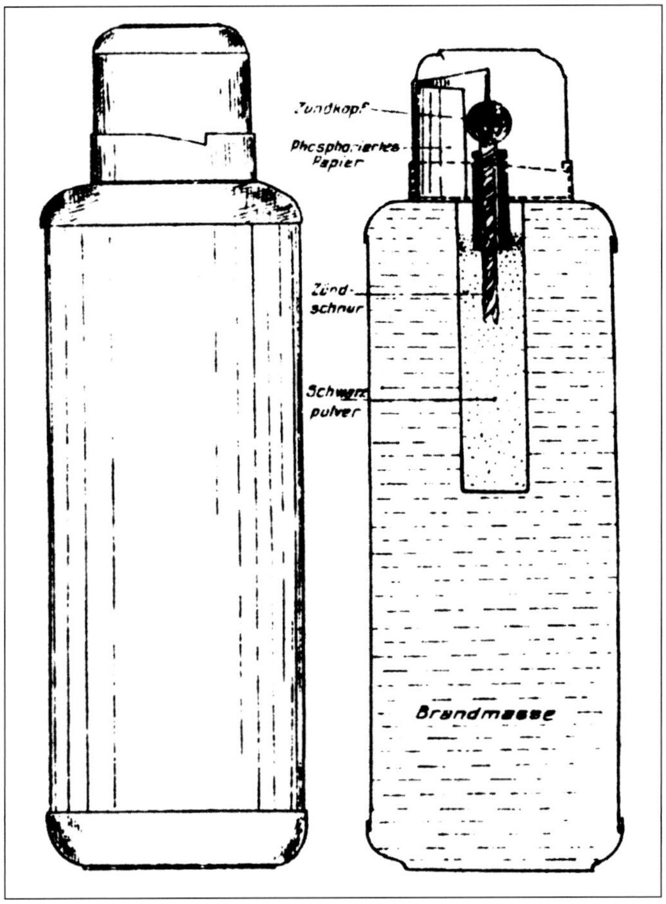

Italian Carasco incendiary grenade, used by flamethrower sappers as a supplement to friction fuses attached to the nozzles of lances. The igniter was essentially a large match, which was struck against phosphorus-coated paper inside the safety cap. When the cap was removed, the fuse set off a reservoir of black powder inside the grenade, which in turn ignited the combustible filling.

Italian assault troops (Arditi) using a Schilt No. 3 bis during the attack on Mt. San Gabriele, September 4, 1917. Each battalion-sized assault unit (reparto d'assalto) contained one flamethrower section of 27 officers and men, armed with 15 portable apparatuses. On September 21 the number of flamethrower sections was increased to three per assault unit, each composed of one officer and 15 men armed with six apparatuses. The Arditi rejected the Schilt No. 3 bis as too heavy and cumbersome, replacing it with the DLF and the Twin Tank Apparatus in early 1918.

Flamethrower sapper wearing the asbestos overcoat, helmet, and gloves, which were said to be extremely hot and uncomfortable. The flamethrower is the Italian Schilt No. 3 bis, with the protective cover removed from the top. Courtesy Gaetano Niedu.

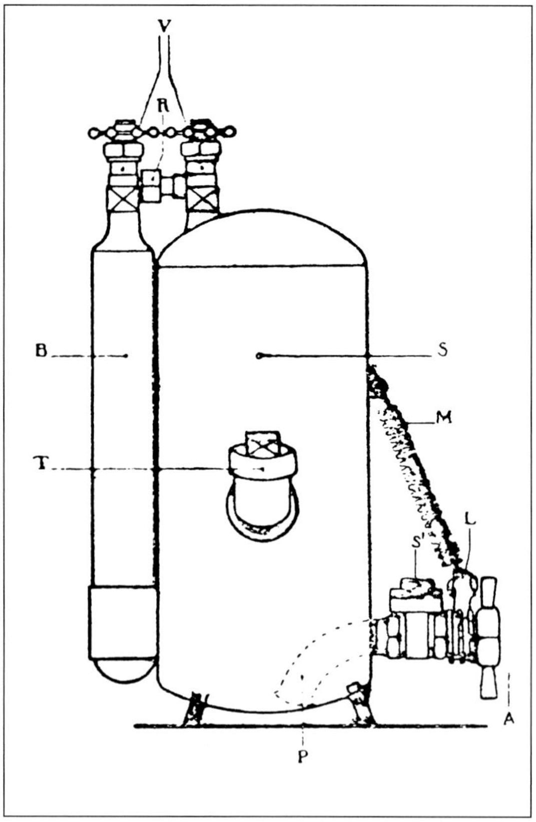

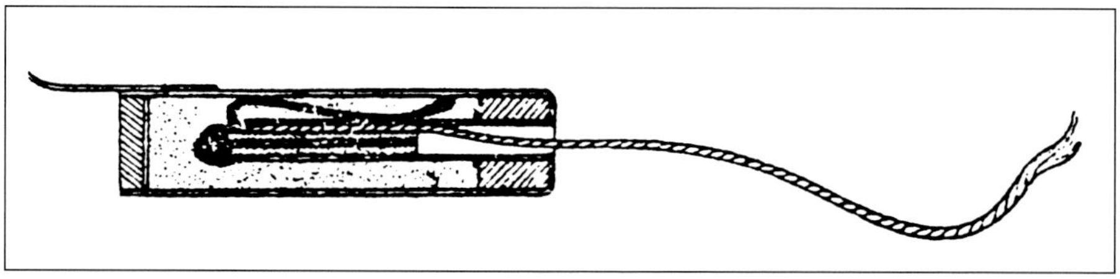

Left: DLF portable flamethrower (Apparato Italiano Modificato Tipo D.L.F.), designed by and named after the Department of Flamethrowers and adopted in early 1918: A) attachment for hose; B) compressed-gas bottle; L) service lever; M) spring; P) outflow pipe; R) connecting lug; S) oil tank; S') gate valve; T) oil-filler tube; V) valves. A two-man squad of sapper-carrier and sapper-mechanic served this weapon.

Above: Friction fuse attached to the nozzles of flamethrower lances. When the string was pulled, the fuse was ignited, burning for several seconds.

October 1917 – The 7th and 8th Flamethrower Companies were established in the 1st Engineer Regiment. Four flamethrower companies were assigned to the Third Army, two to the First Army, and one each to the Second and Sixth Armies.

October 5 – Thirty new portable-flamethrower sections began a 25-day training period, after which six each were assigned to the First and Fourth Armies, eight each to the Second and Third Armies, and two to the Carnia Zone. The commanders of the armies used these sections to complete their assault units or to reinforce their infantry regiments. Each section consisted of a second lieutenant or officer aspirant, one sergeant, one corporal, and 30 men armed with 12 small devices.

October 18 – The Supreme Command established two new static-flamethrower sections assigned as the fifth sections of the 2nd and 6th Flamethrower Companies.

November – After the Battle of Caporetto, the flamethrower depot and the Flamethrower Direction were moved to Montecchio Emilia.

December – The Schilt No. 3 bis arming the two portable sections of the 3rd Flamethrower Company were replaced with Schilt No. 1 static devices.

Late 1917-early 1918 – Four independent flamethrower sections were created. Each consisted of two officers and 60 NCOs and men armed with three Hersent-Thirion and six Schilt No. 1 static devices. The four independent flamethrower sections were employed for special tasks such as defending bridges.

Opposite
Top left: Italian Intermittent-jet Apparatus with Automatic Ignition (Apparato Tipo Italiano a Getto Intermittente con Accensione Automatica), also called the Italian Twin Tank Apparatus (Apparato Tipo Italiano a Due Serbatoi Accoppiati), adopted in December of 1917: B) gas bottle; S) oil tank; T) oil-filler tube; C) protective cover; M) hinged retaining ring; P) connection tube of oil tanks; S') stopcock; L) handle; V) propellant valve; D) shoulder strap; E) reducer. A two-man squad of sapper-carrier and sapper-mechanic served this weapon.

Top right: Gas bottle issued with the DLF portable flamethrower. It could be removed after the oil was pressurized, thus reducing the weight of the flamethrower. The flame oil remained pressurized for 24 hours. This model flamethrower could also be used when the operator was in a prone position.

Bottom: Arditi training with DLF flamethrowers fitted with the lance devised for the Schilt No. 3 bis. Each flamethrower squad consists of an operator and an assistant who opens the propellant-release valve on the weapon.

1918

January 19 – The number of men in each flamethrower section was increased by 25 percent, the reserve of which was to be used by the regimental commander as replacements. In addition, one portable-flamethrower section armed with 12 devices was assigned to each battalion of mountain troops *(Alpini)*.

February – The 9th Flamethrower Company was established in the 1st Engineer Regiment. This was the final flamethrower company created.

February 14 – A portable-flamethrower section was assigned to each regiment of infantry, *Bersaglieri,* and grenadiers, as well as each battalion of *Alpini*. Each section consisted of one officer, one sergeant, two corporals, and 24 men. The number of men was double that required to operate the weapons, in order for the personnel to take extended rest periods. Each section was armed with 12 flamethrowers and enough propellant gas and oil for three fillings of each weapon, as well as 12 asbestos masks and pairs of asbestos gloves.

The nine flamethrower companies were now armed with static devices only.

May – The assault units were expanded from 700 men to 900 men each. A *Reparto* now included three portable-flamethrower sections, each composed of 15 men armed with six devices.[4]

June 15 – In Mure Valley, the Austrians launched a dawn bombardment of an Italian salient, paying particular attention to observation posts of the 9th Flamethrower Company. When the Austrians attacked at 10:00 A.M. the Italians fired their flamethrowers. Fifty Austrians raced toward Observation Post 1676 and skidded to a stop

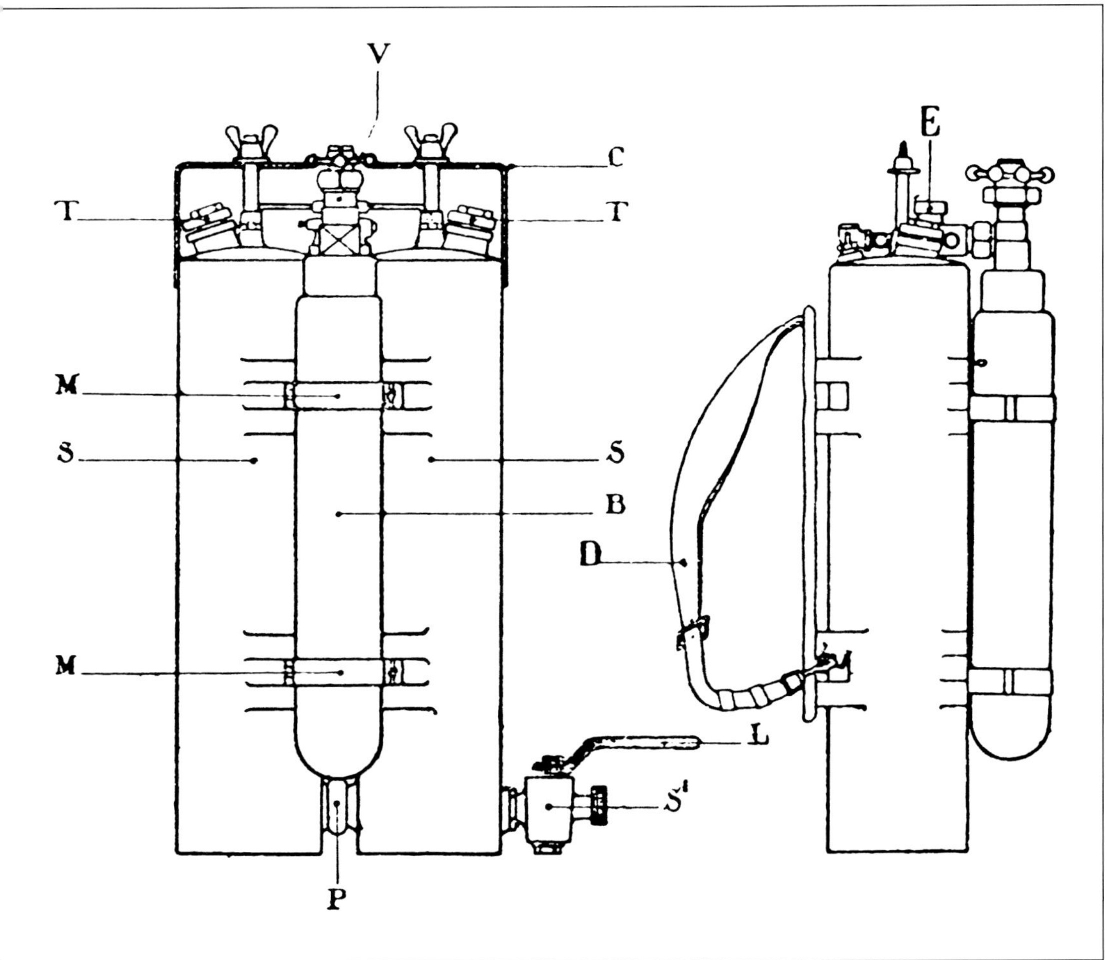
V
C
T
T
E
M
S
S
B
D
M
L
S'
P

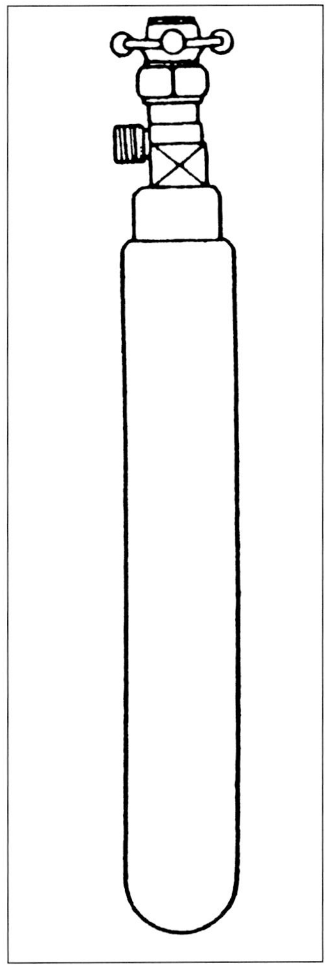

In this second image of Arditi training with DLF flamethrowers, the white smoke from the friction fuses is apparent. Note that in the background the flamethrower operator fires from the prone position, an action that could not be carried out with the Schilt No. 3 bis.

Flamethrower section of the XXIII Reparto d'Assalto. They wear the standard Arditi uniform of gray-green M1910 Bersaglieri cyclist tunic with black collar patches and M1909 Alpini or M1910 cyclist trousers. Instead of flamethrowers, these men are armed with 6.5mm Moschetto '91 Modello Cavalleria carbines and "Petardo Thevenot" hand grenades. Always conscious of style, the Arditi often wore white shirts and neckties into battle.

in front of the burning barbed wire entanglements, exposing themselves to flanking fire from Italian machine guns. The observation post came under heavy bombardment again, and then a gas grenade was thrown inside, killing two of the flamethrower sappers and putting one of the apparatuses out of service. The post was abandoned.

July 7 – In the Cortellazo Woods on the Piave, *Arditi* pole vaulted over barbed wire entanglements into Austrian positions and killed the machine gunners with daggers, while *Arditi* armed with flamethrowers stormed a factory defended by 40 machine guns, blew up an ammunition depot in Quitro Case, and took the entire Austrian garrison prisoner.[5]

August – The number of flamethrower sections per assault unit was increased from three to six.

October – There was a total of 361 portable-flamethrower sections assigned to all regiments of infantry, *Bersaglieri,* and grenadiers, as well as all battalions of *Alpini* and *Arditi*. The first 100 sections were armed with the Schilt No. 3 bis, the next 71 with the Italian twin-tank apparatus, and the rest with the DLF.

November 3 – Italy and Austria-Hungary signed the Armistice of Villa Giusti, which took effect the next day.

From January 1, 1917 to October 30, 1918, approximately 900 officers and 23,000 men were trained as flamethrower sappers. During the war 17 officers and 73 men were killed in action.

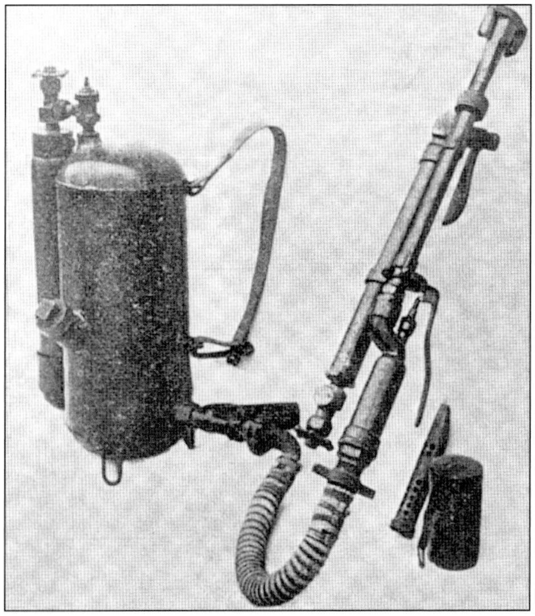

DLF portable flamethrower with automatic-ignition lance. An extra hydrogen bottle has been fitted to the lance to extend the firing duration. This may have been an experimental device that did not see widespread use.

1920

By the beginning of the year the flamethrower companies and sections had been disbanded.[6]

Tactics

Portable flamethrowers were used in assaults against isolated enemy strong points that put up obstinate resistance, machine-gun nests and blockhouses (directing the flame jet at the embrasures), and in a more generalized way of forcing troops from shelters and trenches, generating suffocating smoke, causing fatal wounds, and setting fire to clothing, tables, sandbags, and wooden support structures. They were deployed in pairs.

The element of surprise was necessary for success, as the employment of the flamethrowers had a remarkable influence on the morale of the troops, the mere appearance of flame jets often being sufficient to convince the defenders to surrender. However, it was vital to avoid attributing to flamethrowers results and a combat effectiveness they could not provide. Specifically, flamethrower sections could not act alone, but had to always operate closely with infantry, which protected them with

Official army postcard sent by sapper Alisio Caslani of the 3rd Flamethrower Company on October 2, 1918. The unit stamp is on the left.

Sailors of the Naval Regiment (Reggimento Marina) using a Schilt No. 3 bis as a static defensive weapon. They have placed the flamethrower on the parapet of the trench, exposing it to enemy fire. This dangerous practice was necessary due to the extremely short hose connecting the flamethrower to the automatic-ignition lance. In the background is an American Colt M1914 .30-caliber machine gun.

machine-gun fire, hand grenades, and smoke screens. The employment of flamethrowers was very useful for combat in populated areas and in forests, and also for the reclamation of trenches hit by chemical weapons and for the effective dispersion of toxic gas clouds by heat.

Flame jets were influenced by weather conditions; in particular it was imprudent to employ flamethrowers with a headwind, due to the danger of backfires, heat, and the disturbance created by the smoke.

Static flamethrowers were effective in defense; if used in a surprise action they contributed to the demoralization of the enemy and remarkably slowed his sudden attacks.

Since the continuous flame jet had a relatively short duration, Schilt No. 1 bis and No. 2 apparatuses were used in groups, so as to always have a ready apparatus and allow the others to be recharged. The Hersent-Thirion flamethrowers, capable of a longer duration, were employed alone or protected by two Schilt No. 1 or No. 2. To have a significant effect the static apparatuses had to be deployed en masse, with numerous flamethrowers lined up approximately 165 feet apart. They were used to protect important positions, necessary routes, and networks of crossroads.

For frontline positions the Schilt static flamethrowers were preferred, while the Hersent-Thirion – which was heavy and had a complicated refueling process – was generally used to defend positions in the rear. Only in particularly favorable cases, when the distance from the enemy trenches was greatly reduced and it was possible to line up the apparatuses in forward positions without attracting attention from the enemy, were static flamethrowers used in offensive actions.

Left: Emplaced Hersent-Thirion flamethrower used defensively, without its wheeled carriage. Each Hersent-Thirion covered a front of about 200-330 ft.

Right: Detail of emplaced Hersent-Thirion flamethrower lance and hose. The vertical device is a geared lift for raising and lowering the lance.

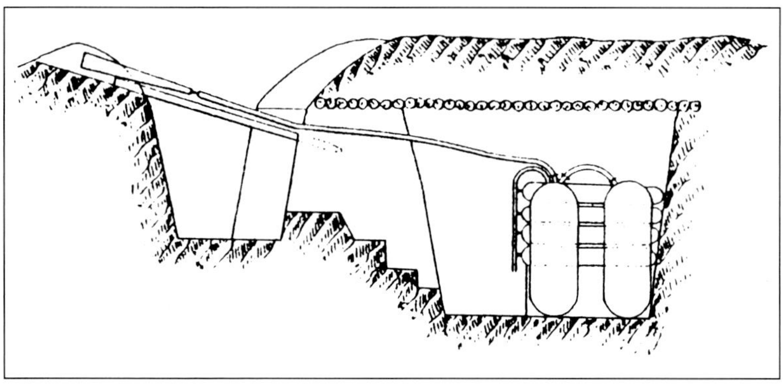

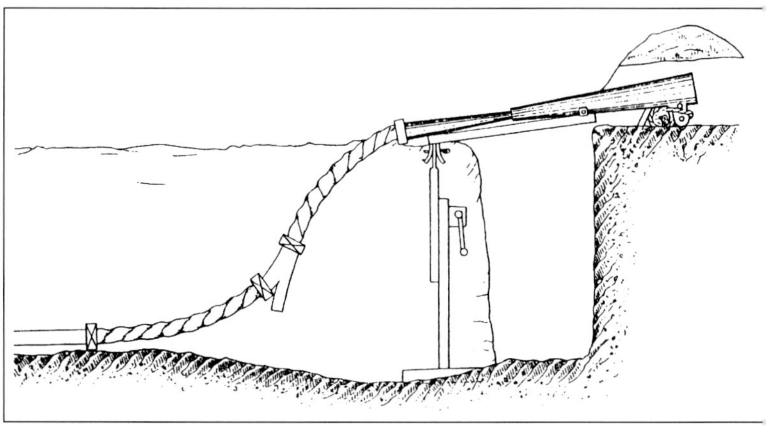

Flamethrower sapper firing a DLF portable device connected to an automatic-ignition lance fueled by hydrogen. In addition to the M1909 gray-green uniform he wears the round-topped M1915 cap (cupelino). Courtesy Gaetano Niedu.

More commonly the large Schilt flamethrowers were employed in the defense of captured enemy lines, in order to neutralize counterattacks. Medium-flamethrower sections were armed with 12 Schilt No. 2, organized into six combat posts of two apparatuses each; static-flamethrower sections were comprised of six combat posts, each armed with one Schilt No. 1 bis; and static-mixed sections had ten Schilt No. 1 bis and two Hersent-Thirion.

In July of 1918 the Third Army Command wrote that flamethrowers, especially the portable type, found optimal employment at the head of counterattacking columns and inside enclosed spaces, where surprise and shock were amplified. However, they were to be used only with great initiative, by enterprising personnel and the *Arditi*. In the counteroffensive they were somewhat cumbersome and deteriorated easily; their employment was sometimes hindered by thick vegetation.

Three flamethrower posts firing their six large devices, either the Schilt No. 1 or the Lagunari. The sappers all wear cotton fatigues and the round M1915 cap. Each flamethrower firing post is protected by low piles of stones.

GREAT BRITAIN

Young private of the Middlesex Regiment, which in the summer of 1915 provided the NCOs who became Britain's first flamethrower operators. They were sent to the Wembley Experimental Station, a secret establishment set up outside London by the Ministry of Munitions. This infantryman wears the khaki 1902 Pattern Service Dress with stiff peaked cap and the 1914 Pattern belt in leather.

1915

April – The Trench Warfare Department of the Ministry of Munitions began researching flamethrowers. Colonel Lucius Jackson, Royal Engineers, supervised the work at Wembley Experimental Station, a secret establishment set up outside London by the Ministry of Munitions.[1] At around this time American inventor Joseph Menchen approached Col. Jackson with his idea for a flamethrower consisting of several oil tanks connected to a single lance, with compressed air as propellant. The Master-General of the Ordnance approved the construction of Menchen's weapon.[2]

Late April – After the first German gas attack of April 22, Lieutenant William Howard Livens of the Royal Engineers began his own flamethrower experiments as a means of retaliation. He turned his bedroom at Chatham into a laboratory and built small flamethrowers that achieved ranges of 30-40 feet.[3]

Summer – The Trench Warfare Department contracted Pedrail Transport, Ltd., to design a mechanized flamethrower with a capacity of 12,000 gallons.[4] One tracked chassis was completed and tested at Salisbury Plain. Powered by two 100 hp Astor engines, it weighed 32 tons empty and achieved a top speed of 15 miles per hour. No weapon was ever fitted to the vehicle, as the plan to build mechanized flamethrowers was abandoned in the fall.

July – Col. Jackson sent Captain F. V. Vincent of the Ministry of Munitions to France to observe trials of the Hersent-Thirion flamethrower. After Vincent returned from France, Captain P. S. Hay of the Ministry of Munitions was assigned to him as his chief technical assistant, with direct control over experimental work on flamethrowers.[5]

Late July – Menchen's flamethrower was completed and readied for trials at Wembley.[6]

In the same month Lt. Livens transferred to the Special Companies, the gas troops of the Royal Engineers. In August he sailed to France and took part in the first British gas attack, carried out at Loos on September 25, 1915.

August – Menchen's flamethrower was successfully tested at Wembley in the presence of military officials, but it was deemed too complicated and cumbersome for active service. The first flamethrower crews were NCOs and men lent by the Middlesex Regiment; from August 1915 the Admiralty provided men from 20th Squadron, Royal Naval Armored Car Division, as flamethrower operators. Col. Jackson chose them because he had an idea of mounting flamethrowers and machine guns on tractors that would be fitted with armored-car fighting compartments.[7] Only one prototype armored tractor was built. The men Jackson handpicked from 20th Squadron to work at Wembley were called the "Guns Crew."[8]

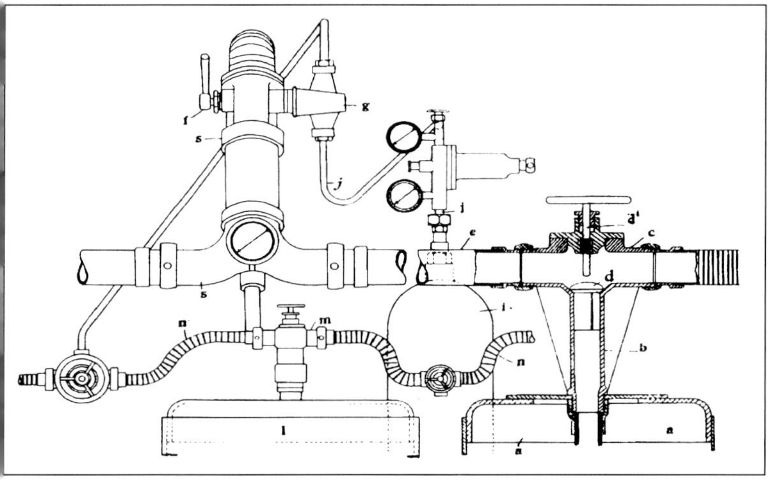

September – After Menchen's flamethrower was rejected, Capts. Vincent and Hay began work on a simpler, lighter battery flamethrower. The Vincent flamethrower was designed, constructed, and delivered to Wembley in only ten days. Alley and MacLellan, Ltd., Engineers, of Glasgow, built the weapon, and Capt. Hay trained the Guns Crew in its operation.[9]

September – The eight-man Vincent battery flamethrower was exhaustively tested with the goal of extending the weapon's range. Different oil mixtures, nozzle diameters, and ignition devices were tested; the ignition turned out to be the most difficult problem to solve. By December the Vincent had been perfected, and General Headquarters ordered 50 batteries.

The Trench Warfare Department designed and tested about 12 different models of portable flamethrower, settling on the Norris. In December an order was placed for 50, which would be used in France.[10]

October-November – Lt. Livens and Colonel Charles H. Foulkes, commander of the Special Companies, had several discussions on flamethrowers.[11]

December 15 – The Trench Warfare Department demonstrated the Vincent battery flamethrower, the Vincent semi-portable, and the Norris portable at Wembley. Col. Foulkes and Lt. Livens were present, having returned from France to see for themselves how the flamethrower work was progressing. During the demonstration a Vincent semi-portable device exploded. Joseph Menchen and Capts. Vincent and Hay were severely burned and sent to hospital. Among the Guns Crew, minor injuries such as burns and flash blindness were daily occurrences.[12] One reason was that the British originally used compressed air as a propellant, which was later changed to deoxygenated air or nitrogen.

The two-man Vincent semi-portable weighed 230 lbs. Transported by wheeled hand truck, it had a capacity of 15 gallons, a duration of 20 seconds, and a range of 40-60 yards. It was not adopted.[13]

Above

Left: Drawing from British patent No. 14,715, "Improvements Relating to Flame or Liquid Discharging Apparatus Applicable for Cremating and for Warlike Purposes." American inventor Joseph Menchen filed the application on October 18, 1915; the patent was granted March 20, 1919. Menchen's flamethrower was the basis for all subsequent British static designs. It consisted of multiple oil containers and propellant bottles connected together by pipes and/or hoses, the entire assembly feeding into a single lance. The device was rejected as too complicated and cumbersome for combat.

Right: Sailors of the Royal Naval Air Service Armored Car Division, the 20th Squadron of which supplied men for the flamethrower "Guns Crew" at Wembley Experimental Station in August of 1915. Like these men the Guns Crew wore a mixture of navy blue and army khaki, retaining their Royal Navy rank insignia. Although sailors, they were under the direct command of the Ministry of Munitions.

Below

Left: Vincent battery flamethrower, consisting of four oil tanks and propellant bottles connected in series by flexible metal pipes to a single lance. This weapon was served by a five-man squad and was designed for use in trenches, as shown, or in bombproof dugouts. Note that each oil tank and propellant bottle has its own pressure gauge, unusual for flamethrowers. Courtesy Dr. Mikhail Supotnitskiy.

Right: Lance of the Vincent battery flamethrower. Ignition was provided by gasoline squirted into the cup around the nozzle and lit with two spark plugs connected to a magneto generator. Compressed air was initially used as a propellant, replaced by deoxygenated air or nitrogen. The four wooden posts brace a steel heat shield; note the wires leading to the spark plugs at the nozzle. Courtesy Dr. Mikhail Supotnitskiy.

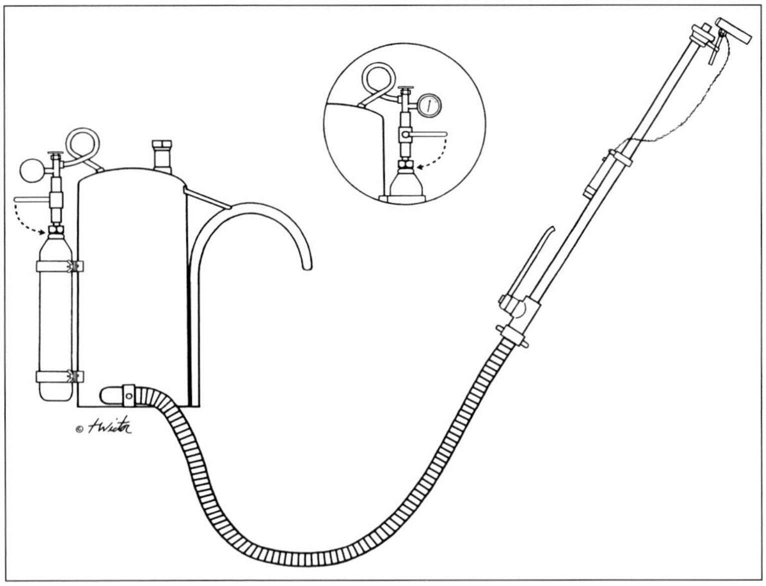

Norris portable flamethrower fitted with Menchen lance. The prototype was equipped with a triggerless lance similar to the one used on the Schilt No. 3. However, when the British army adopted the apparatus in December of 1915, a safety valve was added on the propellant bottle and the lance was replaced with American inventor Joseph Menchen's design. The new lance included an oil-release lever and an ignition system comprised of a dry-cell battery that set off a portfire under the nozzle. Note the leather-padded steel arms of the carrying harness, curved to fit over the operator's shoulders. Fifty Norris-Menchen portable flamethrowers were sent to France, where they were used for training purposes at gas schools. One sapper carried the flamethrower and fired the lance while an assistant opened the valve of the propellant bottle. Inset: left side of flamethrower, showing propellant-release valve and pressure gauge.

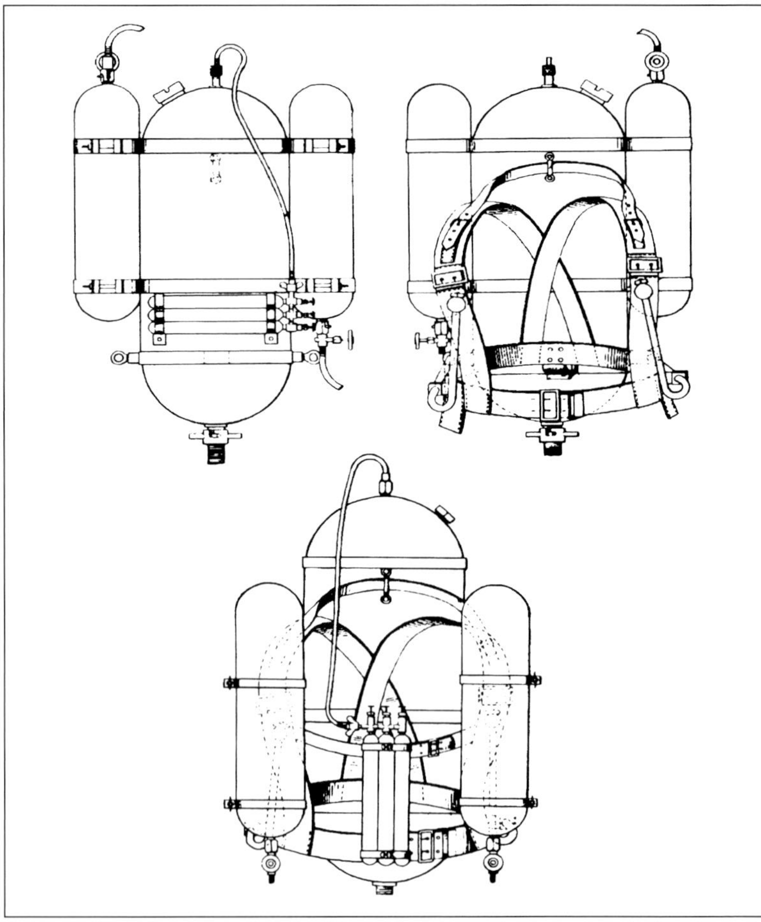

Lawrence Knapsack Flame Projector Model 1915, designed by Lieutenant Percy H. Lawrence of the Royal Engineers. Since Lawrence neglected to pay a sealing fee, no British patent was granted, although the device was assigned the number 17,696 on December 17, 1915. This weapon was a flamethrower that could also spray poison gas. The large cylinder held the oil, while the two smaller tanks held oxygen and chlorine respectively. Carbon dioxide was used as the propellant, stored in three small bottles. From top right: rear view of the flamethrower; front view of the flamethrower attached to a carrying harness; front view of the flamethrower with the propellant bottles and the oxygen and chlorine tanks worn on the front of the harness to protect the operator. Although not adopted by the British, this weapon influenced a Russian design. (See Russia.)

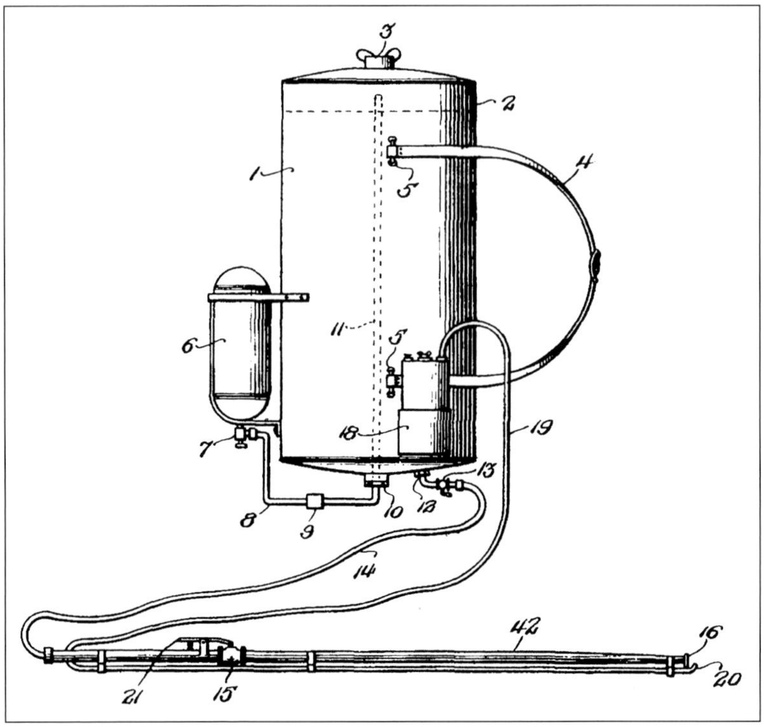

Portable flamethrower designed by William A. Hall; American patent application No. 1,220,103 filed December 29, 1916, and granted on March 20, 1917. Hall applied for British patent No. 15,288 on October 29, 1915. The success of this device is unclear. Some sources claim that Hall flamethrowers were given combat trials in France. The weapon was not adopted by the British but influenced American flamethrower development. It used a pilot light at the lance nozzle to ignite the oil stream, a feature incorporated into both models of American portable flamethrower tested overseas. A small container on the side of the flamethrower was filled with two parts calcium phosphide and one part calcium carbide, which generated the gas for the pilot light.

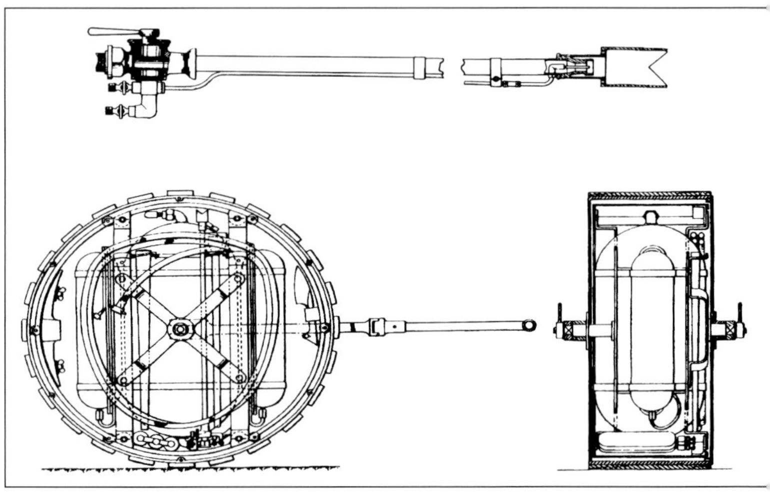

Lance (top) and transportation "roller" of the Lawrence Knapsack Flame Projector Model 1915. The roller allowed the weapon to be pulled like a toy wagon through trenches, while the lance was connected to an armored hose. Different nozzles were used to discharge flames, poison gas, or poisoned flames.

1916

January-June – After witnessing the December 15 flamethrower demonstration at Wembley, Lt. Livens took six months to design two flamethrowers: a six-man large battery model and a two-man semi-portable. He had the assistance of his father, Frederick Howard Livens, chief engineer of Ruston, Proctor and Co., Ltd., of Lincoln.[14] During this period Col. Foulkes placed four 70-man gas sections under Livens's command for him to train in the operation of what were eventually called the "Large Gallery" and the "Semi-portable."[15] The British often referred to their own flamethrowers as *Flammenwerfer,* even in official reports.

January – The Special Brigade was formed as a chemical warfare unit, comprised of 21 engineer companies under the command of Col. Foulkes. Flamethrowers were assigned to four Special Sections that later became Z Special Company, No. 5 (Mortar) Battalion, which had a compliment of 18 officers and 300 men. The new flamethrower sappers began training at a field in Hatfield, Hertfordshire.[16]

June 13 – Ten men of the Wembley Guns Crew disassembled a Vincent battery flamethrower in 4 1/2 minutes, carried it a short distance, then reassembled, filled, and fired it in 14 1/2 minutes.[17] Around this time the Trench Warfare Department demonstrated portable and battery flamethrowers to British government officials, including Prime Minister Herbert Asquith, David Lloyd George, Winston Churchill, and military representatives from Russia, Canada, France, Italy, Belgium, and Japan.[18]

June 19 – The Army Council wrote that "Flame Projectors already demanded will be used whenever an opportunity offers until they become unserviceable; they will not, however, be replaced."[19]

June 21-24 – Lt. Livens and the 254 men of the four Special Sections departed from Southampton and steamed to Le Havre with four disassembled Large Gallery *Flammenwerfer* and 24 Semi-portables. From Le Havre, they travelled by train and truck to Bronfay Farm, in the area of the Fourth Army, a few miles from the Somme front lines. Section 2 took the Semi-portables to the front lines of X, XV, and XIII Corps.[20]

June 27 – Section 1 picked up one Large Gallery *Flammenwerfer* from Bronfay Farm and took it to the front lines of the 7th Division, XV Corps, opposite Fricourt. Men from the Devonshire Regiment, 20th Infantry Brigade, helped carry the parts to the front line, where most of the flamethrower was assembled in a shallow mine gallery. The next day German shelling caused most of the mine gallery to collapse, burying the flamethrower. Section 1 returned to Maricourt with a few salvaged parts.[21]

Well-turned-out young sapper of the Royal Engineers in 1902 Pattern Service Dress in khaki with stiff peaked cap and waist belt of the 1903 Pattern bandolier equipment. Flamethrower sappers of the Special Sections (later Z Company), Special Brigade, were uniformed identically, with no distinguishing insignia. This man may belong to the Special Sections or Z Company, as indicated by his expensive, non-regulation leather gloves. Flamethrower sappers often purchased such gloves as protection against the heat and spatter of their weapons.

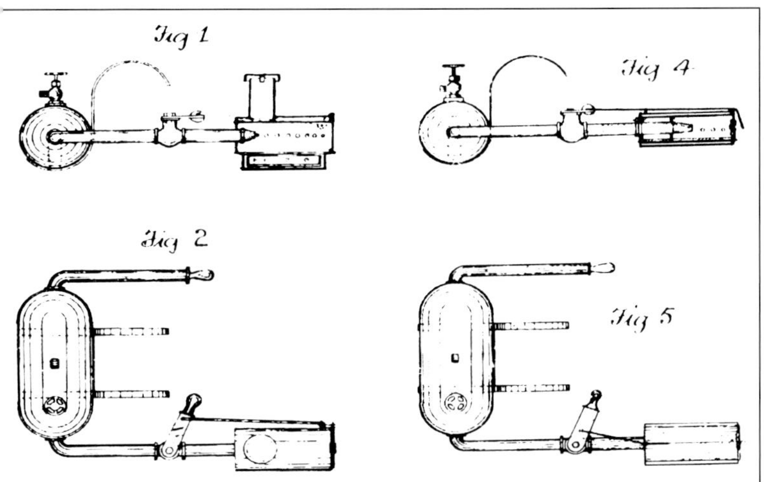

Portable flamethrower designed by Arthur Kitson, of the Kitson Empire Lighting Company. It was assigned British patent No. 18,119 on December 29, 1915, although no patent was granted because Kitson did not pay the sealing fee. Figures 1 and 2 are the side and plan view of one version, and Figures 2 and 3 are a modification. The flamethrower was worn horizontally on the back and fired with the right hand, while the left hand held a steadying handle. The igniter consisted of a container filled with methylated spirit, which was lit with a match. Although the British army tested the design, it was not adopted. From British Patent No. 18,119.

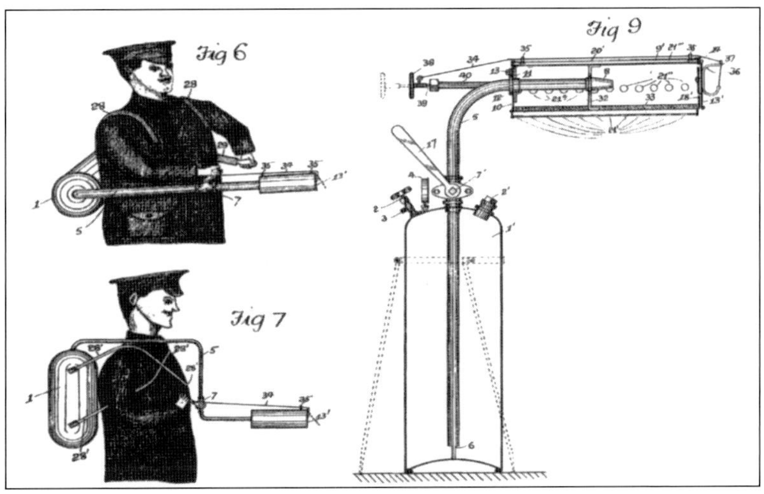

Figure 6 depicts the Kitson portable in action, while Figure 7 is a modification of the weapon, which may have influenced a Russian design called the Tilly-Goskin. Figure 9 is a static version of the Kitson device, which was clearly the basis for the Livens Semi-portable flamethrower. The Kitson static weapon included support poles to prevent the weapon from tipping over backward when fired. All Kitson flamethrowers used either ordinary crude oil or five parts coal tar and five parts methyl alcohol, pressurized in the tank with a mixture of compressed air and carbon dioxide. From British Patent No. 18,119.

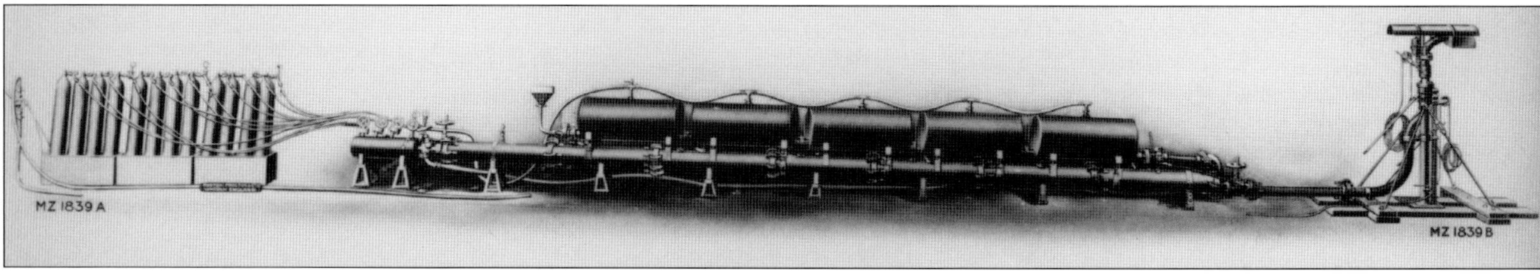

Livens Large Gallery Flammenwerfer, a weapon nearly 50 ft. long. On the left are the propellant bottles; the five oil tanks containing 160 gal. of oil are in the center, above the 9in. bore discharge pipe containing 80 gal. of oil; and the "monitor" containing the nozzle and acetylene ignition system is on the right. A crew of six or seven served the weapon. Imperial War Museum Q.55060

June 29-30 – Section 3 deployed three Large Gallery *Flammenwerfer* in three mine galleries between the Carnoy-Montauban Road and Kasino Point, on the front of the 18th Division and to the left of XIII Corps. Under heavy shellfire, Section 3 assembled the three flamethrowers. The one furthest to the left was destroyed by artillery and abandoned.[22]

July 1 – Opening day of the Battle of the Somme. At 7:15 A.M. the two surviving Large Gallery *Flammenwerfer* were fired at the German trenches. The shots lasted only ten seconds each; the flame jets achieved estimated lengths of 87 and 94 yards and killed about 40 Germans.[23]

July 1 to July 18 – Semi-portable flamethrowers were deployed on 12 occasions, but fired only twice.[24] Because of the weapons' limited range, the men had to carry them deep into No Man's Land,[25] struggling under their weight of 150 lbs.

July 10 – Five Semi-portable Detachments were assigned to the 36th Brigade for the attack on White Trench, but they never fired their flamethrowers. On the same day the weapons of two Semi-portable Detachments taken to Pommiers Redoubt were destroyed by artillery while the men waited for the assault to begin.[26]

July 14 – Lt. Livens reported to Chief of Staff XV Corps:

> If a Flammenwerfer is required which can be moved long distances in crowded trenches it must be either
>
> a) A small apparatus of not more than half the weight of the present one (i.e. a charged weight not exceeding 80 lbs.) or
>
> b) an apparatus quickly assembled from comparatively small and light parts.[27]

On the same day Lt. Livens and 2nd Lieutenant Harry Strange, commander of Section 3, begin experimenting with what became the Livens projector: "Oil drum (10 gallon)

Livens Large Gallery Flammenwerfer being test fired. In combat it was assembled in a mine gallery 10-20 ft. underground; a hydraulic jack pushed the monitor up through the earth like a submarine periscope. Five Large Galley Flammenwerfern were shipped to France, three of which were used four times in 1916 and 1917. British National Archives MUN-385.

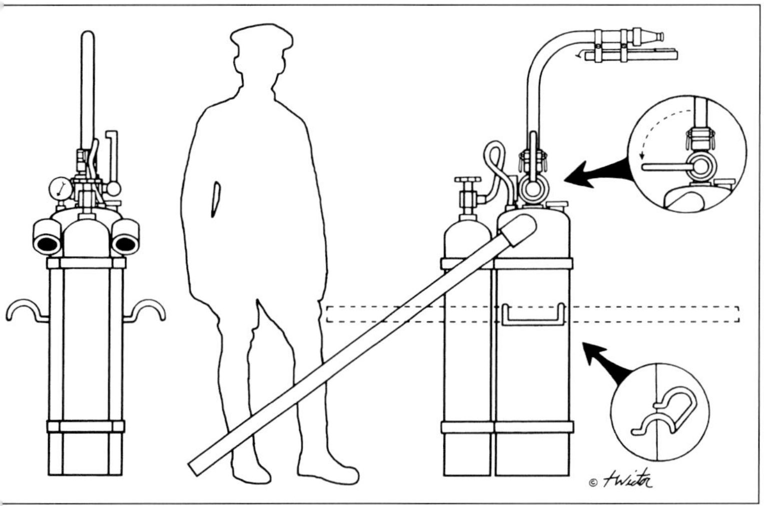

***Left:** Provisional rendering of Livens Semi-portable flamethrower, based on written descriptions. Adopted by the British army in June of 1916, it was operated by a two-man squad that carried it into battle with the aid of poles slipped under curved brackets on the side of the oil tank (lower inset). Once the flamethrower was in position, the carrying poles were used as braces, since the weapon would flip over backward when used. To fire the device, the sapper pressurized the oil by opening the valve of the propellant tank and then pulled downward on the handle of the oil-release stopcock (upper inset). The curved evacuation pipe was fitted with the nozzle of a fire hose, and the igniter consisted of a friction primer that touched off a portfire.*

***Right:** Livens projector, originally designed to replace flamethrowers. The Special Brigade used Livens projectors to fire both oil and gas drums (left and in background), which were ejected by means of an electrically detonated explosive charge (center and right) placed in the rounded base of the tubes. Note the wires, which were connected to a blasting machine. Livens projectors were deployed in batteries of 25 and came in three sizes: Mark I (2 ft., 6 in. long, 65 lbs.), Mark II (2 ft., 9 in. long, 105 lbs.) and Mark III (4 ft. long, 150 lbs.). All had an internal diameter of 8 in. and were used with the 28-lb. steel base plate shown. Maximum range was about 1850 yards. The most effective oil mixture was one part heavy Mexican petroleum residue and three parts Persian distillate. A percussion or time fuse ruptured the drum and both spread and ignited the contents.*

used as Minenwerfer to through*[sic]* another drum (3 gallon) filled with oil which bursts and spreads burning oil."[28] The large steel drum was 12 in. in diameter by 20 in. tall and was used to transport flamethrower oil. A charge of black powder inside the large drum fired the oil-can projectile and ignited the sacking streamers that served as the fuse. The Livens projector would eventually replace the flamethrower.

July 16 – Reports by the Semi-portable Detachments stated:

> [I]t was nearly impossible to negotiate trenches with these weapons at any but a very slow pace indeed that in the chance of the trenches being encumbered by mud or other obstacles progress was nearly impossible. This apparatus was designed for:
>
> a) Attacks on and domination of Mine Craters
> b) Very close fighting in Redoubts and Keeps
> c) Defense of Strong Points.
>
> No type of Portable Flammenwerfer is possible which can be used for open fighting because 40 yards is the present maximum range of such apparatus.[29]

July 17 – Two Semi-portable Detachments fired their weapons in support of the 1/7th Battalion, Worcestershire Regiment, of the 144th Brigade, 48th (South Midland) Division. During this action three flamethrower sappers were killed and nine wounded.[30]

July 23 – Detachments under Lt. Strange and Lt. Barr fired 40 "oil Minenwerfers" for the first time, with the 1/4th Battalion, Gloucestershire Regiment, 144th Brigade, 48th (South Midland) Division.[31]

July 24 – The bulk of the Special Sections began training with the "oil throwing Minenwerfer."[32] In reports the weapon was called the "oil can mortar," "oil mortar," or "oil projector." When used it was buried in the ground at a 45-degree angle with only the muzzle exposed.

End of July – Lieutenant E. Tribe of the Trench Warfare Department arrived in France with a Vincent battery flamethrower. In mid-August, the fifth Large Gallery was sent from Britain.[33] According to another source Tribe accompanied three Vincent battery models to France, but they were never used.[34]

Mid to late 1916 – Russia ordered several sets of Vincent and Livens battery flamethrowers; at Wembley Capt. Hay and Lt. Tribe trained 300 Russian soldiers for about one month in the use of the weapons.[35]

August 9-10 – No. 4 and No. 6 Subsections of Z Company, armed with two Large Gallery flamethrowers, were attached to F Company of the Special Brigade at Treux. They began preparations for installing the weapons at High Wood.[36]

August 19 – The Special Brigade put on a large demonstration of flamethrowers, Livens projectors, and other devices at Toutencourt. Two experimental incendiary

Above: Vincent battery flamethrower fitted with a lattice-type monitor so that the flamethrower could be assembled underground in a mine gallery. Before the device could be fired, a jack pushed the monitor up to the surface, exposing the acetylene-fed igniter to the air. The monitor had a traverse of 30 degrees. Courtesy Simon Jones.

Below: The lattice-type monitor, which raised the nozzle 3 ft. 6 in. above the support framework. The lifting device was known as a "lazy tongs" jack. Courtesy Simon Jones.

"crates" measuring 4 ft. 9 in. square and 3 ft. 7 in. square respectively were packed with tins of oil and fired from underground shafts 20 ft. long, dug at a 45-degree angle. The explosives used to eject the crates caused them to catch fire too early.[37]

September 3 – One Large Gallery and one Vincent battery flamethrower were fired near High Wood. On September 8, the Large Gallery *Flammenwerfer* was fired once, taking out a machine-gun nest.[38] Another source attributed the September 3 flamethrower attacks in High Wood to Semi-portables; the Large Gallery was instead used at Arrowhead Copse, southwest of Guillemont.[39] In a third account, provided by Col. Foulkes, the High Wood attacks were carried out with three Semi-portables and one Vincent battery, while one Large Gallery *Flammenwerfer* was fired at Arrowhead Copse.[40]

October 1 – A Court of Enquiry deemed the Semi-portable unsafe for use due to the tendency of the flame tube to come apart at the Morris coupling.[41] This particular accident had happened three times, spraying sappers with burning oil.

On the same day men of a Special Section fired 36 oil mortars at Flers, in support of an attack by the 2nd Battalion of the 1st Canterbury Infantry Regiment, New Zealand Expeditionary Force. Thirty of the drums were observed to explode on the German position 400 yards away, enveloping it in smoke and flame:

> When the trench was captured several groups, one of 20 and one of 15, of enemy dead were found badly scorched and charred by the oil flames. Some of the prisoners, as might have been expected, complained bitterly of the use of burning oil, and told of the terror excited by the fear of being caught by the flames.[42]

October 5 – Two Semi-portables were fired from a salient near Nieuport, the last flamethrower shots of the year. Z Company continued training and experimenting with Semi-portables but did not use them in combat again.[43]

November 8 – A large battery flamethrower exploded at Wembley, killing one operator and fatally injuring another. Four other men were seriously wounded.[44] At around the same time an experimental Semi-portable was built of riveted Duralumin rather than pressed, welded steel. It exploded due to cracks caused by the riveting process.[45]

Late 1916-most of 1917 – In France, Z Company put all large flamethrowers in storage at Toutencourt, where they rusted and deteriorated for almost a year. One was used once in late 1917.[46] (See October 26, 1917.)

After the Battle of the Somme, General Headquarters "decided to wash out all Flame Projectors as the amount of damage they did in offensive warfare did not

Above: Corporal of the Royal Engineers as he would appear in the field, wearing the khaki 1902 Pattern Service Dress and 1915 Pattern trench cap. The distinctive engineer's cap badge and metal "RE" on the shoulder straps are clearly seen.

Right: Corporal John S. Heaton (right) of L Company, the Special Brigade. He and his companion wear 1914 Pattern Infantry Equipment, including a holster for the .455 caliber six-shot Webley revolver issued as a side arm to gas and flame sappers. The 1914 Pattern equipment supplemented the 1908 Pattern Web Equipment and was made entirely of leather for speed of manufacture. Both versions consisted of haversack, pack, ammunition pouches, water bottle and carrier, and entrenching tool with separate carriers for the head and helve. Like Corporal Heaton, many gas and flame sappers retained their .303 caliber Lee-Enfield rifles. Courtesy Andrew Heaton.

Norris portable flamethrower being demonstrated to Serbian officers at a British gas school near Albert, February 2, 1918. Although the Norris was approved for manufacture, it never saw combat. The operator wears a protective flame-resistant suit that has been camouflaged in wide bands of color applied with a spray gun. Imperial War Museum Q.6493.

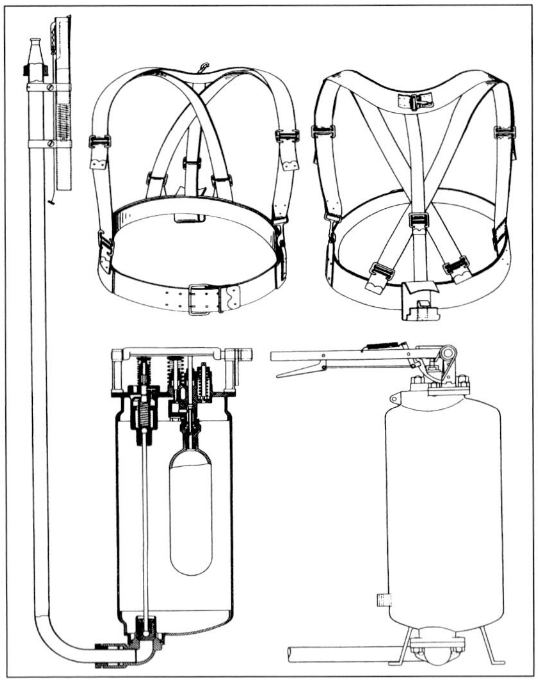

Lawrence Knapsack Flame Projector Model 1917. Designed by Lieutenant Percy H. Lawrence of the Royal Engineers, it was assigned the British patent No. 128,275 on July 10, 1917, although no patent was granted. A swiveling rigid lance was fitted to the right side of the oil tank, and the propellant bottle was suspended inside the flamethrower. To pressurize the oil, the operator used his left hand to pull downward on the firing lever fitted to the top of the weapon. This motion pierced the sealing cap of the propellant bottle, allowing the gas out into the oil. The operator fired the weapon by squeezing the grip at the end of the firing lever. Ignition was provided by a portfire with a friction fuse attached beneath the nozzle of the lance. The British did not adopt this flamethrower. From drawings in British patent No. 128,275.

warrant the vast amount of labour required to instal*[sic]* them in first line trenches or galleries."[47]

ca. late 1916 – Lieutenant G. C. O. Usborne, 40th Squadron, Royal Flying Corps, conceived of mounting a small flamethrower above the rudder of his RAF FE8 fighter to fire backward in flight and burn enemy aircraft on his tail. A button in the instrument panel would operate the device. Usborne – known as the "Gadget King" in his squadron – demonstrated the idea to his superiors, using a small signal rocket fixed to his aircraft. The "Brass Hats" were unimpressed, one of them remarking, "This isn't cricket."[48]

1917

The Trench Warfare Department thoroughly tested captured German flamethrowers and concluded that they were very inferior to the British designs.[49]

At the beginning of the year Col. Foulkes formally redesignated the Special Sections as Z Company, although the name had already been in use for some time.[50]

Mid-1917 – Lt. Percy H. Lawrence of the Royal Engineers was sent to Russia to demonstrate his Knapsack Flame Projector Model 1917. The weapon was manufactured in Britain, but shipments to Russia were halted after the revolution.[51] Branch III of the Russian Chemical Committee, Main Artillery Administration, also manufactured the Lawrence Knapsack Flame Projector Model 1917 under license.[52] (See Russia.)

Night of June 3 – As preparation for the Battle of Messines, O and K Companies of the Special Brigade used Livens projectors to fire 1500 drums of oil into the Bois de Wytschaete, Grand Bois, and Unnamed Wood, the largest such operation of the war.[53]

Night of October 26 – At 2:40 A.M. Section 2 of the Special Brigade fired a Large Gallery *Flammenwerfer* at Dixmunde, in support of the Belgian 2nd Division. This was the last use of the large British flamethrower on land.[54]

1917-1918 – At the request of the Air Board and Admiralty, the Trench Warfare Department carried out a great deal of experimental work on aircraft-mounted flamethrowers and large flamethrowers mounted on fast motor boats.

In addition, American flamethrower experts from the American Headquarters in France paid several visits to Wembley and studied the British flamethrower efforts.[55]

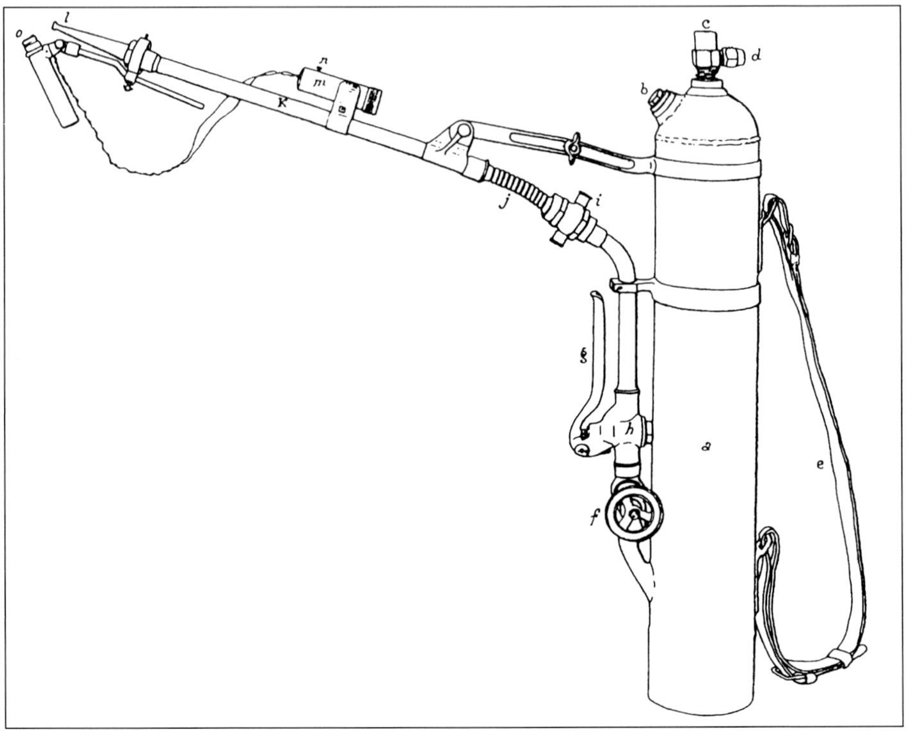

Portable flamethrower designed by Captain P. S. Hay of the Ministry of Munitions in early 1918. Called the "Hay Flame Gun," it was used either standing on the ground or hanging from a shoulder strap. The ignition system consisted of a dry-cell battery mounted on the lance, which set off a portfire positioned under the nozzle. Only about 40 were produced, 36 of which the Admiralty ordered for use during the Zeebrugge raid of April 24, 1918.

***Left:** Soldier of the Ministry of Munitions, wearing the Suit, Anti-liquid Fire, Pattern 3023/1918 and modeling a Hay Flame Gun at the Wembley Experimental Ground outside London. This suit was not used in combat. Courtesy Simon Jones.*

***Right:** Second photo taken at the same time as the pervious, showing the Hay Flame Gun in firing mode. Note the leather shoulder strap and the lowered visor of the fire-resistant suit. The sapper aims the lance with his left hand and holds the trigger lever with his right. Apparently the Hay Flame Gun was the only portable British flamethrower used in combat. Courtesy Simon Jones.*

December – Capt. Hay produced a portable flamethrower called the "Hay Flame Gun," which he offered to the Americans as well as the British.[56]

1918

February – Capt. Hay was lent to the Admiralty to develop flamethrowers for use in naval warfare. At around this time men from Wembley and naval ratings from the Royal Naval Experimental Station at Stratford installed two Vincent battery flamethrowers in HMS *Vindictive*. One device was connected to 18 oil tanks below decks, and the other to 12. Both were built into armored housings fore and aft, called "Flamethrower Huts." The Admiralty also ordered 36 Hay Flame Guns. At Wembley, Capt. Hay and Lt. Tribe trained 40 Stratford naval ratings as flamethrower operators.[57]

April 24 – The British carried out a blocking raid at the German-occupied port of Zeebrugge. As the *Vindictive* drew alongside the Mole, Lieutenant A. L. Eastlake, attached Royal Engineers and the sole army officer on the ship, gave the order to fire the Vincent flamethrower in the fore hut, not knowing that the oil feed pipe had been severed by a shell burst.[58] The moment the order was given, the flamethrower nozzle was shot off. Flammable oil sprayed all over the decks but did not ignite.

In the aft flamethrower hut, Commander Frank Brock lit the ignition system and ordered the weapon fired. As in the case of the forward flamethrower, the nozzle was shot off at that instant and the flamethrower sprayed its entire load of unlit oil.

The Experimental Party, also called the Pyrotechnic Party, was the detachment of 34 volunteers from the Admiralty Experimental Station. They worked the Vincent flamethrowers on *Vindictive* and the Hay Flame Guns in the naval and marine storming parties that landed on the Mole.[59] In addition they were armed with phosphorus grenades and operated the signal flares and smoke machines. Lieutenant Graham S. Hewett, R.N.V.R., commanded the Pyrotechnic Party. Air Mechanic W. H. Gough was one of the Hay Flame Gunners:

Above: HMS Vindictive after the Zeebrugge raid of April 24, 1918. The aft flamethrower hut is clearly visible as a large box on the port side of the stern; the fore flamethrower hut is below and slightly to the left of the crow's nest in front of the forward funnel. Each hut housed a Vincent battery flamethrower, one connected to 18 oil containers and the other to 12. The Pyrotechnic Party of Wembley Experimental Station – sailors commanded by a Lieutenant of the Royal Naval Volunteer Reserve – manned the weapons.

Left: Foredeck of the HMS Vindictive; note the bullet-riddled flamethrower hut on the right. Neither Vincent battery flamethrower was used in the raid, as the nozzles of both were shot away by enemy fire, soaking the decks with flame oil that luckily did not ignite.

Sailors and Royal Marines celebrating their safe return from the Zeebrugge raid. In the center-left foreground, members of the Pyrotechnic Party hold a Hay Flame Gun on their shoulders. The Admiralty ordered 36 such flamethrowers for the operation.

> Shortly after the seamen went over, I followed, but as the flamenwerfer*[sic]* I carried was very unwieldy, I could not keep up with the platoon, but followed them over the brows and across the mole. Here I found a shed which was open and on going inside found a stack of rifles and two dead men. Coming out I observed a party with weapons, including I believe a machine gun, just landing from a destroyer alongside the mole. I discharged my flamethrower on them and they ceased firing and our men who were near put them finally out of action. The flamethrower now being discharged, I was myself out of action and therefore went back to the *Vindictive*. I used my revolver once on one of three men who tried to get to the scaling ladders to wrench them.[60]

This was the final combat use of flamethrowers in the war.

May 6 – The War Office prohibited Lt. Lawrence from demonstrating his flamethrower to American officers in France. Brigadier General C. M. Wagstaff of the British Mission to the American Expeditionary Force (AEF) sent an explanation to Colonel Amos Fries, commander of the American 30th Engineer Regiment (Gas and Flame):

> The first reason is that Lawrence has given a lot of trouble to the War Office, and they are not going to let him give any more, to themselves or anybody else.
>
> The second reason is that although this particular invention is not bad, the whole principle is objected to, and it is not recommended that Flame-Projectors be seriously taken up.[61]

Norris portable flamethrower demonstration at a gas school, November of 1918. The lance operator wears flame-resistant coveralls, while the assistant opens the valve on the propellant bottle. These demonstrations were intended to reduce the troops' anxiety over flamethrowers and show how to defend against the weapons.

June – Capt. Hay took three of his Flame Guns to France and demonstrated them to General John J. Pershing, Commander-in-Chief of the AEF. Hay then exhibited his weapon to French and Italian officials in Paris. Inspired by Hay's design, the Americans and British cooperated on a new portable flamethrower that was completed just before the Armistice.[62] The unidentified device may be the Knapsack Flame Projector, Mark I, accepted by the U.S. Army on December 9, 1918. (See United States.)

During the war the British produced 50 Norris-Menchen portable flamethrowers, 50 Vincent Battery models, 54 Livens Large Gallery flamethrowers, 24 Livens Semi-portables, and 36 Hay Flame Guns, for a total of 214 devices.[63] Twelve British flamethrower sappers were killed in action or died of wounds, accident, or gassing.[64]

1919

Summer – The Special Brigade was demobilized.[65]

Tactics

The British did not develop formalized flame tactics. All of their flamethrowers were used offensively in infantry assaults without the protection of riflemen and/or hand-grenade throwers.

In 1915 the plan had been to use flamethrowers in conjunction with poison gas, smoke, and Stokes mortars, but this coordination never panned out.

Brig. Gen. Foulkes seems to have spoken for most of the British military establishment when he wrote, "I did not consider [portable or semi-portable flamethrowers] to be of any value in an assault, because if an infantry attacking party ever succeeded in carrying such a dangerous and cumbersome machine to within close range of a German trench, it would only be for the reason that there was little or no opposition to overcome; while for clearing trenches and dug-outs, hand grenades would be equally effective, and would require no specially trained troops or special apparatus for their use."[66]

RUSSIA

1915

May 17 or 18 – A Mr. Bratoliubov, whose father-in-law was a general on the Artillery Committee, announced to the Commission for the Preparation of Explosives *(Komisiia po Zagotovke Vzryvchatykh Veshchestv)* that for 30 million rubles he could equip the Russian army with a flamethrower *(ognemet)* manufactured in the United States.[1] The chairman of the CPE, artillery general and professor of organic chemistry Vladimir N. Ipatieff, turned down the offer after testing the inflammable liquids and finding them worthless.

Bratoliubov then approached Grand Duke Mikhail Aleksandrovich, brother of Tsar Nicholas II. The Grand Duke conferred with the Tsar and, rather than refer the weapon to the Special Council for Defense for investigation, noted on Bratoliubov's report that the invention should be pursued. Bratoliubov was thus able to secure an advance of 2 million rubles from a local bank. By the time the Assistant War Minister got wind of the project and questioned Ipatieff, Bratoliubov and the money had vanished.

Spring – The CPE began researching flamethrowers.[2]

July – The War Ministry ordered the establishment of the Commission for the Production of Asphyxiating Gases *(Komisiia po Izgotovleniiu Udushaiushchikh Sredstv)*. Among its many duties the CPAG was to organize chemical-warfare units.[3]

Above: Russian soldier posing with an Austrian 50l M. 15 Flammenwerfer. The Russians based some of their own flamethrower designs on captured Austrian and German weapons and may have used the original devices in combat. This soldier wears the flamethrower accessory box, and there is a flame-oil can on the bench next to the weapon. The apparatus is essentially ready for action.

Left: German civilians demonstrating a Fiedler portable flamethrower to the Russians at Izhora on March 14, 1909. The top-hatted man on the right is almost certainly inventor Richard Fiedler, who tried to interest the Russian army in three sizes of flamethrower in 1909 and 1911. Both his attempts were rejected on the grounds that flamethrower operators and their weapons were vulnerable to rifle and artillery fire; flamethrowers were too inaccurate; and the logistics of providing oil and preparing the devices for use was not worth the effort. Courtesy Dr. Mikhail Supotnitskiy.

Undated photo of Russian soldier modeling a Kleif M.1912 captured from the Austrians or Germans. Spurred by such acquisitions, the Russians began researching flamethrowers in the spring of 1915. In this photo the igniter holder displays an unidentified attachment that is likely a special nozzle for spraying poison gas. Many Russian reports also claim that Central Powers' troops sprayed acid with flamethrowers, although neither German nor Austrian records have confirmed this. Courtesy Russian State Military-Historical Archives.

August 3 – The Main Artillery Administration *(Glavnoe Artilleriiskoe Upravlenie)*, which acquired munitions for the army, formed the CPAG. It was comprised of five engineers who had studied at the Artillery Academy.[4]

September – The first 20 flamethrowers manufactured by a Professor Gorbov were tested by the CPE.[5] Flamethrowers were to be produced by the Main Military Technical Administration *(Glavnoe Voenno-Tekhnicheskoe Upravlenie)*.

October – The CPAG began organizing Chemical Detachments *(Khimicheskie Komandy)* to carry out gas attacks. Composed of artillerymen, the detachments were subordinate to the general of artillery of the army to which they were attached.[6] Initially two detachments were established, followed in the next few months by five more.[7]

1916

January – The Supreme Headquarters established the Directorate of the Field Inspector-General of Artillery *(Upravlenie Polevogo General-Inspectora Artillerii pri Stavke)*, which would control supplies, weapons, and equipment of the artillery and Chemical Detachments in the field.[8]

February – The General Staff *(Glavnyi Shtab)* ordered the creation of a War-Chemical Committee *(Voenno-Khimicheskii Komitet)* to supervise the production of gas masks and the training of troops in defense against chemical weapons. On February 16 the War Minister wrote to the Tsar supporting the new committee.[9]

March – The Main Military Technical Administration ordered the production of 1500 Gorbov portable flamethrowers.[10]

March 2 – The Tsar approved the War-Chemical Committee of the General Staff. Soon afterward, the General Staff established a Council for the War-Chemical Committee, adding yet another layer of bureaucracy to the chemical-warfare effort.[11]

March 21 – The Fifth Army, under the command of General Vasily Gourko, used flamethrowers and gas hand grenades in savage fighting against a German salient at Jacobstadt, 80 miles southeast of Riga.[12] No other details of this operation are known. The flamethrower troops may have been artillerymen of a Chemical Detachment using captured Austrian and/or German devices.

April – The British trained 300 Russian officers and men in the use of large static flamethrowers at Wembley Experimental Station outside London. The month-long course was taught by Captain Hay and Lieutenant Tribe of the Ministry of Muni-

Private first class (Yefreitor) of the 13th Field Artillery Brigade, uniformed in the khaki M1916 shirt-tunic (gymnastiorka) in wool. On his stiff, detachable shoulder straps (pogoni) he wears privately purchased crossed metal cannon barrels and the single red stripe of his rank; the straps are reversible, colored khaki on one side and crimson on the other for artillery and sappers. The first Russian gas and flame troops were artillerymen who served in the seven Chemical Detachments (Khimicheskie Komandy) of the Commission for the Production of Asphyxiating Gases (CPAG), organized in late 1915. Artillerymen saw themselves as an elite, referring to the infantry as the "cattle."

These Russian soldiers, captured by the Germans on the eastern front, escaped from prison camps on the French border while doing road work during the Battle of Verdun. Photographed in France, they wear Russian, German, and French uniforms. In April of 1916 the British trained 300 such Russian escapees as flamethrower operators and repatriated them. Some of these men joined the Flame-Chemical Training Battalion (Uchebnogo Ognekhimicheskogo Batalyona), which instructed sappers in chemical and flame warfare.

tions, and the men were inspected by Grand Duke Michael before sailing for Russia.[13] These flamethrower operators were former prisoners of war[14] who had escaped from German camps on the French border while doing road work for their captors during the Battle of Verdun.

April 16 – Tsar Nicholas II ratified the creation of a Chemical Committee in the Main Artillery Adminstration.[15] General Ipatieff was appointed chairman of the Chemical Committee, which was supervised by the Council of the War-Chemical Committee of the General Staff. The War-Chemical Committee of the General Staff continued to operate, often as a competitor of the new Chemical Committee.

The Chemical Committee of the Main Artillery Administration had five branches: I. Explosives; II. Poison Gases; III. Incendiaries and Flamethrowers; IV. Gas masks; and V. Acids. Members of the Committee included military officers, academics, scientists, and representatives of private nongovernmental organizations. With the creation of the Chemical Committee, responsibility for producing flamethrowers was relinquished by the Main Military Technical Administration.

To instruct the troops in gas and flame warfare, the Chemical Committee formed the Flame-Chemical Training Battalion *(Uchebnogo Ognekhimicheskogo Batalyona)*, based in Petrograd. A technical battalion, it likely had a strength of about 9 officers, 20 NCOs, and 645 men organized into three companies.[16]

Private (Ryadovoi) of the 42nd Field Artillery Brigade. On the shoulder straps of his khaki M1910 cotton shirt-tunic, the branch-of-service distinction and unit number are stenciled in red paint, regulation for enlisted men. Note the artillery belt buckle, dark-green trousers, M1910 fleece cap (papakha), holstered seven-shot 7.62mm M1895 Nagant revolver on his right hip, and M1881 saber. The men of the Chemical Detachments formed by the CPAG wore artillery uniforms with no special insignia.

Instructors of the Flame-Chemical Training Battalion arresting government loyalists in Petrograd during the November Revolution of 1917. The men of the battalion wore a crossed hammer-and-wrench badge on their caps, shoulder boards, and the collars of their greatcoats. Cap bands and collar patches were black with light-green piping, while shoulder straps had no numeral or cipher. The battalion instructed sappers of the 14 Chemical Detachments in flame and poison-gas warfare, as well as the generation of smoke screens. Disarmed of their flamethrowers and poison gas by the Provisional Government in July of 1917 for harboring Bolshevik sympathies, the flame-chemical instructors took part in the November Revolution on the side of the Reds, fighting as infantry.

Metal hammer-and-wrench badge of the Flame-Chemical Training Battalion. It was based on the symbol of the Practical Technological Institute in Petrograd.

The flame-chemical troops trained by the battalion were designated sappers *(sapery)* rather than artillerymen. They were assigned to 13 Chemical Detachments, one for each army at the various fronts. These new units replaced the seven artillery Chemical Detachments created by the CPAG. Their mission was to engage in gas and flame warfare and lay down smoke screens. Comprised of about three officers, 12 NCOs, and 150 sappers who would be equipped with gas cylinders, flamethrowers, and smoke-generating equipment, Chemical Detachments were subordinate to the commander of the army to which they were attached. For combat operations the army commander would separate gas, flame, or smoke sections from his Chemical Detachment and provide them to individual divisions or brigades.[17]

Each army formed one chemical-warfare school, one chemical laboratory, and one depot of gas weapons and smoke generators, smoke pots, and smoke candles. Flamethrowers would be added to the arsenal when they became available. Although the artillery generals of the respective armies no longer directly controlled the Chemical Detachments, the Inspector of Artillery of each army still supervised the units.

Engineer officers (left and right). The 2nd lieutenant (pod-poruchik) on the right wears the M1881 greatcoat (shinel) with black collar patches (petlitsi) piped in red. His shoulder straps are adorned with metal engineering badges of crossed pick and shovel and the crossed cannon barrels of the artillery, almost certainly identifying him as a flame-chemical sapper. The ensign (praporshchik) on the left wears a shirt-tunic with shoulder boards that display metal engineering badges and the number "4," indicating either the 4th Engineer Battalion or the Chemical Detachment of the Fourth Army. His M1907/10 visor cap (furazhka) has the engineers' black band piped in red and his awards include a shoulder-strap jetton (pogonchik) hanging from his tunic button and the badge of the Nicholas Engineering School. Note the unusual reinforcing patches on the knees of his trousers.

Above: Sapper Robert Vitolu, a Latvian. He wears the belt buckle of the engineers – a double-headed eagle surmounting crossed axes – and shoulder straps stenciled with the engineer badge and the unit number 1, both in brown oil paint. Since he also displays the breast badge of the 1st Vyborg Fortress Artillery Battalion, he is likely a flame-chemical sapper. After April of 1916 the artillerymen of the Chemical Detachments were redesignated sappers, but many continued to wear the insignia of their former units. In addition a large percentage of flame-chemical sappers continued to be drawn from the artillery. Vitolu is armed with a Japanese M1897 bayonet, issued due to shortages of Russian weapons.

Left: Sapper private wearing a khaki M1910 shirt-tunic in cotton; the unit number 13 and engineer badge of crossed pick and shovel on the soft shoulder straps are stenciled in brown oil paint, regulation for enlisted men. The band of his visor cap is khaki instead of black, and the stamped-tin cockade is painted the imperial colors of orange and black. This sapper may belong to a Chemical Detachment, as the latter units wore no distinguishing insignia.

The Directorate of the Field Inspector-General of the Artillery devised gas and flame tactics and supplied weapons, equipment, poison gas, and flame oil.[18] The Chemical Detachments first saw combat as gas troops. (See September 18.)

At the end of April, Branch III of the Chemical Committee, under the direction of Colonel L. V. Martiushev, commander of the Flame-Chemical Training Battalion, began researching flamethrowers.[19]

Early May – In response to a request from the Russian government, the British shipped one Vincent battery flamethrower to Russia. Twenty more were sent by the end of the month.[20]

Mid May – Branch III of the Chemical Committee produced a portable flamethrower *(ranchevyĭ ognemet)* which was demonstrated to the Tsar.[21] This weapon was probably the Tilly-Goskin, a highly unusual British design:

> The apparatus consists of one large reservoir, into which is welded another reservoir of a smaller diameter. The large reservoir is for flammable liquid and the smaller for compressed air. A manual air pump is used to fill this reservoir through a pneumatic valve placed in the lid of the oil tank. The two reservoirs are connected by means of a tube through the pneumatic valve, which is used to pass the compressed air from the small reservoir into the large before the apparatus is used. The oil reservoir is equipped with: a) an elbow-shaped tube for the ejection of flammable liquid under pressure; b) a disk spring valve for regulating the liquid jet and terminating the action; c) an iron tube with a nozzle; d) a bayonet; e) an igniter.[22]

May 21 – Col. Martiushev reported to the General Staff on the progress of training personnel for ten flamethrower batteries, a plan that never came to fruition. Two of-

Flame-chemical sapper of the First Army Chemical Detachment. He wears a quilted jacket called a "body warmer" (telogreika) and an M1910 fleece cap. His tunic, trousers, and boots appear deeply stained with oil.

Tsar Nicholas II (left) observing the demonstration of a portable flamethrower. The date is said to be May of 1916; the weapon is almost certainly the Tilly-Goskin. Note the long handle on the top of the tank, attached to an internal hand pump that provided the compressed-air propellant. Under the prominent igniter is a mounting for a bayonet, unique among all known flamethrowers. Courtesy Nik Cornish.

ficers and 38 soldiers, former prisoners of war trained as flamethrower operators by the British, joined the battalion soon afterward.[23]

June – The Russian engineers Stranden, Povarnin, and Stolitsa invented the first explosive-piston flamethrower *(fugasnyĭ porshnevoĭ ognemet),* which used the pressure of an explosive charge to eject the oil.[24] It was known as the SPS. At around the same time Branch III of the Chemical Committee produced two models of portable flamethrower, the Tovarnitskiy and the Aleksandrov, both of which were accepted by the Russian army.[25]

Another flamethrower made available to the Chemical Detachments in very small numbers was the Arkhangelysk System, an apparatus of undetermined size manufactured at the Kiev arsenal and the Kiev wire and nail plant. Tovarnitskiy flamethrowers were manufactured at the Kiev automobile plant and the wire and nail plant, and the Tilly-Goskin was produced at a plant run by an engineer named Korsak.[26] Like the Tilly-Goskin the Arkhangelysk flamethrower was a British design made in Russia under license.[27] No information about this device has yet been located.

Completed flamethrowers were shipped to the front-line weapons depots of the Chemical Detachments. Flame-chemical sappers were rotated in groups back to Petrograd for training in the use of the devices.

General Ipatieff, chairman of the Chemical Committee, wrote in his memoirs that the Tovarnitskiy portable flamethrower was a copy or modification of an Austrian model,[28] likely the *kleine 22l M. 15 Flammenwerfer.* However, schematic drawings of the Tovarnitskiy bear little resemblance to any Austrian flamethrower. It is possible that the Aleksandrov was a copy of an Austrian apparatus.

June 15 – The Chemical Committee reduced the number of Gorbov flamethrowers ordered by the Main Military Technical Administration from 1500 to 1000. On the same day it ordered 6000 Aleksandrov portables, 6000 Tovarnitskiy portables, and 200 Tovarnitskiy trench flamethrowers *(transheĭnymi ognemety).* The Committee also purchased 65 Vincent battery and 50 Livens Large Gallery flamethrowers,[29] the latter obtained directly from the contractor with the approval of the British Ministry of Munitions. Fifty of the Vincent devices were the new type, which used oil tanks

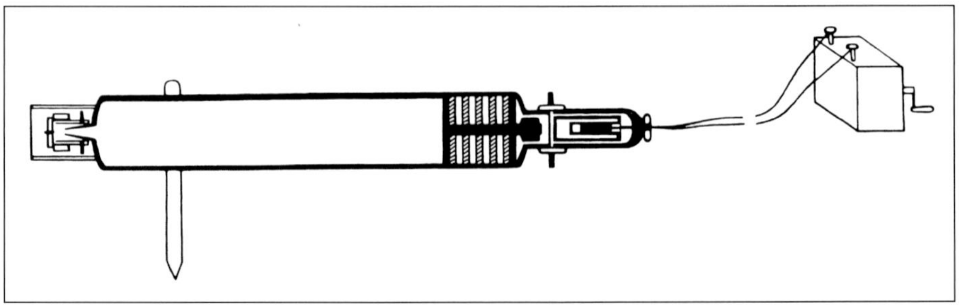

Right: SPS explosive-piston flamethrower, accepted by the Russian army in early 1917. On the right is the electric blasting machine, which detonated the explosive cartridge in the base. The explosion pushed the piston (in black) through the flamethrower, ejecting the oil in a 1-2 second burst. The ignition system consisted of four cartridges mounted around the nozzle, the friction primers of which were attached by heavy threads to a steel plate. The jet of oil struck the plate, ejecting it and pulling the primer threads of the ignition cartridges, which produced a circle of flame through which the oil sprayed. The SPS was a static defensive flamethrower held fast to the ground with a stout metal stake.

Below: Unidentified model of portable Russian flamethrower almost certainly based on the Lawrence Knapsack Flame Projector Model 1915. It may be the Gorbov or the Aleksandrov. The lance is apparently fitted with an elongated bottle for hydrogen, indicating a burner as the ignition source. To date no information has been located about the Gorbov or the Aleksandrov, other than the fact that they had limited ranges and were not successful.

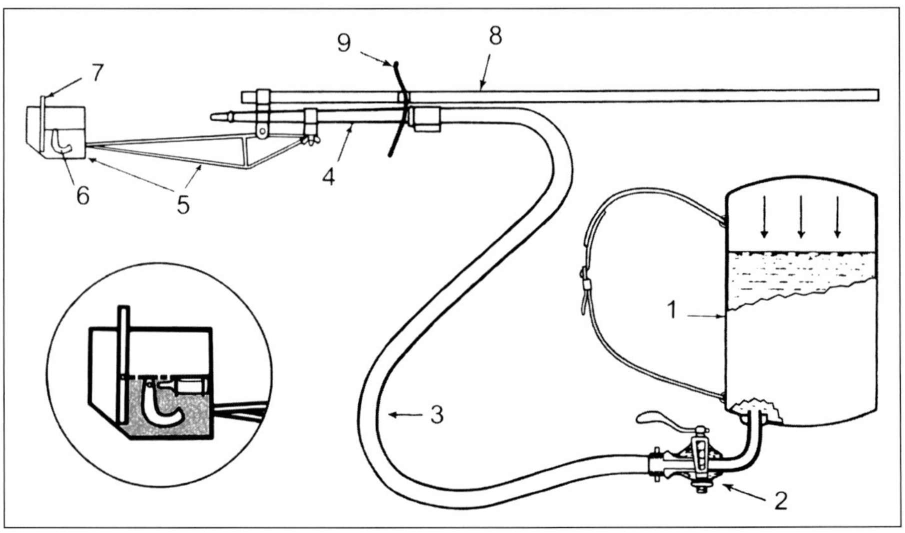

Bottom right: Tovarnitskiy portable flamethrower, adopted by the Russian army in late 1916. It was operated by at least two sappers, one who wore the flamethrower and opened the valve, and the other who aimed the nozzle: 1) oil tank, which was filled 3/4 of the way with oil and the remainder with carbon dioxide; 2) oil release valve, which also served as oil filler tube; 3) 2-meter hose; 4) nozzle; 5) tin igniter and support brace; 6) curved striker; 7) hinged flap; 8) wooden rod; 9) steel heat shield. Inset: detail of igniter. When the stream of oil hit the hinged metal flap, it activated the striker, which broke a glass ampoule of sulfuric acid and ignited gasoline-soaked hemp or jute fiber sprinkled with "igniting powder," a mixture of 75% potassium chlorate and 25% sugar. From the work of Yakob Moiseevich Fishman, Director of the Soviet War Chemical Administration. Courtesy Dr. Mikhail Supotnitskiy.

Vincent battery flamethrower served by sappers of the Red Army in the late 1920s. The British sent 36 Vincent battery flamethrowers to the Russians, who modified them according to unknown specifications. Both sides used flamethrowers extensively during the Russian Civil War, although the Soviets had more of the weapons. In 1923 Red Army flamethrower troops were redesignated chemical troops.

14 inches in diameter, made of steel 1/8th of an inch thick. This reduced the empty weight of each container by 68 lbs. The Tsar abdicated before the flamethrower could be developed, and the order was canceled.[30]

July 28 – The General Staff submitted a report to the Directorate of the Field Inspector-General of Artillery, recommending the formation of permanent Flamethrower Detachments *(Ognemetnye Komandy)* to be merged with the trench-gun batteries already planned for each infantry regiment. Each of these new infantry subunits would be armed with 12 portable flamethrowers and four 37mm Rosenberg M1915 trench guns (*Transheĭnaya 37mm Pushka obr. 1915 g.).*

A Flamethrower Detachment was to be comprised of one officer, three corporals, five privates first class, and 21 sappers. The General Staff stressed the necessity of proceeding immediately with the creation of the Flamethrower Detachments and the training of their personnel by the Flame-Chemical Training Battalion. Enough sappers for the first 20 Detachments should be sent to Petrograd in about one and a half weeks.[31]

August 10 – The Directorate of the Field Inspector-General of Artillery acknowledged to the General Staff that infantry Flamethrower Detachments would be created, beginning with one per division. In order of priority Flamethrower Detachments would be established on the Caucasian front, the western front, the southwestern front, and finally the northern front.[32]

September – The British shipped 15 Vincent battery flamethrowers to Petrograd, bringing the total number of devices the Russians received to 36. All were modified in Russia to meet the conditions of active service.[33]

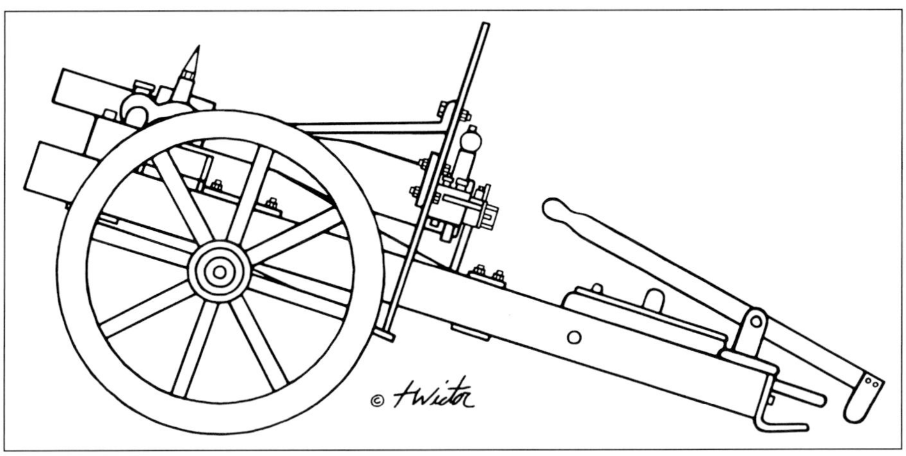

The 37mm M1915 trench gun (Transhe naya 37mm Pushka obr. 1915 g.), designed by Colonel M. F. Rosenberg of the Artillery Committee. On July 28, 1916, the General Staff recommended creating Flamethrower Detachments and merging them with trench-gun batteries. The new units would each be armed with 12 portable flamethrowers and four Rosenberg guns. One such flamethrower-gun detachment would be attached to each infantry regiment, a plan that was never carried out. Equipped with a steel shield 6-8mm thick, the Rosenberg weighed 397 lbs. and could be broken down into the barrel, carriage, and wheels. The 29-in. barrel made it accurate up to about 1200 paces.

17/511F

September 18 – The Second Army Chemical Detachment became the first of these units to see action, launching a cloud-gas attack at Smorgoni.[34]

September 24 – Order No. 1270 of the Chief of Staff of the Supreme Commander-in-Chief established the material state of the Flamethrower Detachments. Flamethrower Detachments would be comprised of one officer and 29 combatant soldiers and junior commanders, as recommended by the General Staff, with the addition of three noncombatant soldiers. Each Detachment would be armed with 12 portable flamethrowers.[35] The Russian army had 208 line-infantry regiments, 12 Guard, and 16 Grenadier, for a total of 236.[36] Each of the 236 Flamethrower Detachments would be permanently attached to its infantry regiment, an approach adopted by the Italians in 1917. (See Italy.)

November 9 – The General Staff reported to the Directorate of the Field Inspector-General of Artillery and to General Ipatieff of the Chemical Committee that it did not share the view of the Directorate of the Field Inspector-General of Artillery that portable flamethrowers should be used only for defense. Instead, the General Staff saw flamethrowers as highly destructive weapons best suited for offensive operations. Furthermore, it was necessary to quickly deploy sappers to Petrograd for instruction by the Flame-Chemical Training Battalion so that the regimental Flamethrower Detachments could be sent to the front.[37]

December 18 – The Chief of Staff of the Supreme Commander-in-Chief approved the plan of the General Staff to form three flamethrower batteries *(batareĭ ognemeta)* that would be used defensively on the various fronts. Each battery consisted of six officers and 128 sappers and was armed with four trench flamethrowers.[38] Three models of trench flamethrower would be issued: the Tovarnitskiy, the British Vincent, and the General Ershov System.[39] Information on the latter has yet to be found.

Opposite

Top: Livens Large Gallery Flammenwerfer assembled on a railroad siding prior to being shipped to Russia. One of 50 such weapons, it is fitted with oil tanks stenciled "This side up" in Russian. The British trained 300 Russian soldiers to operate the Livens Large Gallery Flammenwerfer and the Vincent battery flamethrower. British National Archives MUN-385.

Bottom: These sappers of the First Army Chemical Detachment are preparing gas cylinders for a cloud attack in Illuksta, Lithuania, date unknown. They wear M1881 and M1911 greatcoats with no collar patches. The number of flame-chemical sappers attached to army divisions or brigades depended on the mission. In late 1916 portable flamethrower sections armed with 12 devices each were to be permanently attached to infantry regiments. This plan was canceled due to the revolution of February 1917. Note the Zelinsky-Kumant gas masks worn by three of the men in the trench. Flame-chemical sappers were issued M1891 7.62mm Moisin Nagant rifles, carbines, or M1895 Nagant revolvers as personal weapons. Courtesy Russian State Military-Historical Archives.

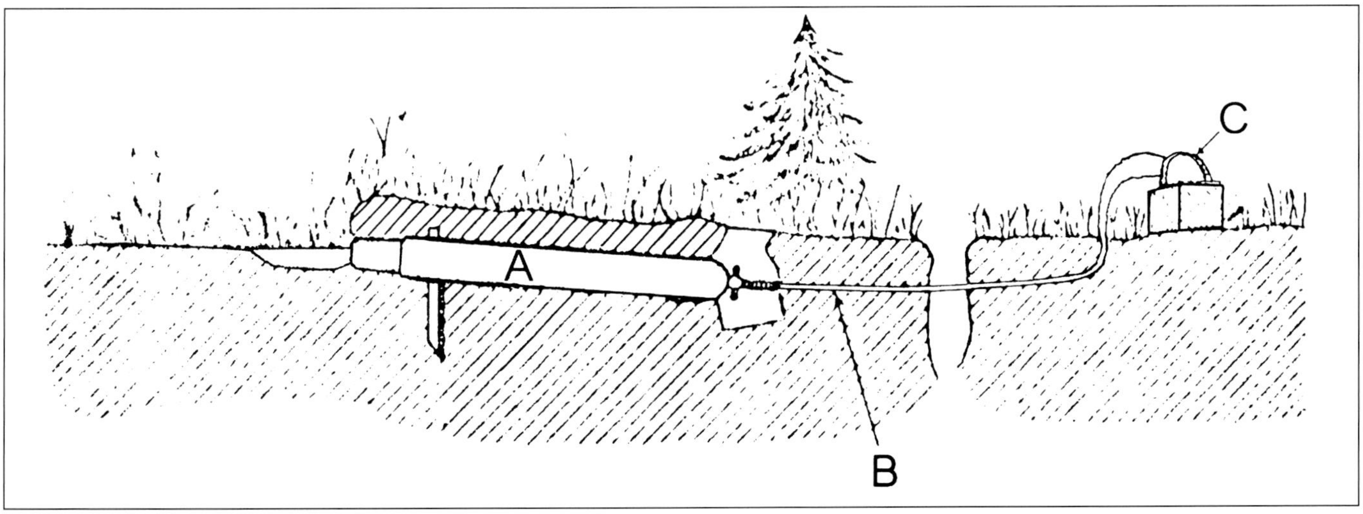

Above: SPS explosive-piston flamethrower in position, covered with a shallow layer of earth for concealment: A) flamethrower; B) electrical leads; C) electric blasting machine. The SPS was used in batteries of up to 25. From the work of Yakob Moiseevich Fishman, courtesy Dr. Mikhail Supotnitskiy.

Left: Poor-quality photo of a portable flamethrower in action. On the lower left, the steel-helmeted sapper is seen firing his weapon. The French M1915 Adrian helmet and Russian M1916 version were not issued to sappers in large numbers. Since no oil tank is visible in this image, the weapon is a two-man device. Photos of imperial Russian flamethrower troops in action are virtually nonexistent.

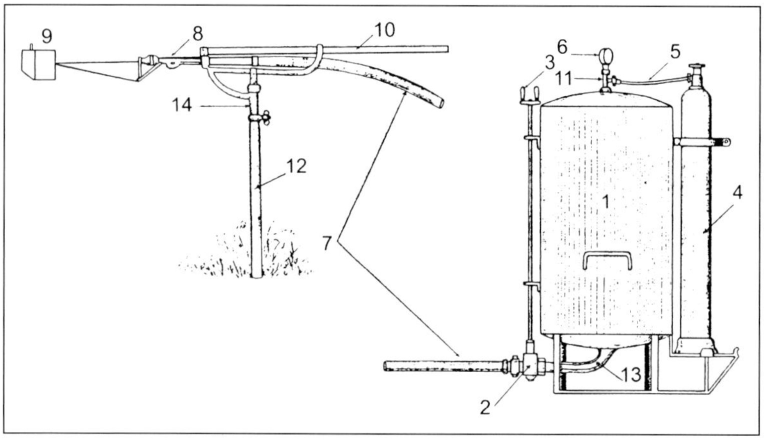

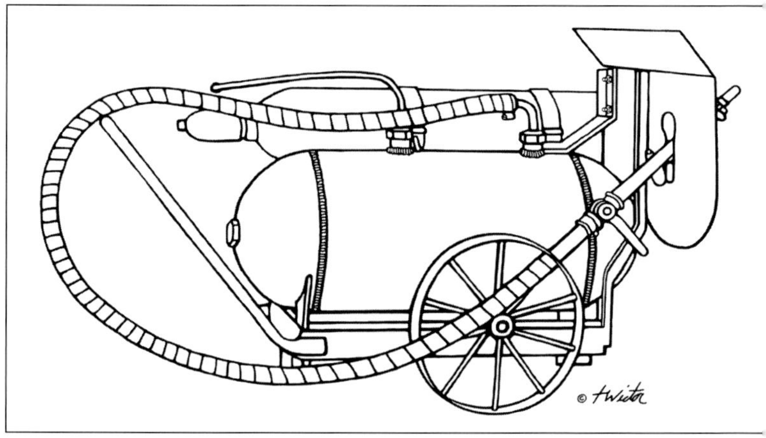

Left: Tovarnitskiy trench flamethrower, adopted by the Russian army in late 1916. Operated by a nine-man squad, it armed three independent heavy-flamethrower batteries: 1) oil tank; 2) outflow valve; 3) oil-release handle; 4) propellant bottle; 5) propellant tubing; 6) pressure gauge; 7) 28 ft. canvas hose; 8) nozzle; 9) igniter; 10) wooden rod; 11) T-junction; 12) pintle; 13) outflow tube; 14) swiveling support. The Tovarnitskiy trench flamethrower was used singly and in batteries of four. From the work of Yakob Moiseevich Fishman, courtesy Dr. Mikhail Supotnitskiy.

Right: Trench flamethrower, possibly the "General Ershov System." The oil tank was permanently fixed to a wheeled carriage that included a horseshoe-shaped handle for pulling (left) and a shield that also served as a support base (right) when the weapon was tipped upright in a trench. In this illustration the propellant-feed line has been disconnected, and a protective cover has been screwed over the valve on the propellant bottle. The lance nozzle includes an attachment point for the igniter and its support. No data on weight, capacity, duration, or range of the Ershov have yet been discovered.

1917

By January 1, the Main Military Technical Administration had produced 180 Gorbov flamethrowers. The Chemical Committee of the Main Artillery Administration had produced 140 Alexandrov portables, 5000 Tovarnitsky portables, and 50 Tovarnitsky trench flamethrowers. It had also received 21 British Vincent battery flamethrowers.[40]

January – The 14th Chemical Detachment was formed.[41]

Early 1917 – After much testing, the explosive-piston SPS flamethrower was accepted by the Russian army and used in batteries as a static weapon. As many as 25 could be connected to a single electric blasting machine and fired simultaneously.[42]

February – The Flame-Chemical Training Battalion completed its instruction of the infantry Flamethrower Detachments. Before the 236 new units could be deployed, however, political upheaval threw the armed forces into chaos.

March 2 – The February Revolution. Following civil unrest in Petrograd from February 22 to March 1, Tsar Nicholas II abdicated.

Unable to dispatch the Flamethrower Detachments to the fronts, the General Staff and Directorate of the Field Inspector-General of Artillery reverted to the previous plan for waging gas and flame warfare: Ad hoc flamethrower sections of flame-chemical sappers were formed in Chemical Detachments and temporarily attached to infantry regiments for particular offensive or defensive missions. After the operation, the flamethrower contingents returned to their parent units.[43] Portable-flamethrower sections saw combat in 1917,[44] during the summer and fall.

March 12 – The Provisional Government was established in Petrograd. It viewed the Flame-Chemical Training Battalion with suspicion, as many of the unit had begun openly expressing Bolshevik sympathies.

May – New Minister of War Alexander Kerensky began organizing special all-volunteer assault units in preparation for the coming summer offensive. Over the next six months 39 infantry "shock battalions" *(udarnye batalyony)* were raised.[45] A shock battalion was comprised of four companies of three platoons each.[46] Also called "battalions of death" *(batalyony smerti),* they were similar to German and Austrian assault battalions but did not include flamethrower sections. As of yet no records have been found indicating that flamethrower sappers of the Chemical Detachments were assigned to shock battalions, although the Directorate of the Field Inspector-General of Artillery devised flame tactics that included the use of infantry assault troops.

Mid-1917 – Lt. Percy H. Lawrence of the British Royal Engineers traveled to Russia to demonstrate his Knapsack Flame Projector Model 1917. The Russians ordered a consignment of several hundred devices manufactured in Britain, but shipments were halted after the November revolution.[47] Branch III of the Chemical Committee also produced the Lawrence under license, until the Russian civil war.[48]

Flame-resistant asbestos suit worn by Russian flamethrower sappers in 1916. It appears to be nearly identical to the British "Suit, Anti-liquid Fire, pattern 3023/1918." Although thoroughly tested the suit was not adopted. Courtesy Dr. Mikhail Supotnitskiy.

Mid-1917 – Sappers of the three trench-flamethrower batteries completed their training and were sent to the northern, western, and southwestern fronts.[49] Records of their combat experiences have not yet been located.

Lawrence Knapsack Flame Projector Model 1917; the operator aims the lance with his right hand and fires the weapon with his left, which grips the discharge lever beside his ear. Note the white smoke from the portfire under the lance nozzle. In mid-1917 inventor Lieutenant P. H. Lawrence of the Royal Engineers traveled to Russia to demonstrate his weapon. The Russians placed an order with the British, and Branch III of the Chemical Committee began manufacture of the flamethrower under license. Following the revolution of November 1917, the British ceased shipments of the Lawrence to Russia. British National Archives MUN-385.

Undated photo of a flame-chemical sapper uniformed in a high-quality wool M1910 shirt-tunic, the stiff shoulder boards of which display privately purchased officers' metal engineering badges and numbers. His visor cap features a wire stiffener in the brim to improve its appearance, and he wears an officer's belt. The unusually expensive outfit indicates the elite status of his unit, the Ninth Army Chemical Detachment or Chemical Company (Khimicheskie Rota).

June 19 – The Supreme Commander-in-Chief ordered that one regiment of each infantry division form its own flamethrower detachment for combat. The remaining three regiments of the division would establish one flamethrower detachment each, strictly for the purpose of evaluating the weapon. Each of the 14 Chemical Detachments organized a course for training infantrymen in the use of flamethrowers. Instructors from the Flame-Chemical Training Battalion were sent to each army to teach the courses.[50]

June 30 – In preparation for the final Russian offensive of the war, the Seventh Army Chemical Detachment carried out a flamethrower attack against German Reserve Infantry Regiment No. 104 on the Lysonia Heights near Brzezany, Galicia.[51] After a one-hour artillery barrage the flamethrower sappers advanced at 4:00 P.M. under cover of a smoke screen, followed at 4:10 by a wave of infantry. The Germans repulsed the attackers with heavy fire from artillery, trench mortars, grenade launchers, and machine guns. At 4:25 the Russians attempted a second assault but were unable to leave their trenches. Finally at 6:00 P.M. the Russians bombarded the German positions with artillery and unleashed poison gas from cylinders, the latter causing

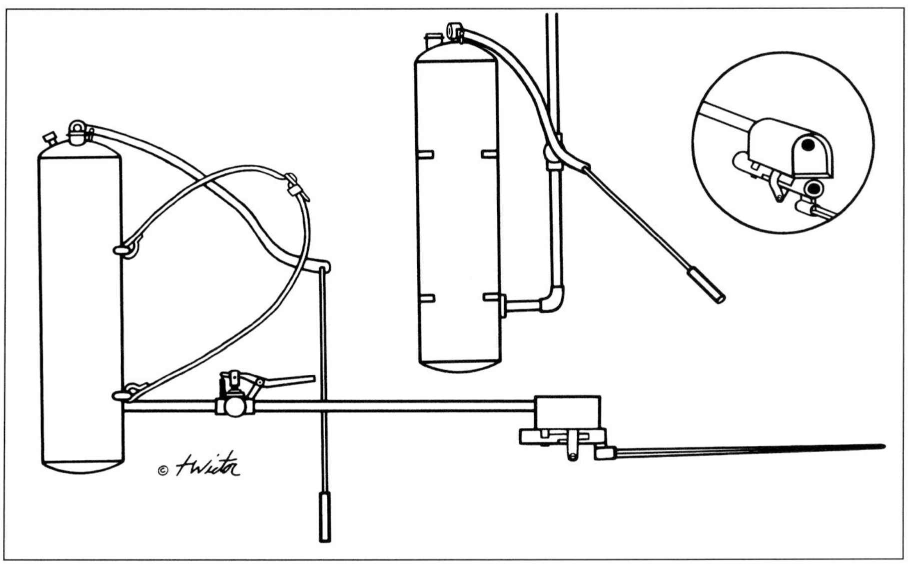

Provisional rendering of the Tilly-Goskin portable flamethrower, based on the photo and written description provided earlier: side view (left) and front view without shoulder straps (center). A British design, the Tilly-Goskin was a hand-pumped device that used compressed air as the propellant, which was stored in an internal reservoir. Both the air-pump handle and rigid, swiveling lance were on the left side of the weapon, requiring that the operator reach across his body with his right hand and hold the lance while he compressed the air. The lance was also fitted with a bayonet, for when the sapper ran out of oil. In action the sapper moved the rod attached to the air-pump handle out of the way by laying it on his left shoulder. Very few of these weapons were produced. Inset: Igniter and mounting lug for bayonet. The igniter is similar to the British Kitson design, which was a container of methylated spirit.

the Germans to experience only a slight watering of the eyes. In this operation the Chemical Detachment used all three weapons in its arsenal: smoke, gas, and flame.

July 1 – The "Kerensky Offensive" began when the Russian Seventh and Eleventh Armies attacked Austro-German positions in Galicia. Although flamethrowers were certainly used, no specific accounts of such actions have yet been discovered. After two weeks Russian morale and discipline collapsed. By July 23 the Russians had retreated 150 miles.

July – The Flame-Chemical Training Battalion was disarmed by the Provisional Government and confined to its barracks after the instructors demanded that all governmental power be given to the emerging Soviets.[52]

September – By order of the Chief of Staff of the Supreme Commander-in-Chief, the Chemical Detachments were redesignated Chemical Companies *(Khimicheskie Roty)* and expanded with newly trained personnel[53] to about 240 men each. Commanders of Chemical Companies were artillerymen or engineers; senior officers were recruited from all branches of service and trained in gas and flame warfare. Officers assigned as chemical chiefs of fronts and armies, as well as their assistants, were recruited from all branches of service and given extensive training in gas and flame warfare.

November 7 – Vladimir Ilyich Lenin led a Bolshevik coup in Petrograd that overthrew the Provisional Government. The instructors of the Flame-Chemical Training Battalion took part in the fighting as infantrymen, since their flamethrowers and gas had been confiscated. As a communist unit, the battalion became one of the most reliable in Petrograd.[54] It was effectively disbanded after the fall of the Provisional Government.

November 20 – People's Commissar for Foreign Affairs Leon Trotsky formally notified the Allies of Russia's change of government and its Decree of Peace.[55]

Russian infantrymen armed with Japanese M1905 6.5mm Arisaka Type 38 rifles with M1897 bayonets. Note the wartime canvas ammunition bandoliers and M1915 Adrian helmet with double-headed eagle badge on the front. The thin straps across their chests are attached to metal boxes containing Zelinsky-Kumant gas masks. On June 19, 1917, the Supreme Commander-in-Chief ordered that all infantry regiments form their own flamethrower detachments. One detachment of each division would engage in combat, and the others would evaluate the weapons. Each Chemical Detachment established a course for infantrymen in the use of flamethrowers, taught by instructors of the Flame-Chemical Training Battalion.

1918

January 28 – The Workers' and Peasants' Red Army was formed.[56] Due to the near-universal collapse of industry, institutions, and public order, the Red Army was not able to immediately organize a flame-chemical arm.[57] Reserves of Tsarist weapons were relatively small, and men trained in their use had to be identified, located, and induced to join the Bolsheviks. This process took several months.

March 3 – Russia signed the Treaty of Brest Litovsk and withdrew from the war.[58]

During World War I Russia manufactured 10,000 Tovarnitskiy portable flamethrowers, 200 Tovarnitskiy trench flamethrowers, 362 SPS flamethrowers, and a combined total of fewer than 900 Gorbov, Aleksandrov, Ershov, Arkhangelysk, and Tilly-Goskin flamethrowers. The British supplied 36 Vincent battery flamethrowers, 50 Livens Large Gallery *Flammenwerfer,* and an unknown number of Lawrence Knapsack Flame Projectors. By the end of the war Russian troops in the field had received 11,446 flamethrowers.[59] Very few Russian devices were built because of shortages, labor disputes, and apathy generated by the knowledge that Russia would soon leave the conflict.

June 1 – The Chemical Committee in Petrograd was abolished, replaced by a chemical branch of the Main Artillery Administration that relocated in Moscow.[60]

June 8 – The "White" counterrevolutionary Peoples' Army of the Members of the Constituent Assembly (*Komitet Uchreditelnogo Sobraniya* or *Komuch*) was formed in Samara. It included the 1st Flamethrower-Chemical Battalion,[61] armed with weapons left over from the Tsarist army. After several defeats at the hands of the Reds, the Peoples' Army of the *Komuch* disbanded on September 23. Other White forces had flamethrower detachments, but they were small and relatively ineffectual.

Summer – The Chemical Section (*Khimicheskiĭ Otdel*) was formed in the 9th Division of the Red Army. Directly supervised by the Main Artillery Administration, it was tasked with collecting and storing all flame-chemical documentation, equip-

An instructor of the Flame-Chemical Training Battalion (standing). Seated on the right is an ensign of railway troops wearing a black privately purchased "French" tunic, named after British general Sir John French. The flame-chemical instructor and the engineer officer in the center have removed their shoulder straps, perhaps indicating that this photo was taken after the March Revolution of 1917. The Provisional Government saw shoulder boards as Tsarist and introduced cuff rings as rank devices. This system was not widely adopted.

Below: Bolsheviks in 1918. Communists wore civilian clothes or Tsarist uniforms stripped of imperial cockades and shoulder boards. In this photo the man standing on the right wears a cap with a red star, the symbol soon adopted universally by the Bolsheviks. During this period there were no formalized flame-chemical troops. Individual Red armies organized their own detachments, recruiting former members of the Tsarist army and arming them with weapons of the old regime.

Left: Men of an unidentified "White" army unit, photographed in 1918. The Whites battled the Bolsheviks or Reds during the Russian civil war of 1917-1923. Initially most Whites wore Tsarist uniforms and civilian clothing, as in this image. The man on the right is a sapper private first class who wears metal shovel-and-pick insignia on the shoulder straps of his cotton shirt-tunic. White armies had a small number of flamethrower detachments, comprised of sappers who had served in the Chemical Companies.

Right: This photo of Red Army sappers shows the basic appearance of Russian flamethrower operators from 1919 until December of 1926, when the shovel-and-pick engineer badge was replaced with the crossed gas canisters and gas mask of the chemical troops. Most of these men wear the M1924 overcoat and M1919 cap (budenovka) in khaki, while the sapper standing in the center rear is uniformed in the M1924 shirt-service jacket (rubakhi-frencha). The overcoats display black collar patches; from 1924 chemical troops wore black patches piped in light green instead of red. Seated from left to right are an assistant platoon commander (pomoshchnik komandira vzvoda), a squad leader (komandir otdeleniya), company deputy commander (starshina roty), and another assistant platoon commander. The others are "Red Army men" (krasnoarme tsy), the equivalent of privates.

ment, weapons, and raw materials left over from the Tsarist army. During this period there was no centralized flame-chemical authority that issued cohesive plans. Instead, individual armies at the fronts were ordered to use their own initiative in creating flame-chemical units to be deployed locally.

1919

January – The first of two Red Army flamethrower companies was formed in the Moscow military district; it was called simply the Flamethrower Company. At this time the Red Army separated flamethrower troops from chemical units and made them subordinate to the Main Engineering Administration.

Consisting of four platoons, the Flamethrower Company manufactured flamethrower parts, trained operators, and studied and tested the apparatuses. The Red Army retained only the Tovarnitskiy portable and trench devices, the British Vincent battery model, and the SPS explosive-piston flamethrower. Gorbov and Aleksandrov flamethrowers were withdrawn from service because they achieved only very short ranges of 45-60 feet. In addition, charging the Gorbov with carbon dioxide derived from carbonic acid was a complicated process that could only be carried out in warm weather, making the weapon useless in the winter.[62]

Late 1919 – The Flamethrower Company was transformed into the Experimental-Research Company, which contained four platoons. The 1st Platoon was armed with two Vincent battery flamethrowers; the 2nd Platoon had eight Tovarnitskiy trench flamethrowers; the 3rd Platoon held 20 SPS explosive-piston flamethrowers; and the 4th Platoon was armed with 30 Tovarnitskiy portable devices.

October – Former Tsarist army flamethrower sappers serving in the 1st Tula (subsequently 48th) Rifle Division on the western front were formed into an additional flamethrower company of four platoons armed with two Vincent battery flamethrowers each. This company was intended for positional defense in the most important sectors of the western front.

1920

Summer – A flamethrower detachment was formed on the southern front, using elements of the 51st Rifle Division. When the division defended the Kakhovka bridgehead in October, this detachment was armed with 25 SPS explosive-piston flamethrowers.

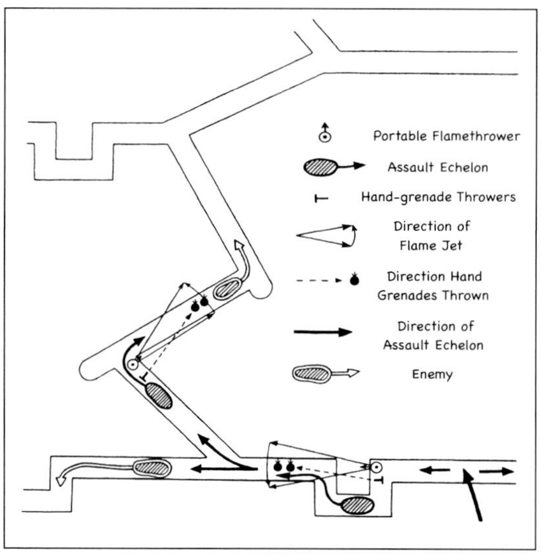

Russian method of executing an attack with portable flamethrowers, hand-grenade throwers, and infantry assault troops. From the work of Yakob Moiseevich Fishman, courtesy Dr. Mikhail Supotnitskiy.

Undated photo of a defensive flamethrower post on an artillery training field; the portable weapon cannot be identified. An ensign (left) reads a map spread over the oil tank, while two enlisted men clear the lance nozzle with a stick. In the background an officer wears a leather box that likely contains igniters, He displays a gas-warning rattle to an enlisted man carrying a rolled flag used to determine wind direction, vital for preventing accidental blowback that could burn the flamethrower squad or cause the weapon to explode. None of the men wear gas-mask containers, indicating the posed nature of the photo.

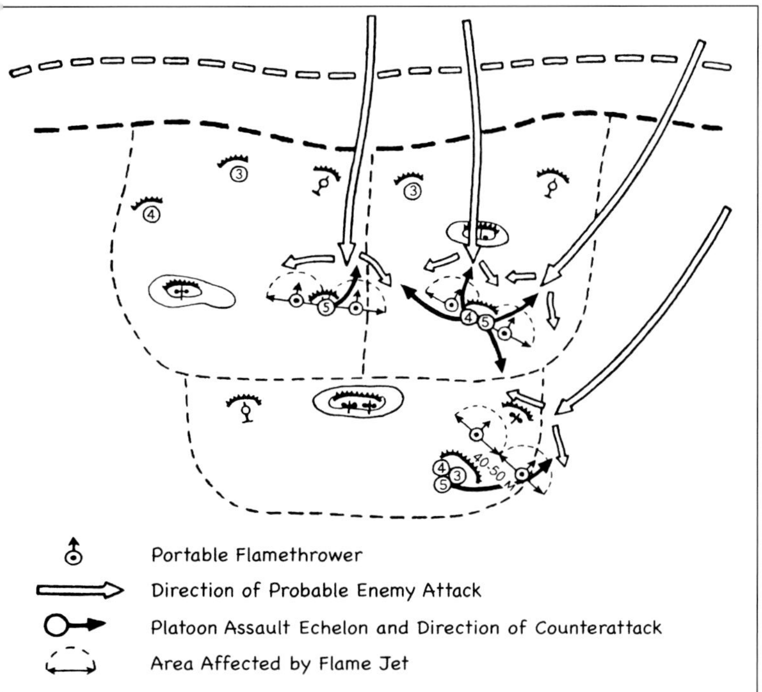

Russian method of defense with portable flamethrowers. From the work of Yakob Moiseevich Fishman, courtesy Dr. Mikhail Supotnitskiy.

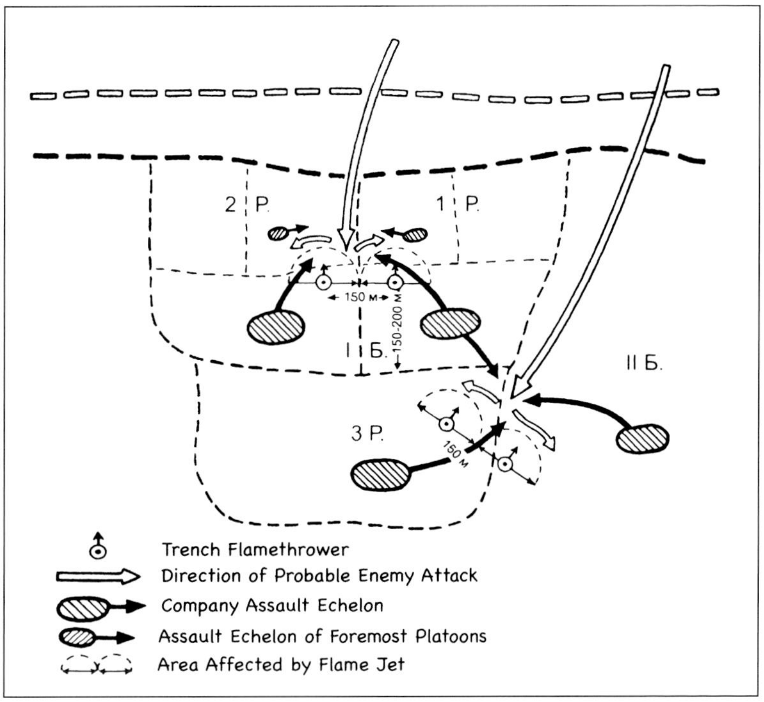

Russian method of defense with trench flamethrowers and infantry assault troops. From the work of Yakob Moiseevich Fishman, courtesy Dr. Mikhail Supotnitskiy.

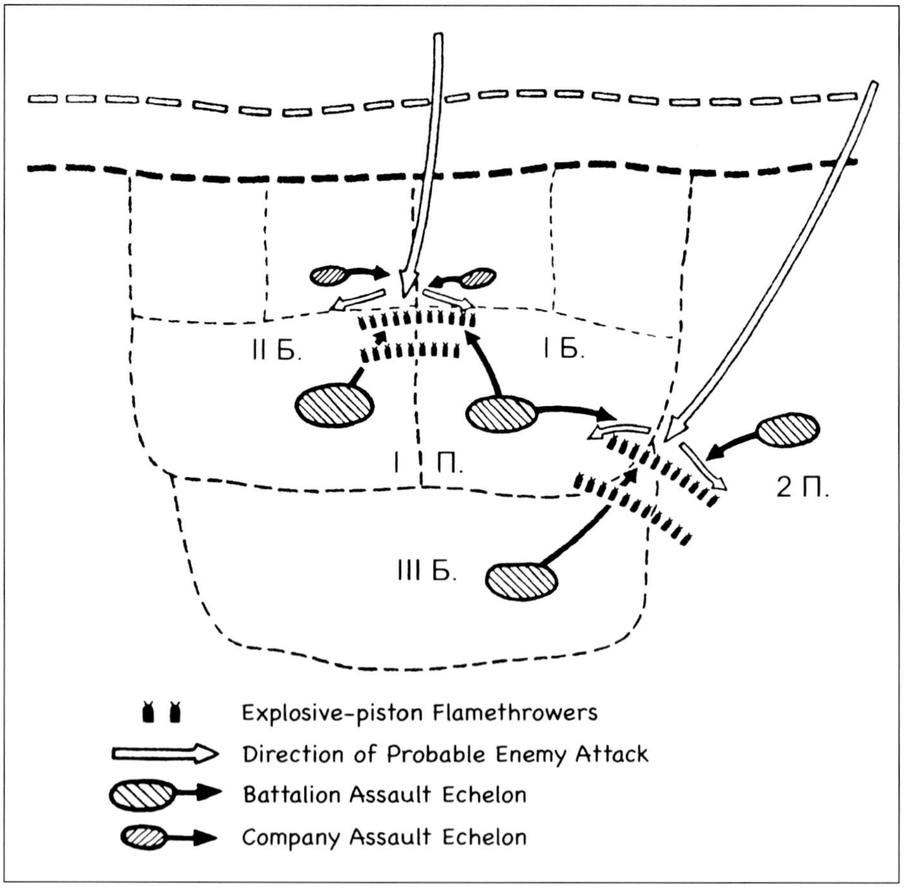

Russian method of defense with SPS explosive-piston flamethrowers and infantry assault troops. From the work of Yakob Moiseevich Fishman, courtesy Dr. Mikhail Supotnitskiy.

1923

All flamethrower troops were redesignated chemical troops under the command of the Main Artillery Administration.

Tactics

Portable flamethrowers were used in shock troops modeled on the German example. In an offensive role, flamethrower squads and hand-grenade throwers rolled up trenches in concert with infantry. Defensively, pairs of flamethrower squads covered a front of 130-165 feet and were teamed with assault echelons in order to carry out small-scale counterattacks. (See Germany.)

Trench flamethrowers were used exclusively for defense. As in the case of portable flamethrowers deployed defensively, they were used in pairs, covering a front of approximately 500 feet. Assault echelons were detailed to launch small-scale counterattacks after the flamethrowers fired.

The SPS explosive-piston flamethrower was a defensive weapon, used in the same way as the trench flamethrower. It was deployed in batteries of up to 25, in conjunction with battalion and company assault echelons that carried out small-scale counterattacks.

UNITED STATES

1917

This young engineer of an unidentified regiment is outfitted in the olive-drab M1912 uniform with bronze collar disks, the left displaying the castle motif of his branch and the right marked with "US." Gas and flame engineers wore the castle collar disk until June of 1918.

April – The Bureau of Mines established the American University Experiment Station in Washington, D.C. and began researching chemical warfare.

June – American University created the Pyrotechnic Division, the Flaming-liquid Section of which studied and developed flamethrowers.[1]

July 5 – General Order 8 of the American Expeditionary Force (AEF) organized the General Headquarters (GHQ) of the AEF. The Administrative and Technical Staff included the Chief of the Gas Service, who was responsible for offensive and defensive gas and flame operations. He supplied personnel and material, supervised the training of gas troops, and oversaw experiments with new gases, delivery systems, and protection.[2]

July 19 – Henri Chapal, of C. and E. Chapal Brothers and Company, Dyers of Skins and Furs, offered the U.S. Army 25 flamethrowers invented by his son, Sergeant Léon Chapal of the French 1st Engineer Regiment.[3]

August 15 – War Department General Order 108 declared that each army would organize a Gas and Flame Service of one regiment.[4] This order established the 30th Engineer Regiment (Gas and Flame) of the National Army. It was organized from August 30 to November 28 at Camp American University, District of Columbia.

August 22 – Lieutenant Colonel Amos A. Fries of the Corps of Engineers was assigned Engineer in Charge of Gas in France.[5] He was about to be named director of roads when his orders were changed and he was put in command of gas instead.[6]

August 24 – Lt. Col. Fries wrote to the Chief of Staff of the AEF, recommending that the 25 Chapal flamethrowers be accepted so that they could be tested at the Gas School in France. Fries added, "the use of liquid fire or flame projectors is rapidly going out of date in all the armies. The labor, expense, and danger to the troops themselves using the apparatus are so great as to make other means of attack preferable in practically all cases."[7]

September 3 – AEF General Order 31 established the Gas Service of the AEF, with Lt. Col. Fries as Chief and the 30th Engineers providing its personnel.[8] It was also known as the AEF Gas Corps.

September 4 – Fries was promoted to full colonel and placed in titular command of the 30th Engineers. He established its headquarters at Chaumont, close to the GHQ of the AEF.[9] The actual commander of the regiment in the United States was Major Earle J. Atkisson.[10] Col. Fries obtained over 200 officers from the Engineers, Ordnance, Cavalry, and Infantry. Although assigned to the AEF Gas Service, they continued to hold commissions in their previous branches.[11]

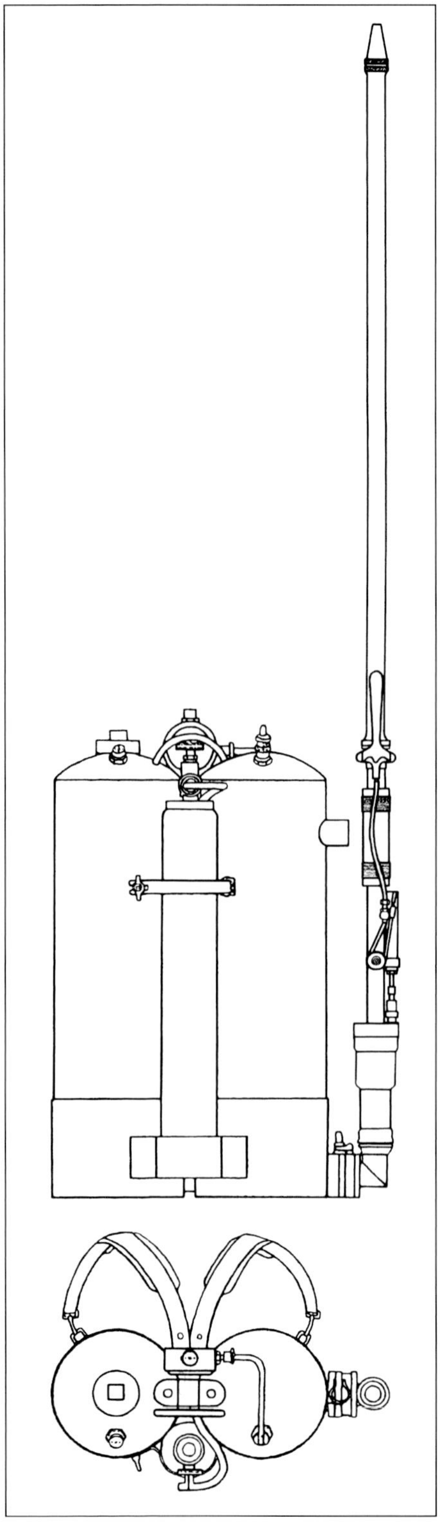

Rear and overhead view of the Chapal portable flamethrower, designed by Sergeant Léon Chapal of the French 1st Engineer Regiment. It appears to have been produced in relatively significant numbers but was not adopted. In August of 1917 Chapal's father Henri offered 25 of the weapons to Amos A. Fries as a gift to the U.S. Army, "in admiration of your noble nation which I have learned to love during the 27 years of my stay in New York." Chapal's design influenced subsequent American efforts.

Hard-faced men of the 30th Engineer Regiment (Gas and Flame) photographed at Camp American University, Washington, D. C., in December of 1917. All volunteers, the 30th Engineers were chemists, gas engineers, plumbers, electricians, pipe fitters, mechanics, explosives experts, carpenters, and blacksmiths between the ages of 18 and 40, with above-average physical strength. These men wear the M1917 olive-drab overcoat and M1912 campaign hat with scarlet-and-white engineer cord, and they are armed with the .30-cal. M1903 Springfield rifle.

October – Fries organized the AEF Gas Service into the Defensive Branch and the Offensive Branch. He commanded the Offensive Branch, which would direct operations of gas and flamethrower troops modeled on the British Special Brigade.[12]

October 15 – The War Department ordered that the 30th Engineers form a battalion of two companies (A and B) of 250 men each, as well as a Battalion Headquarters of 24 men and 16 officers. The army and the press cooperated in a publicity campaign, which led to syndicated articles in over 350 newspapers nationwide. "The time has gone by for any ethical discussion as to the propriety of using gas and flames against the enemy," said one. "The Germans started the practice and are keeping it up."[13]

Gas and flame regiments were to be all-volunteer units with six battalions of three companies each, a total of 210 officers and 4,873 men per regiment. Five battalions were combat units and the sixth was a replacement battalion of fully trained personnel. Each company was organized into a headquarters section and four platoons; each platoon was divided into two sections. A section consisted of two Stokes mortar gun-teams and a carrying party, for a total of sixteen mortars per company. All personnel were also trained in the use of gas cylinders and Livens projectors.[14]

Mid October – The Gas Service of the National Army was set up in Washington as the coordinating agent between the many bureaus and laboratories engaged in chemical-warfare activities. All communications from abroad dealing with gas and flame warfare were routed through the Gas Service, U.S. Army.[15] It had no authority to control research, policy, or production.[16]

October 16 – The Chemical Service Section, National Army, was created to provide an experimental gas and flame laboratory for General Pershing in France. It traveled to Puteaux, near Paris, in January of 1918.[17]

November – About 300 American infantry officers underwent training by the French at the AEF Infantry Officers' School at Chaumont. These first and second lieutenants were allowed to choose from various specialties, distinguished by colored hat bands: white for bayonet experts, yellow for machine gunners, red for rifle grenadiers, orange for hand-grenade throwers, green for riflemen, and blue for flamethrower operators.[18] The training was to familiarize American officers with French weapons and tactics.

French sappers of a Compagnie Schilt demonstrating Schilt No. 3 bis flamethrowers to American infantry officers in France, September 26, 1917. The Americans were trained in the use of the weapon but never saw combat. Note that the French flamethrower lance was operated with only one hand, unlike most other designs. During the demonstrations, one of the American officers remarked, "This sure ain't no place for a nervous man." U.S. National Archives 111-SC-3274.

Soldier of the Incendiary Unit of the Trench Warfare Section, Engineering Division, Ordnance Department, testing a Boyd No. 3 portable flamethrower. The Incendiary Unit experimented with French and British flamethrowers and developed the American models that were tested overseas but not adopted. U.S. National Archives 111-SC-54890.

12

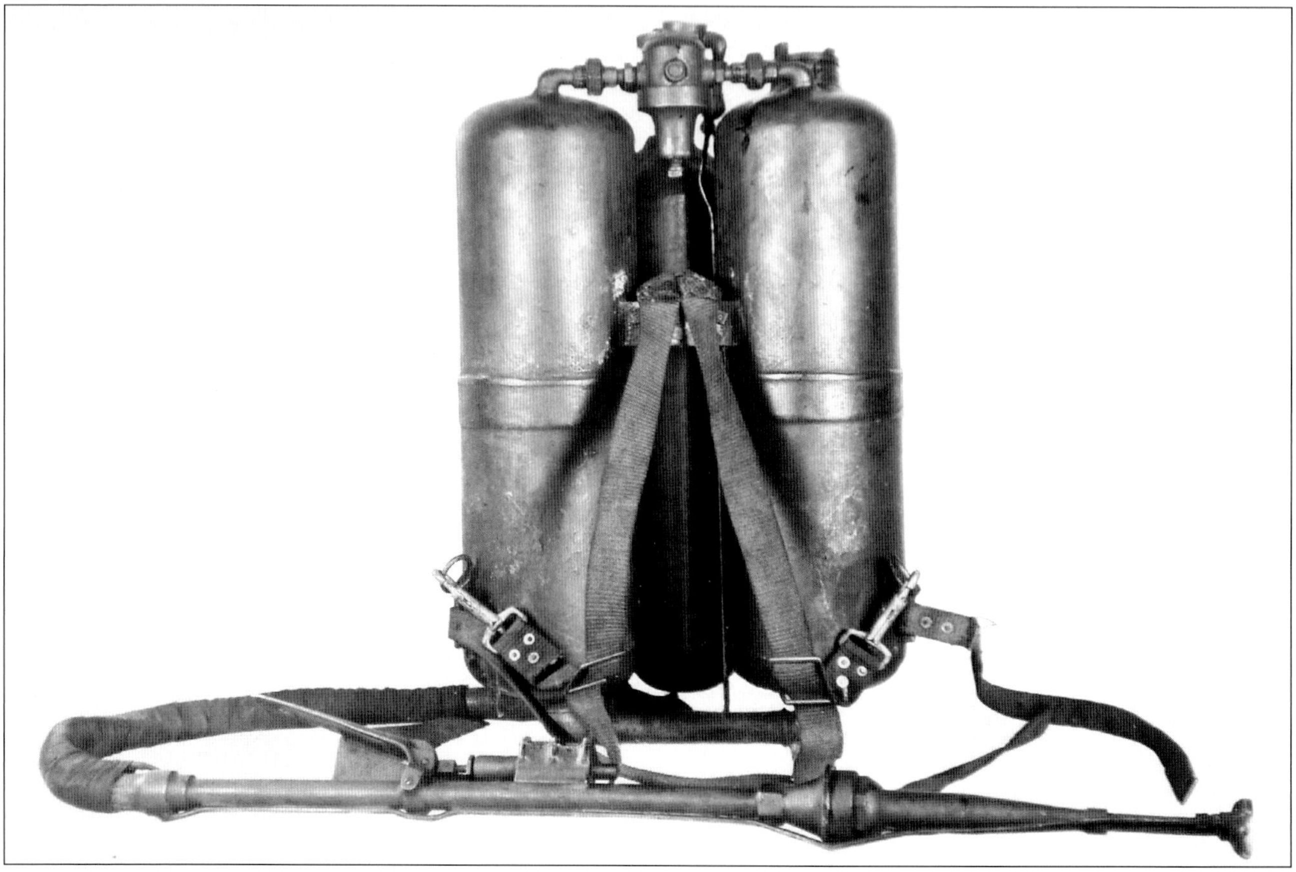

Opposite
Top: Rear view of Boyd No. 3 portable flamethrower, known officially as the Overseas Model Flame Projector. Two were tested in France in March of 1918, but the weapon was abandoned in accordance with Colonel Fries's dictum that flamethrowers were useless. The two tanks on either side were filled with oil, while the center tank held the hydrogen propellant. Hydrogen was also used in the pilot light of the lance, which ignited the oil jet. The hydrogen feed line can be seen emerging from under the cloth sleeve encasing the hose. Courtesy American University.

Bottom: Front view of Boyd No. 3. Note the webbing shoulder straps. Details of the lance include a hand-lever trigger and the prominent hydrogen feed line for the pilot light. Courtesy American University.

Far left: Rear view of the D-B (for "Davis-Bournonville") No. 2 portable flamethrower, which served as a test bed for a later, smaller model. Like the Boyd No. 3, it used hydrogen both as the propellant and as the fuel source for the pilot light that ignited the oil. Note the hydrogen feed line snaking from the propellant bottle around the hose and lance and ending in the pilot-light housing over the nozzle. Courtesy American University.

Left: Front view of the D-B No. 2 portable flamethrower. It lacks shoulder straps and fittings because it was never actually worn, but tested instead as a static weapon. At 80 lbs., it was deemed too heavy for use. Courtesy American University.

November 1 – Col. Fries ordered 100 P_3 and 100 P_4 flamethrowers from the French, which would be tested against American flamethrowers sent to France.[19]

November 8 – The Incendiary Unit of the Trench Warfare Section, Engineering Division, Ordnance Department, conducted tests with American flamethrowers at Marlin Aviation Field, New Haven, Connecticut.[20] These weapons were developed by the Flaming-liquid Section of the Pyrotechnic Division, American University, for use by the 30th Engineers.

November 14 and 20 – The Incendiary Unit tested Davis-Bournonville (D-B) flamethrowers,[21] likely the No. 1 and/or No. 2 models.

December 4-5 – Companies C and D, 30th Engineers, were organized.[22]

December 15 – The Incendiary Unit tested D-B and Boyd portable flamethrowers at Marlin Aviation Field.[23] These were almost certainly the D-B No. 3 and the Boyd No. 3, "overseas" models sent to France for trials in 1918.

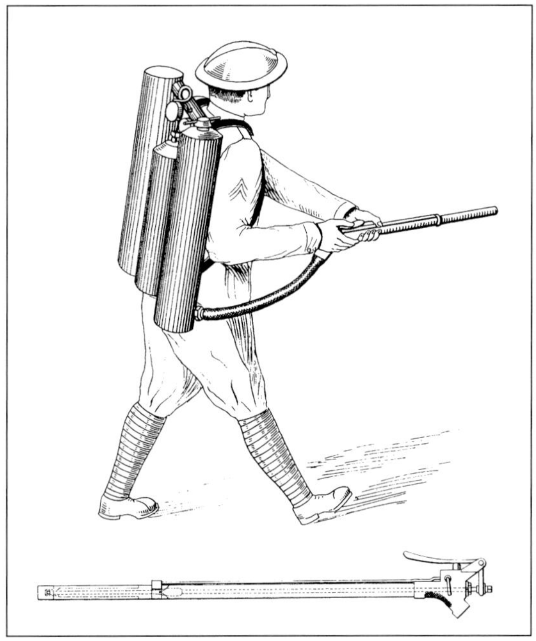

Left: First Lieutenant of the 30th Engineers, date and place unknown. He wears the M1912 officers' service dress including Sam Browne belt, Small Box Respirator, and steel helmet. The small sign reads "Regimental Gas Office": note gas-warning klaxon.

Above: D-B No. 3, a second portable flamethrower designed by the Incendiary Unit of the Trench Warfare Section, Ordnance Department. Two examples were completed on March 18, 1918, and shipped to France for tests. Drawing taken from U.S. patent No. 1340012.

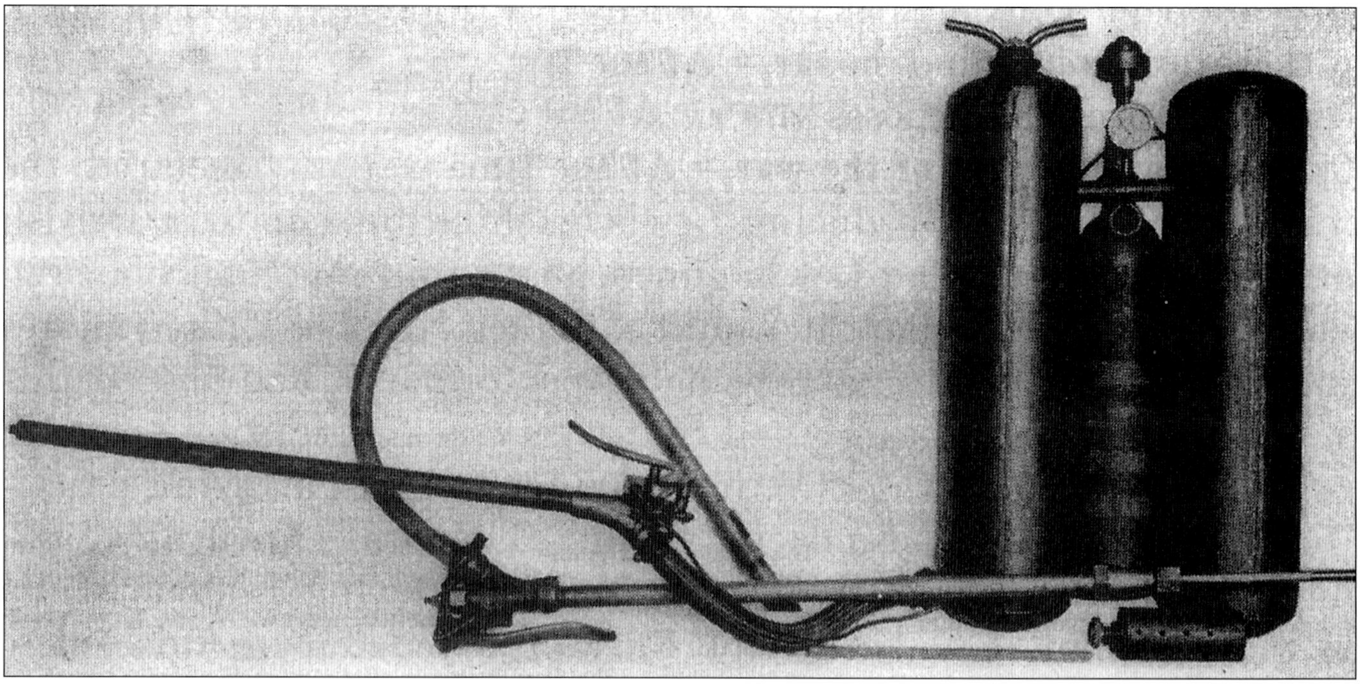

D-B No. 3 with two models of lance and various attachments. This flamethrower had a quick-release attachment point for the shoulder straps that allowed the operator to instantly drop the weapon in the event of puncture or leakage. The lances included hydrogen pilot lights and self-closing valves. On November 11, 1918, the same day the armistice was declared, one D-B. No. 3 was completed out of an order of 10. The remainder of the order was canceled, as the budget to the postwar Chemical Warfare Service was slashed dramatically. Courtesy Bruce Canfield.

The Schilt No. 3 bis used by American engineers in the photo shown opposite. The lance nozzle, protective metal cover of the flamethrower top, and padded knapsack harness have been removed to facilitate cleaning. A multicolored patchwork camouflage has been painted over the original blue-gray finish.

1918

January 28 – Companies A and B, 1st Battalion, 30th Engineers, arrived in France. Although Col. Fries ordered his troops to test portable flamethrowers in combat (see June 29, 1918), the vast majority of the Gas and Flame engineers fought with Livens gas projectors and Stokes mortars that fired high-explosive, phosphorus, or thermite shells. The 1st Battalion was known in the AEF as the "Hell Fire Battalion," and its men were called the "Hell Fire Boys."[24]

February 18 – Lt. Percy H. Lawrence of the Royal Engineers demonstrated his Knapsack Flame Projector Model 1917 to the Americans in France, telling them that it was far superior to the Norris device adopted by the British army. The Americans noted that the range of the Lawrence was 18 yards longer than any other type in use, and it was simple and relatively safe to operate.[25] Lawrence appears to have arranged the demonstration on his own initiative, without informing his superiors.[26]

March 10 – Companies C and D, 30th Engineers, landed at Brest.[27]

March 18 – Two D-B No. 3 portable flamethrowers were completed by the Incendiary Unit and shipped to France for tests.[28]

March 26 – Col. Fries requested of the Officer in Charge of the Gas Service, London, that two Lawrence Knapsack Flame Projectors Model 1917 be sent to the Incendiary Unit, Trench Warfare Section, Engineering Bureau, Ordnance Department, Washington, D.C.[29]

March 28 – Two Boyd No. 3 portable flamethrowers were completed by the Incendiary Unit and shipped to France for tests.[30]

April 5 – Company F, 30th Engineers, was organized.[31]

Spring 1918 – 1st Lieutenant L. I. Shaw of the Ordnance Department was sent to France to research foreign portable flamethrowers in order to incorporate their best features into an American design. The AEF officers he interviewed were uniformly unenthusiastic about flamethrowers, citing their limited capacity and the danger they posed to their operators.[32]

May 5 – Lt. Shaw wrote to the Production and Supply Division of the AEF Gas Service, requesting that six of the 96 P_3 flamethrowers ordered by Col. Fries be delivered to him at the Experimental Field in Chaumont.[33]

May 6 – After a few hours of examining the P_3 flamethrowers, Shaw recommended that the 30th Engineers not adopt the weapon or even use it for training purposes, as it seemed to him a "decidedly inferior" apparatus.[34]

Rare image of a French instructor (center) training two Americans of the 30th Engineers in the use of a Schilt No. 3 bis flamethrower. This photo and the next were taken in France in 1918, by a member of the American Field Service, a volunteer ambulance corps. The 30th Engineers tested portable flamethrowers in combat, but details of the weapons and circumstances are unknown.

On the same day Brigadier General C. M. Wagstaff of the British Mission to the AEF wrote to Amos Fries, explaining that Lt. Percy H. Lawrence, R.E., could not be spared to conduct further demonstrations of his flamethrower. He had caused a lot of trouble for the War Office, and they would not let him cause more. In addition, even though Lawrence's weapon was not bad, the War Office rejected the entire principle of flamethrowers and recommended that they not be seriously considered.[35]

May 8 – Col. Fries replied to Brig. Gen. Wagstaff, stating, "The views you express regarding the whole principle of Flame Projectors is*[sic]* entirely in accordance with my own."[36] Despite this memo, the 30th Engineers remained committed to creating an American portable flamethrower. Lt. Shaw of the Ordnance Department continued his research in France.[37]

May 9 – Col. Fries wired Lt. Salisbury of the AEF Gas Service, London, informing him that it was not advisable for the U.S. to manufacture the Lawrence flamethrower under license.[38]

May 10 – The Incendiary Unit reported on the progress of the "flaming bayonet,"[39] a small, rifle-mounted flamethrower never used in combat.

Sleeve patch of the Chemical Service Section, adopted in December of 1917. Privates first class wore it on the middle of the right sleeve. The backing was olive-drab wool, and the benzene ring and crossed retorts were embroidered in yellow-gold thread. Bronze collar disks bearing this symbol were also issued. The Chemical Warfare Service used the insignia beginning in June of 1918, but it was not popular with the men of the 30th Engineers, many of whom felt it resembled crossed golf clubs.

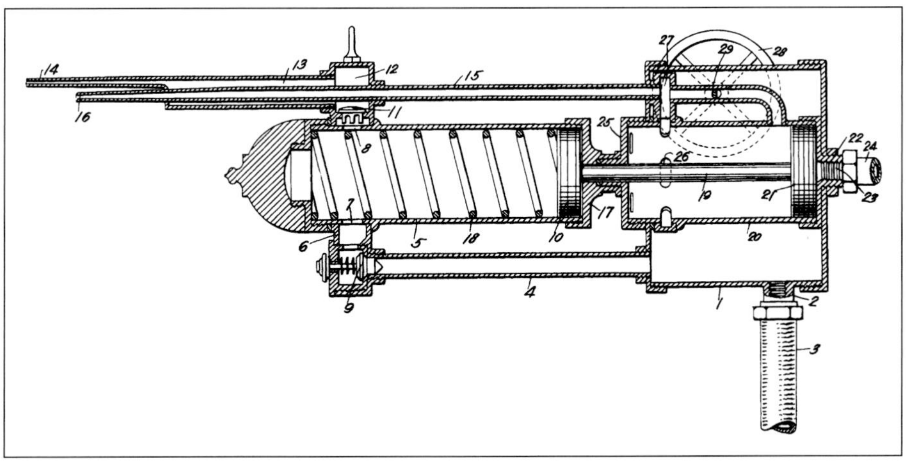

"Automatic Fire Thrower," a device for converting a rifle or machine gun into a flamethrower. Inventor Alexander E. Seidler of New York filed an application on April 20, 1918, and was granted American patent number 1,304,710 on May 27, 1919. The device was threaded onto the barrel of a rifle or machine gun (24), which was loaded with blank cartridges. Each time a cartridge was detonated, the gases forced a piston (21) forward, drawing oil from a separate tank through a tube (3) into a chamber (5). From here it passed through a valve into the barrel (13) and out the nozzle (14). The flame of the blank cartridge passed through a pipe (15) and ignited the jet of oil. A spring (18) forced the piston back to its original position, ready for the next detonation, while a wheel (28) regulated the pressure of the expanding gases. The device could be attached to a machine gun to produce a continuous flame. It is not known if Seidler presented his "Automatic Fire Thrower" to the U.S. Army.

Right: Men of the CWS using a British Lawrence Knapsack Flame Projector Model 1917 to melt snow from a New York City sidewalk in 1920. It has been fitted with a hydrogen pilot light attached under the nozzle. A length of slender tubing runs from the burner to a small gas container on the top rear of the oil tank. Note the oil-release lever on the top of the flamethrower. This photo contradicts the claim of Brig. Gen Fries that the CWS had discarded all of their flamethrowers by 1919. Library of Congress LC USZ62.

Below: American lieutenant of engineers demonstrating the Flaming Bayonet, Cartridge Type, Mark III, a miniature flamethrower attached beneath the muzzle of an M1917 Enfield rifle. The box-shaped case contained six cartridges packed with an incendiary filling, each of which could project a burst of flame up to 15 ft. in length. To fire the weapon, the rifleman pulled a trigger on the rear of the box with his left forefinger while holding the rifle butt with his right hand.

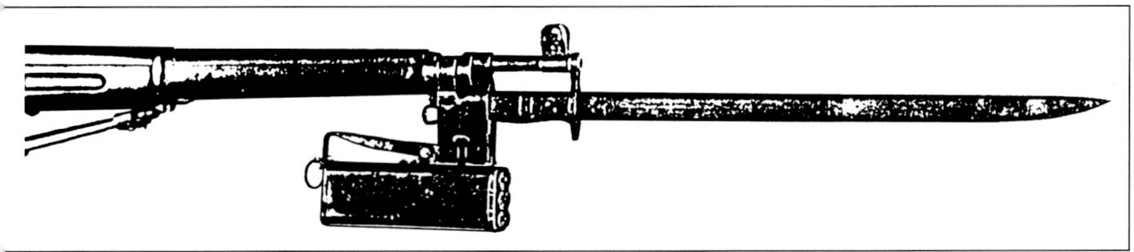

Flaming Bayonet, Cartridge Type, Mark III. The flaming bayonet was designed to create tactical surprise, but none appear to have been sent overseas. Research into the concept stopped with the end of the war.

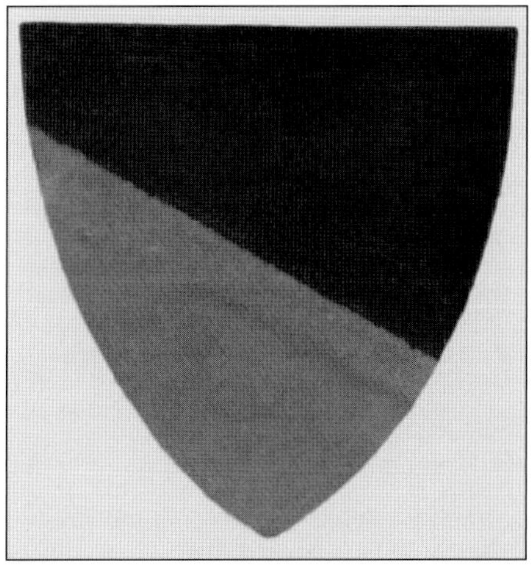

Shoulder patch of the Chemical Warfare Service, a shield divided diagonally into cobalt blue on top and golden yellow below. It was worn by gas and flame troops after July 13, 1918, when the 30th Engineer Regiment was transferred to the Chemical Warfare Service and became the 1st Gas Regiment.

May 11 – Major General William L. Sibert was made chief of the Gas Service, U.S. Army. He was ordered to bring about better coordination between the Bureau of Mines, the Medical Department, the Ordnance Department, the Signal Corps, the Corps of Engineers, and the AEF, all of which were working on chemical and flame warfare.[40]

Summer 1918 – The Incendiary Unit developed the Parapet Type Flame Projector. Similar in principle to the Russian SPS explosive-piston flamethrower, it used a slow-burning pressure cartridge of celluloid. The firing chamber was located inside the oil reservoir, which was placed either at the bottom of the trench or in a niche and covered with sandbags. A flexible hose carried the oil to the nozzle, which was built into the trench wall or attached to the parapet.

To operate the flamethrower the engineer pulled a cord to remove a safety pin and either struck a firing pin with the palm of his hand or used an electric blasting machine. Pressure from the burning celluloid forced a piston through the reservoir, expelled the liquid, and activated a mechanical pilot light that ignited the jet. The flamethrower had a range of 80 feet and could be deployed in batteries. Only two examples were completed.[41]

June 19 – A telegram from Lt. Higbee and Col. Fries to Lt. Salisbury in London, acknowledged that the AEF Gas Service in France had ordered 48 Lawrence Knapsack Flame Projectors Model 1917.[42]

June 25 – Control of the American University Experiment Station, Washington, D.C., was transferred from the Bureau of Mines to the War Department.[43] Research on flamethrowers was thus removed from the hands of civilians.

On the same day the Adams flamethrower (see July 2) and the British Hay Flame Gun were demonstrated to American, British, French, and Italian officers at the Gas Service Experimental Field in Chaumont.[44]

June 28 – The U.S. Army Gas Service was transformed into the Chemical Warfare Service (CWS), U.S. Army, under the command of Maj. Gen. Sibert. Also called the Chemical Warfare Service of the National Army, it was given control over all facilities and functions applying to toxic chemicals.[45] The CWS was organized into the following divisions: Overseas, Research, Development, Gas Defense Production, Gas Offense Production, Medical, Proving, Training, Administration, and Gas and Flame.

The Research Division was divided into Sections: the Pyrotechnic Section experimented with Livens projectors and flamethrowers, including foreign models and those developed by the Ordnance Department.[46] Although the Americans copied the British incendiary drum for Livens projectors, it appears that the AEF did not use it in combat.

On the same day that the CWS was established, the AEF Gas Service became the Overseas Division, Chemical Warfare Service, also called the Chemical Warfare Service AEF. Fries was made Chief of CWS AEF and promoted to brigadier general.[47]

June 29 – Lt. Shaw of the Ordnance Department recommended that all types of British, French, Italian, and American flamethrowers be tried out at once, in a single demonstration at the CWS AEF Experimental Field in Chaumont. Shaw had inspected most models of flamethrower and saw positive elements in all of them. He

Engineer private displaying the patch of the Chemical Warfare Service on the upper left shoulder of his olive-drab M1917 tunic. He also wears the castle insignia disk on the right side of his collar. The three chevrons on his lower left sleeve indicate eighteen months of service overseas, and the red chevron above them show that he was honorably discharged from the army. As an engineer, he could belong to one of several research, combat, training, or production units that comprised the CWS.

This engineer of an unknown regiment wears the shoulder patch of the First Army with a small shield of the CWS beneath the crossbar of the "A." Clearly a man who follows his own rules, he gives a double thumbs up to the small boy aiming a trophy Kar 98AZ carbine. The photo was probably taken soon after the engineer arrived home from France.

suggested that after the demonstration there be a conference of flamethrower experts from each nation involved.

Shaw requested the demonstration and conference because "it has been decided by the commanding officer of the 30th Engineers to at least try out the flame projector of the portable type in actual warfare."[48] Details of the combat trials have not been located.

July 1 – The American University Experiment Station became the Research Division of the CWS, U.S. Army.[49]

July 2 – The Director of Experiments at the Headquarters of the Experimental Field, CWS AEF, described the two-man static flamethrower invented by engineer Major Henry Adams. Oil supplied by a centrifugal pump was atomized by a blast of steam from a boiler and ignited as it sprayed through a projector. The range of the flamethrower depended on the velocity of the steam jet rather than the inertia of the liquid oil. Boiler (30 in. by 48 in.), burner, kerosene tank, oil pump, water tank, oil tank, and projector together weighed almost 1800 lbs.[50]

July 10 – Brig. Gen. Fries informed Lt. Salisbury in London that no effort should be made to bring Lt. Lawrence to France to demonstrate his flamethrower.[51]

July 12 – Second Battalion Headquarters and Companies E and F, 30th Engineers, landed at Brest.[52]

July 13 – The 30th Engineer Regiment was transferred to the Chemical Warfare Service and redesignated the 1st Gas Regiment.[53]

July 15 – Engineer Captain Zanetti requested a report on the Boyd and D-B portable flamethrowers that would be tested later in the month.[54]

July 23 – A test of all models of American, British, French, and Italian flamethrowers was held at the CWS AEF Experimental Field in Chaumont.[55]

July 25 – Lt. Shaw of the Ordnance Department submitted his report on the test. Beginning in August, the Engineering Corps and Ordnance Department ceased reporting on flamethrowers, with the exception of the Adams device.[56] (See next entry.)

Early October – A steam-driven tank named the "America," officially known as the "Flame Projector, Tractor Type, Mark I," was demonstrated for General Persh-

Above: Although these men are identified as belonging to the 41st "Sunset" Division, many display CWS shoulder patches. By the end of the war, chemical troops wore one each of three different collar disks, two arm badges, and at least eleven shoulder-patch combinations if they had served in the First Army. These soldiers are equipped with the M1910 haversack with meat can pouch, M1917 steel helmets, M1918 overseas caps instead of the campaign hat, and M1917 Small Box Respirators.

Left: Two engineers photographed after their discharge from the army, as indicated by the red chevrons on their upper left sleeves. The seated private first class wears an unidentified patch on his left shoulder and a specialist badge on his right upper arm, while the standing soldier displays the shoulder patch of the First Army with a CWS inset of cobalt blue over golden yellow, the same colors of the cord and acorns of his M1917 campaign hat. He wears no collar insignia, and he has tied his puttees cavalry style, at the ankles.

Right: Sleeve patch of private first class, 1st Gas Regiment, in olive-drab wool and embroidered yellow-gold thread. On August 12, 1918, Major General William Sibert, Chief of the Chemical Warfare Service, requested the "dragon-over-shells" motif. It was to replace the crossed retorts of the CWS, which were seen as "not sufficiently warlike" by the troops. By the time the dragon-over-shells insignia was rejected by the Secretary of War as frivolous, many soldiers had already received their new patches or collar disks. It was worn on the middle of the right sleeve until the end of the war.

Postwar illustration of men from the CWS melting snow banks with a modified Adams steam-powered flamethrower. The steam both propelled the oil jet and atomized it so that it could be ignited at the nozzle. Pipe from the boiler was coiled into a tank of oil, which was kept at a temperature of 90° F. The steam-driven centrifugal pump that fed the oil into the lance is not pictured.

ing at the CWS AEF Experimental Field in Chaumont. Conceived in March, it was armed with Maj. Adams's steam-powered flamethrower. During the demonstration heat waves and glare from the flamethrower blinded the crew, allowing Brig. Gen. Fries to crawl up undetected and show how easily infantrymen could destroy the tank. The project was abandoned.[57]

November 11 – On Armistice Day, one D-B No. 3 flamethrower was completed out of an order of ten. No more were built.[58] During the war the 30th Engineer Regiment (Gas and Flame) and 1st Gas Regiment carried out a total of 152 operations with Stokes mortars and Livens projectors.[59] Thirty-nine officers and men from both regiments were killed in action or died of wounds, accident, gassing, or disease.[60]

December 9 – The Incendiary Unit completed its design for the Knapsack Flame Projector, Mark I, based on the research from Lt. Shaw and specifications drawn up by the 1st Gas Regiment. Nothing is known about this model, other than its weight of 50 lbs.[61] The total number of American flamethrowers manufactured during the war was around twelve, including: one Knapsack Flame Projector, Mark I; two Boyd No. 3; one D-B No. 1; one D-B No. 2; three D-B No. 3; two Parapet Type Flame Projectors; and one Adams steam-powered flamethrower.

Private Evan Jones, 1st Gas Regiment, uniformed in the M1912 wool tunic and semi-breeches in olive drab, with M1910 dismounted cartridge belt and canvas leggings. Although he still displays the castle collar disk of the 30th Engineers, the cord and acorns of his M1912 campaign hat are the cobalt blue and golden yellow of the CWS. He is armed with the .30-caliber M1917 Enfield rifle and M1905 bayonet.

The "America," a steam-powered tank, which in September of 1918 was shipped to AEF headquarters in France for testing. It was armed with the Adams steam-driven flamethrower mounted in the bow and two .30 caliber machine guns in each side sponson. Two two-cylinder steam engines provided 500 horsepower, for a top speed of four miles per hour. A 35-hp gasoline engine allowed for the 1600psi boiler pressure required to operate the flamethrower. The "America" weighed 50 tons and had length of 39 ft. 9 in., a width of 12 ft. 6 in., and a height of 10 ft. 4.5 inches.

The "America" in France, fitted with a turret for the flamethrower. In this configuration the weapon had a range of 90 yards. During its demonstration to American officers in October of 1918, CWS Chief Brigadier General Amos A. Fries showed how he was able to crawl close enough to the tank to destroy it with an explosive charge, due to the fact that glare and shimmering heat waves from the flamethrower blinded the crew. Only one example of the Steam Tank was built; the project was soon abandoned.

Second Lieutenants of Company H, 1st Gas Regiment, photographed in Chillicothe, Ohio, in late 1918. They are in shirtsleeves order, wearing the M1916 olive-drab wool shirt with bronze collar pins of the infantry and cavalry; officers in the 1st Gas Regiment kept their commissions in their original units. Note the leather gaiters and the M1912 campaign hats with cords and acorns of cobalt blue and golden yellow.

Patch of the 1st Gas Regiment, a yellow shield with a dark-blue "1." Adopted after July 3, 1918, it was worn on the upper left shoulder. Several variations existed.

1919

February 2 – The 1st Gas Regiment arrived back in the United States.

March 2 – The regiment was mustered out.

Brig. Gen. Fries declared the flamethrower "one of the greatest failures among the many promising devices tried out on a large scale during the war."[62] As head of the peacetime CWS, he eliminated virtually all research and development of flamethrowers. However, flamethrowers remained in the Chemical Warfare Service arsenal for some time, as evidenced below.

1920

January 1-March 30 – The Baltimore recruiting district of the U.S. Army spent $6.40 on three 5-gallon cans of benzene, used to fill flamethrowers designated "recruiting novelties."[63]

Tactics

It is likely that French tactics were used during the limited combat trials of the portable flamethrower. (See France.)

Chapter Ten

Czech Legion

1918

April 21 – Italy amalgamated its Czech Labor Corps – Czech prisoners captured from the Austro-Hungarian Army – and other units into the Autonomous Czech Corps, also called the 6th Czech Division, comprised of the 31st through 34th Rifle Regiments. At least 10,000 Czechs served.[1]

The four infantry regiments of the 6th Czech Division had three battalions each. One portable-flamethrower section of one officer, one sergeant, two corporals, and 24 infantrymen armed with 12 devices was raised in each battalion. These sections were numbered 217 to 228, a total of 12.[2] In Czech, the flamethrower was the *ohňomet*.

Czech Legions of the French and Russian armed forces had no flamethrower troops, as those nations had their own dedicated flame and flame-chemical units. (See France and Russia.)

Flamethrower squad of the Czech Legion (eskoslovenské Legie). These are veterans of the Czech Corps or 6th Czech Division, raised by the Italians in April of 1918. The sign between the late-model Schilt No. 3 bis flamethrowers reads "39th 'Vysocansky' Regiment, C. S. [eskoslovensko], Flame Projectors, 17 February, 1919." Note the Italian M1909 gray-green uniforms, Alpini hats and boots, and daggers (pugnali). Rifles are the Austrian Mannlicher M1895 8mm Short Rifle "Stutzen," and ammunition pouches are a mixture of Austrian and Italian manufacture. On the upper left arms, the men wear the shield of the Czech Corps and the Italian flamethrower qualification badge, a black dragon puffing out red flames. The flamethrowers are missing the protective cover for the top of the fuel tank; the lances are Italian automatic-ignition models.

Infantrymen of the Czech Corps. At least two flamethrower squads are present, armed with Italian Schilt No. 3 bis with automatic-ignition lances. On the right are two grenadiers, rifles slung across their backs. With the exception of the British, flamethrower troops of all the combatants paired flamethrowers with hand-grenade throwers during the assault. Brown Reference Group.

These assault troops of the Czech Corps train with flamethrowers and Bangalore torpedoes for breaching barbed-wire obstacles. The men wear Italian Adrian steel helmets and are armed with M1891 Moschetto carbines. As in the previous two images, the flamethrowers are the Italian Schilt No. 3 bis with automatic-ignition lance. Brown Reference Group.

Flamethrower operator of the Czech Corps photographed in Prague, date unknown. He wears the Italian M1909 uniform and is armed with a dagger symbolizing his status as an assault trooper. The protruding edges of the purple-and-silver Czech Corps shield and the Italian flamethrower-qualification badge can be seen on his upper left arm.

June 10 – The Italian Supreme Army Command ordered the formation of an Assault Army Corps comprised of an Assault Division (called "A" Division) and the 6th Czech Division. After the Battle of the Piave (June 15-24), the Czech Division was removed from the Assault Army Corps and replaced with another Assault Division.[3]

August 10 – Great Britain recognized all three Czech Legions as parts of an independent army; the United States and Japan soon followed suit.[4]

September – The 35th and 39th Rifle Regiments were formed in the 6th Czech Division. Each had three portable flamethrower sections that were not given official numbers, as these regiments did not see combat with the Italians.

October 28 – Czechoslovakia declared its independence.

Tactics

The flamethrower operators of the 6th Czech Division were trained by the Italians and thus used Italian tactics. (See Italy.)

CHAPTER ELEVEN

CANADA

1917

June 28 – The 12th Infantry Brigade of the Canadian 4th Division, Canadian Corps, advanced into Avion, the southern suburb of Lens. As part of the assault, the Canadians fired incendiary weapons:

> The Canadians used flame projectors for the first time and, under cover of an intense barrage, the attacking brigades faced a driving rain and flooded areas to reach the village. It was tightly-locked fighting, as intensely waged as any fighting of the war, but the Canadians hung grimly on to Avion and registered another 500-yard bite into German territory on a mile of front.[1]

A second version of the assault indicates that these were Livens projectors rather than flamethrowers:

> As a preliminary to this attack the Canadians, for the first time in their war experience, used flame projectors – another Hun-devised weapon – pouring the blazing contents of two hundred drums of oil into a section of the enemy's front.[2]

Livens projector. The 4th Canadian Division used Livens projectors as incendiary weapons at Avion on June 28, 1917, firing 200 drums of flammable oil at German positions. Note the leather muzzle cover, the explosive charge on the left, and the metal base plate on the right. Usually Livens projectors were used in batteries of 25.

This Canadian sapper wears the khaki Other Ranks' 1903 Pattern Service Dress Jacket and breeches, 1905 Pattern Service Dress Cap with badge of the Non-permanent Force, ankle boots with spurs, and 1903 Pattern leather bandolier. In late June of 1917 the Canadian 4th Division contained the 4th Canadian Engineer Brigade; men of the 10th, 11th, or 12th Field Companies of the Canadian Engineers may therefore have carried out the Livens-projector incendiary attack at Avion.

Canadian sapper uniformed in the British 1902 Pattern Service Dress in khaki, worn by most of the Canadian Expeditionary Force. His cap displays the badge of the Permanent Force, Royal Canadian Engineers; the brass titles "CANADA" and "CE" are pinned to his shoulder straps.

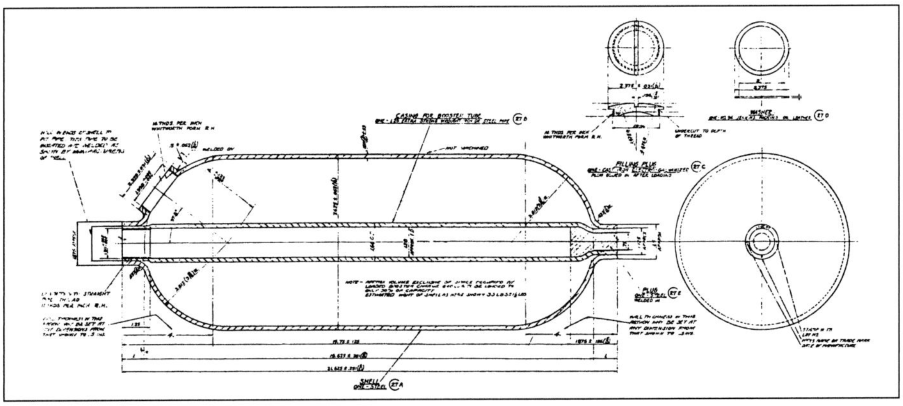

Mark I incendiary drum for Livens projector, which had a diameter of 7.6 in. and a length of 19 in. It was filled through an opening (left) with one part heavy Mexican petroleum residue and three parts Persian distillate; the filling plug and washer are illustrated top right. A steel "gaine tube" running through the center of the projectile held the TNT bursting charge and detonator, which was set off by either a percussion or a time fuse. The explosion created a flash about 40 ft. high, spreading flaming liquid over an area of 40 square yards.

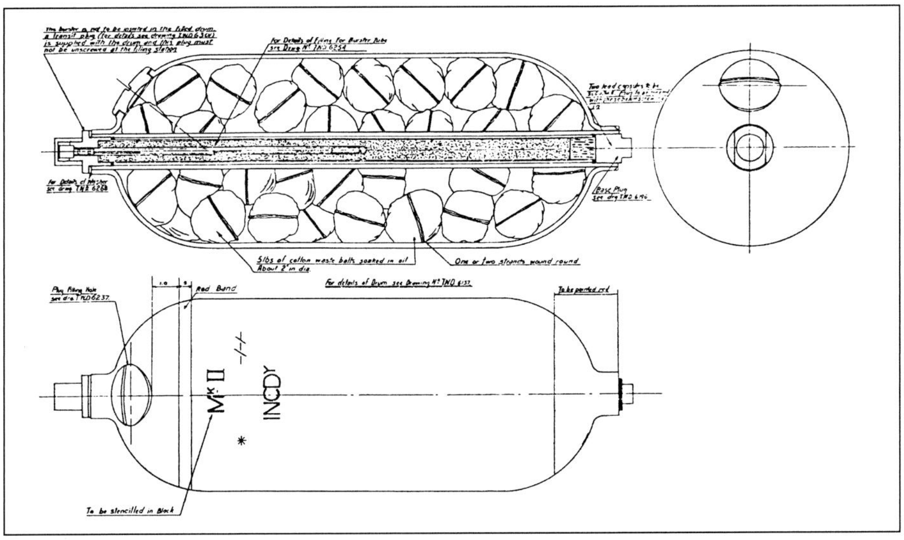

Mark II incendiary drum for Livens projector, produced in 1917. It was loaded with 5 lbs. of cotton waste balls (ca. 60 balls per pound) saturated with different oil mixtures. When the drum exploded, it created approximately 85 patches of fire over an area 35 yards by 22 yards, which burned for about four minutes. Each Mark II incendiary drum weighed 53 lbs. when loaded.

The Canadian 4th Division contained the 4th Canadian Engineer Brigade, comprised of the 10th, 11th, and 12th Field Companies of the Canadian Engineers. However, the war diary of the 4th Canadian Engineer Brigade does not mention the Livens-projector attack of June 28; in fact no official Canadian or British records of this operation have been located. The unit that fired the projectors remains unidentified.

Field Marshal Sir Douglas Haig, Commander-in-Chief of the British Expeditionary Force, indicated in his dispatch of December 25, 1917, that this action was part of a complex feint:

> On the evening of the 28th June a deliberate and carefully-thought-out scheme was put into operation by the First Army, to give the enemy the impression that he was being attacked on a twelve-mile front from Gavrelle to Hulluch.
>
> Elaborate demonstrations were made on the whole of this front, accompanied by discharges of gas, smoke, and thermit, and a mock raid was successfully carried out south-east of Loos.[3]

October 18 – Brigadier General Victor Odlum, commander of the 11th Canadian Infantry Brigade, asked the Canadian General Staff to establish four Special Companies and a Stokes mortar battery in the Canadian Corps to engage in poison-gas warfare. At around the same time the Canadian Gas Services recommended the creation of two gas companies armed with canisters and Livens projectors. Without explanation the Canadian Overseas Ministry rejected all plans for gas units with offensive capabilities.[4]

Tactics

Livens projectors were used much as trench mortars, to bombard the enemy line prior to an assault. They were deployed in batteries of 25.

Appendices

Appendix 1
Flamethrower Data

Country	Model	Dimensions (height x diameter)	Weight when full	Capacity	Range	Continuous Duration
			Central Powers			
Germany						
large	*grosse Flammenwerfer (Grof) M.1912*	40 in. x 20 in.	ca. 650 lbs.	45 gal.	115-130 ft.	45 sec.
	Lichtgrof M.1916	ca. 40 in. x 12 in.	297 lbs.	26 gal.	131 ft.	45 sec.
	Double *Lichtgrof M.1916*	ca. 40 in. x 12 in. (x 2)	594 lbs.	2 x 26 = 52 gal.	131 ft.	70 sec.
	Triple *Lichtgrof M.1916*	ca. 40 in. x 12 in. (x 3)	891 lbs.	3 x 26 = 78 gal.	131 ft.	120 sec.
medium	*mittlere Flammenwerfer (Kleif) M.1917*	23.6 in. x 9.8 in.	68 lbs.	4.2 gal.	(0.2in. nozzle) 72 ft.	(0.2in. nozzle) 15 sec.
					(0.3in. nozzle) 105 ft.	(0.3in. nozzle) 12 sec.
	Double *Kleif M.1917*	23.6 in. x 9.8 in. (x 2)	136 lbs.	2 x 4.2 = 8.4 gal.	66 ft.	15 sec.
small	*kleine Flammenwerfer (Kleif) M.1912*	23.6 in. x 9.8 in.	71 lbs.	4.2 gal.	66 ft.	15 sec.
	Kleif M.1914	23.6 in. x 9.8 in.	71 lbs.	4.2 gal.	(0.2in. nozzle) 50-60 ft.	(0.2in. nozzle) 15 sec.
					(0.3in. nozzle) -	(0.3in. nozzle) -
	Kleif M.1915 (early model)	18 in. x 10 in. (oil tank)	70 lbs.	5 gal.	(0.2in. nozzle) 83 ft.	(0.2in nozzle) 20-25 sec.
					(0.3-in nozzle) -	(0.3-in nozzle) -
	Kleif M.1915 (late model)	18 in. x 10 in. (oil tank)	70 lbs.	5 gal.	(0.2in. nozzle) 83 ft.	(0.2in. nozzle) 20-25 sec.
					(0.3in. nozzle) -	(0.3in. nozzle) -
	Double *Kleif M.1915*	18 in. x 10 in. (oil tank x 2)		140 lbs.	2 x 5 = 10 gal.	(0.4in. nozzle) - (0.4in. nozzle) -
	Kleif M.1916	23.6 in. x 9.8 in.	68 lbs.	4.2 gal.	(0.2in. nozzle) 72 ft.	(0.2in. nozzle) 15 sec.
					(0.3in. nozzle) 105 ft.	(0.3in. nozzle) 12 sec.
	Double *Kleif M.1916*	23.6 in. x 9.8 in. (x 2)	136 lbs.	2 x 4.2 = 8.4 gal.	(0.4in. nozzle) 100-116 ft.	(0.4in. nozzle) 22 sec.
	Wechselapparat (Wex) M.1917	ca. 18 in. (diameter)	55 lbs.	2.9 gal.	(0.2in. nozzle) 82 ft.	(0.2in. nozzle) 20 sec.
					(0.3in. nozzle) 98 ft.	(0.3in. nozzle) 9 sec.
Austria-Hungary						
large	*grosse 200l M. 15 Flammenwerfer*	ca. 42 in. x 22 in.	ca. 700 lbs.	53 gal.	ca. 200 ft.	15 sec.
medium	*mittlere 50l M. 15 Flammenwerfer*	ca. 34 in. x 10 in.	ca. 200 lbs.	13.2 gal.	ca. 98 ft.	15 sec.
	mittlere 50l M. 15a Flammenwerfer	ca. 34 in. x 10 in.	ca. 200 lbs.	13.2 gal.	ca. 98 ft.	15 sec.
	Double *mittlere 50 l M. 15 Flammenwerfer*	ca. 34 in. x 10 in.	ca. 400 lbs.	2 x 13.2 = 26.4 gal.	ca. 98 ft.	30 sec.
small	*Kleif M.1912*	23.6 in. x 9.8 in.	71 lbs.	4.2 gal.	66 ft.	15 sec.
	kleine 22l M. 15 Flammenwerfer	ca. 21 in. x 8 in.	ca. 75 lbs.	6 gal.	(0.16in. nozzle) ca. 80 ft.	(0.16in. nozzle) 15 sec.
					(0.2in. nozzle) – (0.2in. nozzle) -	
	kleine 15l M. 16 Flammenwerfer	ca. 19 in. x 7.5 in.	ca. 60 lbs.	4 gal.	(0.16in. nozzle) ca. 70 ft.	(0.16in. nozzle) 15 sec.
					(0.2in. nozzle) -	(0.2in. nozzle) -
Bulgaria						
large	*Lichtgrof M.1916*	ca. 40 in. x 12 in.	297 lbs.	26 gal.	131 ft.	45 sec.
medium	*Kleif M.1917*	23.6 in. x 9.8 in.	68 lbs.	4.2 gal.	(0.2in. nozzle) 72 ft.	(0.2in. nozzle) 15 sec.
					(0.3in. nozzle) 105 ft.	(0.3in. nozzle) 12 sec.
small	*Wex M.1917*	ca. 18 in. (diameter)	55 lbs.	2.9 gal.	(0.2in. nozzle) 82 ft.	(0.2in. nozzle) 20 sec.
					(0.3in. nozzle) 98 ft.	(0.3in. nozzle) 9 sec.
Ottoman Empire						
medium	*Kleif M.1917*	23.6 in. x 9.8 in.	68 lbs.	4.2 gal.	(0.2in. nozzle) 72 ft.	(0.2in. nozzle) 15 sec.
					(0.3in. nozzle) 105 ft.	(0.3in. nozzle) 12 sec.
small	*Kleif M.1912*	23.6 in. x 9.8 in.	71 lbs.	4.2 gal.	66 ft.	15 sec.

Allied Powers

France						
large	Hersent-Thirion	40 in. x 16 in. (x 4)	3968 lbs.	4 x 33 = 132 gal.	230-260 ft.	20 sec.
	L_1	ca. 28 in. x 12 in. (x 3)	794 lbs.	3 x 12 = 36 gal.	200 ft.	20 sec.
	L_2	ca. 24 in. x 11 in. (x 4)	661 lbs.	4 x 8 = 32 gal.	150 ft.	17 sec.
	Schilt No. 1	47.2 in. x 13 in.	276 lbs.	21 gal.	115 ft.	20-25 sec.
	Schilt No. 1 bis	25 in. x 13 in.	187 lbs.	14.5 gal.	115 ft.	15-20 sec.
medium	Schilt No. 2	24 in. x 11 in.	110 lbs.	8 gal.	50 ft.	20 sec.
small	Chapal	22 in. x 5.5 in (x 2)	ca. 54 lbs.	2 x 2.2 = 4.4 gal.	66 ft.	
	P_3	ca. 20 in. x 8 in.	53 lbs.	3.7 gal.	92 ft.	ca. 15 sec.
	P_4	ca. 18 in. x 8 in.	42 lbs.	2.6 gal.	75 ft.	ca. 10 sec.
	Schilt No. 3 (early model)	23 in. x 7.3 in.	51 lbs.	4.2 gal.	50 ft.	10 sec.
	Schilt No. 3 (late model)	23 in. x 7.3 in.	51 lbs.	4.2 gal.	50 ft.	10 sec.
	Schilt No. 3 bis	22 in. x 8 in.	66 lbs.	4 gal.	66 ft.	5-10 bursts
		ca. 15 sec.				
Italy						
large	Hersent-Thirion	40 in. x 16 in. (x 4)	3968 lbs.	4 x 33 = 132 gal.	230-260 ft.	20 sec.
	Lagunari	25 in. x 13 in.	190 lbs.	15 gal.	115 ft.	15-20 sec.
	Schilt No. 1	47.3 in. x 13 in.	276 lbs.	21 gal.	115 ft.	20-25 sec.
	Schilt No. 1 bis	25 in. x 13 in.	187 lbs.	14.5 gal.	115 ft.	15-20 sec.
medium	Schilt No. 2	24 in. x 11 in.	110 lbs.	8 gal.	50 ft.	20 sec.
small	DLF	17.7 in. x 7 in.	40 lbs.	3.2 gal.	50-66 ft.	ca. 15 sec.
	Intermittent Jet with Automatic Ignition	20 in. x 4.8 in. (x 2)	53 lbs.	2 x 1.6 = 3.2	50-66 ft.	ca. 15 sec.
	Modified Italian Schilt No. 3 bis	22 in. x 8 in.	66 lbs.	4 gal.	66 ft.	5-10 bursts
	Schilt No. 3 (early model)	23 in. x 7.3 in.	51 lbs.	4.2 gal.	50 ft.	10 sec.
	Schilt No. 3 (late model)	23 in. x 7.3 in.	51 lbs.	4.2 gal.	50 ft.	10 sec.
Great Britain						
large	Livens Large Gallery *Flammenwerfer*	ca. 4 ft. high x 50 ft. long	4000 lbs.	80 + (5 x 41.6) = 288 gal.	336 ft.	4 min.
	Vincent battery model	48 in. x 16 in. (x 4)	ca. 950 lbs.	4 x 24 = 96 gal.	270 ft.	11-50 sec., or 16 flame balls over 3 min.
	Vincent new-type battery model	48 in. x 14 in. (x 4)	ca. 687 lbs.	4 x 23 = 92 gal.	270 ft.	11-50 sec., or 16 flame balls over 3 min.
medium	Livens Semi-portable	44 in. x 12 in.	150 lbs.	14 gal.	105 ft.	ca. 30 sec.
small	Hall	-	50 lbs.	4 gal.	100 ft.	ca. 15 sec.
	Hay Flame Gun	35 in. x 5.5 in.	66 lbs.	2.6 gal.	66 ft.	ca. 15 sec.
	Lawrence Model 1917	ca. 19 in. x 8 in.	40 lbs.	3 gal.	135 ft.	ca. 16 sec.
	Norris	ca. 24 in. x 9 in.	85 lbs.	6.5 gal.	105 ft.	18 sec.
Russia						
large	General Ershov	-	-	-	-	-
	Livens Large Gallery *Flammenwerfer*	ca. 4 ft. high x 50 ft. long	4000 lbs.	80 + (5 x 41.6) = 288 gal.	336 ft.	4 min.
	SPS	-	70 lbs.	-	135 ft.	1-2 sec.
	Tovarnitskiy trench model	39 in. x 20 in.	423 lbs.	53 gal.	115-180 ft.	1 min., or 3 min. intermittent
	Vincent battery model	48 in. x 16 in. (x 4)	ca. 950 lbs.	4 x 24 = 96 gal.	270 ft.	11-50 sec., or 16 flame balls over 3 min.
small	Aleksandrov	-	-	-	45-60 ft.	-
	Gorbov	-	-	45-60 ft.	-	
	Lawrence Model 1917	ca. 19 in. x 8 in.	40 lbs.	3 gal.	135 ft.	ca. 16 sec.
	Tilly-Goskin	ca. 22 in x 6 in.	ca. 40 lbs.	-	150 ft.	3 min. intermittent, or 25 seconds continuous
	Tovarnitskiy knapsack model	ca. 21 in. x 6 in.	55 lbs.	ca. 4 gal.	50-100 ft.	50-55 sec.
unk. size	Arkhangelysk System	-	-	-	-	-
United States						
large	Adams Steam Flamethrower	48 in. x 30 in. (boiler)	1800 lbs.	9 gal. per min.	44 ft.	2-3 min.
	Parapet Type	-	-	-	80 ft.	-
small	Boyd No. 3	ca. 21 in. x 7 in. (x 2)	80 lbs.	2 x 2.5 = 5 gal.	90-130 ft.	ca. 20 sec.
	Davis-Bournonville (D-B) No. 3	ca. 20 in. x 6 in.	70 lbs.	ca. 2 x 2.5 = 5 gal.	-	ca. 15 sec.
	Knapsack Flame Projector, Mark I	-	50 lbs.	-	-	-
Czech Legion						
small	Modified Italian Schilt No. 3 bis	22 in. x 8 in.	66 lbs.	4 gal.	66 ft.	5-10 bursts

Appendix 2
Types of Flamethrower Oil

Germany, Bulgaria, and the Ottoman Empire

According to German sources flamethrower oil was composed of a mixture of coal-tar residue with other chemical additions, light and heavy hydrocarbons, coal-tar oil, and carbon disulphide.[1] It had a specific gravity of 1. The light materials heightened combustibility, and the heavy materials increased the range of the flame jet.

French tests done on three different samples of German flamethrower oil showed that each had a different composition. The first sample consisted mainly of wood distillate with acetone, methyl alcohol, ethylene hydrocarbons, carbolic acids, and pyridine bases. The second sample was composed of 42 to 45 percent oil of acetone (the residue of the manufacture of ordinary acetone) and 55 to 58 percent wood tar free of pyroligneus acid (wood vinegar) and creosote. The third sample comprised 30 percent carbon disulfide, 45 percent oil of acetone, and 25 percent pitch.[2]

There were four grades of flame oil, color coded by their thickness.

> A.) Blue oil - The oil most employed in the field. Relatively thick flowing, it produced a heavy flame that heightened the adverse psychological impact on the enemy. Blue oil was susceptible to thickening further in severe cold, which could clog the flamethrower. Under such conditions, Yellow oil was substituted.
>
> B.) Yellow oil - A thin, quick-burning oil that produced little smoke and a very hot flame. When Yellow oil was used, it was imperative that the valves and couplings of the flamethrower be tightened to prevent leakage, the major cause of accidental burns or explosions. Yellow oil was also dangerous to use in enclosed spaces such as dugouts and tunnels because of its strong fumes.
>
> C.) Green oil - A mixture of one part Blue and three parts Yellow oil. It produced a heavy smoke but retained some of the heat of Yellow oil.
>
> D.) Red oil - The cheapest, thickest grade of oil, used for training purposes only and never in the field. It produced more smoke than heat. When Red oil was used, the flamethrower had to be carefully cleaned afterward.

All four grades of flamethrower oil decomposed over time, thickening into clumps and clogging the valves, nozzles, and hoses of flamethrowers. Regular cleaning and inspection of the equipment was vital.

Oil in large flamethrowers was pressurized to 221 psi; oil in medium and small devices was pressurized to 338 psi.

Austria-Hungary

The standard mixture was tar oil and raw benzene. Fuel oil and raw benzene could be substituted in the same proportions, as could oil-gas tar and raw benzene, or petroleum and gasoline or alcohol.[3]

Oil in large flamethrowers was pressurized to 176 psi; oil in medium and small weapons was pressurized to 220 psi.

France, Italy, and the Czech Legion

All used French flamethrower oil, which was composed of 70 percent decanted, dephenolated coal-tar naptha and 30 percent gasoline. In very cold weather pure decanted, dephenolated coal-tar naptha was used.[4]

The Italians also used a mixture of five parts tar oil and one part fuel oil or carbon disulphide.[5]

Oil in the Hersent-Thirion was pressurized to 2204 psi; oil in the Schilt No. 1 and Schilt No. 2 was pressurized to 213 psi; and oil in small flamethrowers was pressurized to 146 or 220 psi, depending on the model.

Great Britain

The Lawrence Knapsack Flame Projector Model 1915 used a mixture of turpentine, carbon disulphide, and phosphorus. For all other weapons, many mixtures of heavy and light oils and spirits were tried, including gasoline, kerosene, turpentine, crude oil, and tar. The most useful mixture was 50 percent heavy fuel oil that had a specific gravity of .9 mixed with 50 percent kerosene that had a specific gravity of .75.[6]

Oil in large flamethrowers was pressurized to 1800 psi; oil in the Semi-portable was pressurized to 250 psi; oil in the Norris and Lawrence Knapsack Flame Projector Model 1917 was pressurized to 200 psi; and oil in the Hay Flame Gun was pressurized to 250 psi.

Incendiary drums for Livens projectors were filled with one part heavy Mexican petroleum residue and three parts Persian distillate.[7]

Russia

Although the composition of the flamethrower oil used by the Russians in World War I has not yet been discovered, the Soviets had two mixtures at the beginning of World War II. The first was 70 percent straw oil (a straw-colored petroleum paraffin oil) and 30 percent raw gasoline, and the second was 25 percent kerosene, 25 percent raw gasoline, and 50 percent straw oil.[8]

Oil in the Tovarnitskiy trench flamethrower was pressurized to 146-191 psi; oil in the Tovarnitskiy portable flamethrower was pressurized to 176-220 psi; oil in the Tilly-Goskin was pressurized to 205 psi; and oil in the Gorbov and Aleksandrov flamethrowers was pressurized to 367-514 psi.

United States

Three mixtures of flamethrower oil were used: the first was 50 percent crude benzene and 50 percent kerosene; the second was 20 percent benzene and 80 percent kerosene; and the third was 33 percent gasoline and 67 percent gas oil. Because of gasoline shortages, the first two mixtures were used most often.[9]

Water in the Adams Steam Flamethrower was pressurized to 70 psi, while oil in the Boyd No. 3 was pressurized to 250 psi.

Canada

It is likely that Canadian Livens projectors fired incendiary drums filled with the same oil mixture used by the British: one part heavy Mexican petroleum residue and three parts Persian distillate.

Notes

[1] Theune, pp. 19-21.

[2] Ministère de la Guerre, *Lance-flammes portatifs étrangers,* p. 17.

[3] *Anleitung für Flammenwerfer,* pp. 4-5.

[4] *Lectures of the French Army Chemical Warfare School, First Lecture,* pp. 16-17, and Ministero della Guerra, *Cenni Descrittivi degli Apparati Schilt,* (Rome: Laboratorio Foto-litografico del Ministero della Guerra, 1916), p. 14.

[5] Pirocchi, pp. 41-42.

[6] "Flame Projectors," pp. 13, 19.

[7] Ray, p. 68.

[8] "Istoriya Ognemetë," http://ss24.nnm.ru/istoriya_ognemjota (accessed February 13, 2009).

[9] Ray, p. 83.

Appendix 3
Colors of Incendiary Weapons

Germany, Bulgaria, and the Ottoman Empire
Metal and pasteboard fire tubes were painted brownish red, while incendiary grenades were field gray. Flamethrowers and lances were factory painted matte or glossy field gray that varied in shade from light green to nearly black. In the field flamethrowers were given camouflage coats of several patterns, the most common being wide, vertical bands of earth tones (yellow ochre, red brown, mid green) separated by black lines, or "lozenges" of any available hue, including blues, purples, greens, yellows, browns, and grays. If the latter approach, either hard-edged or feathered lozenges were applied.

Austria-Hungary
Flamethrowers and lances were factory painted matte khaki brown, the same color as steel helmets. Like German weapons they were also camouflaged in the field, either in wide bands of earth tones separated by black lines, or multi-colored lozenges with hard or feathered edges.

France
Initially French flamethrowers and incendiary grenades were painted a glossy light blue-gray. Lances were unpainted steel and brass. By 1916 flamethrowers were issued in a matte khaki green or olive shade, while the P_3 and P_4 devices appear to have been glossy black. Camouflage was applied in the field, consisting of a single earth tone over the top half of the flamethrower, segmented multicolored patterns with hard edges such as found on artillery pieces, or a stippling of several colors.

Italy
Imported French flamethrowers were glossy light blue-gray, while Italian weapons were glossy mid green or gray-green, the same color used on steel helmets. Lances were unpainted steel and brass.

Great Britain
Flamethrowers were either glossy battleship gray or a very dark color, possibly glossy black. Livens projectors were unpainted metal.

Russia
Flamethrowers were likely painted matte khaki, the same as steel helmets. They may also have been painted glossy olive green. Some large flamethrowers were camouflaged in wide, hard-edged bands of several colors.

United States
American flamethrowers were unpainted metal or matte olive drab, the same as steel helmets. The few French weapons accepted were olive green, black, or camouflaged. British portable flamethrowers were very dark, possibly black, while Livens projectors were unpainted metal.

Czech Legion
Flamethrowers were Italian, therefore glossy mid green or gray-green.

Canada
Livens projectors were unpainted metal.

Appendix 4
Defense Against Flamethrowers

None of the combatants devised particularly effective defenses against flamethrowers. Newspapers reported that French soldiers wrapped themselves in bandages and slathered on handfuls of mud, which when dry armored the men like tortoises. The "wonderful clay baked hard as iron. They had to break it off with a hammer."[1]

In another account, the French deflected the flames with large oblong shields woven from osier, willows with long, straight twigs used in basket making. The shields were covered with clay that dried into a hard shell impervious to burning oil. One problem with this form of defense was that it produced a terrible, suffocating odor that gas masks could not filter out.[2]

Both the British and the French were said to have used asbestos umbrellas that may have been copied from devices used early in the war by German flamethrower pioneers.[3] Contemporary photos of such umbrellas have yet to be located.

The British also trained their men to duck under the flame[4] and then shoot down the flamethrower operator:[5]

> If caught in the open by a liquid fire attack, bayonet men should charge madly at the source of the fire, and the chances are about ten to one that they will not be seriously injured and they will be able to stab the nozzle man.[6]

In addition, rapid fire was opened on all clouds of smoke emitted by flamethrowers,[7] as the Germans used these to cover their advance.

The Russians experimented with fire-resistant clothing for their troops, issued extinguishing liquids, dug trenches with dramatic traverses, and finally took a very direct approach:

> Fire of all types is the most reliable means of protection against flamethrowers.[8]

Most of these methods relied more on luck than genuine countermeasures, and they did not take into account tactics such as curved-trajectory shooting, which a skilled operator could use to reach enemies crouched at the bottom of a trench or foxhole. Flame jets could also be bounced off trench walls in order to reach around corners. When deployed properly in conjunction with machine gunners, grenade-launcher squads, and hand-grenade throwers, flamethrowers were devastatingly effective weapons.

Only the Americans put in writing what the other combatants knew but did not articulate:

> It is impossible to withstand a liquid fire attack if the operators succeed in coming within sixty yards before the garrison can man its parapets.[9]

Notes

1"'Liquid Fire' Most Feared," *The Kansas City Star* (March 13, 1918), p. 11, col. 3.

2"Germans' Liquid Fire Turned Upon Themselves in Their Latest Attack on Verdun Defenses," *The New York Times* (March 22, 1916).

3"Asbestos Umbrellas for Firemen, *Modern Mechanix and Inventions* (January 1933); and "Asbestos Shield Protects Firemen," *Popular Science* Volume 121 Number 4 (October 1932): 19.

4S. A. Dion, *Tanks, Gas, Bombing, Liquid Fire* (New York: George U. Harvey Publishing Company, 1917), p. 154.

5S. M. J. Auld, *Gas and Flame in Modern Warfare* (New York: George H. Doran Company, 1918), p. 201.

6F. Haws Elliott, *Trench Fighting* (Boston, New York: Houghton Mifflin Company, 1917), p. 67.

7"Gases and Flame," Memorandum No. 15, Headquarters Fort Niagra Training Camp (Fort Niagra, New York: Office of Senior Instructor, 1917), p. 62.

8De-Lazari, p. 134.

9Georges Bertrand and Oscar N. Solbert, *Tactics and Dutiers for Trench Fighting* (New York, G. P. Putnam's Sons, 1918), p. 228.

Appendix 5
Extract from the Report of the Commission for the Inspection of the Methods of Application of Flamethrowers by the Germans in Combat on November 9, 1916, in the Region of the Skrobova Stream.

By the morning of October 27[1] our units that had advanced to the west bank of Skrobova Stream and occupied the position were: the 218th Gorbatovsky Infantry Regiment, from the height to 3/4 verst *[1 verst = 3500 feet]* north of the village of Dlonoe-Skrobovo including Folvarka, which was 1/2 verst west of the southern outskirts of the village of Gorny Skrobov; south of the stream that flows through the village of Perevoloki was the 217th Kovrov Infantry Regiment; and finally from the stream to the so-called Triangular Grove, 1/2 verst west of Mark 97.5, one verst south of the Skrobov-Colony group, the 1st and 2nd battalions of the 322nd Soligalichskiy Infantry Regiment occupied the position.[2]

The divisional reserves of the Corps and the Army, along with artillery, were arranged east of Skrobova Stream. The position located on the west bank of Skrobova Stream consisted of several lines of entrenchments, connected by communication trenches. The distance of the entrenchments of our first line from the enemy entrenchments ranged from 200-300 paces to several tens of paces, and in some places wire entanglements were widespread; generally each side had its wire entanglement, although there were small sections (at the 217th Regiment) where wire entanglements were not yet in place.

On the night of October 26-27 the troops were alerted that on the following day, October 27, the Germans would attack with flamethrowers; in some sectors this warning was passed by word of mouth, and company commanders warned the lower ranks of the forthcoming attack with flamethrowers, explaining the device and its effects (according to information from newspapers and drawings from periodicals).[3] In one company of the 322nd Infantry Regiment some were even given supplies of water to extinguish large flames that arose, and the lower ranks were told to take off clothing lit by flamethrowers. In other parts of the company those occupying the first line knew nothing about the forthcoming attack and they did not have information about the flamethrowers. Since nobody saw to intelligently explaining flamethrowers and their actions, as well as measures to combat them, this warning on the whole was hardly beneficial, and likely somewhat increased the nervous state of the men.

From 0600 hours on October 27 the enemy opened artillery fire on the location of the troop housing, directing it predominantly along the eastern bank of Skrobova Stream, on the artillery positions, and from approximately 1000 hours fire was concentrated mostly on our position located on the western bank of the stream.

The enemy systematically destroyed our entrenchments, gradually increasing fire to the level of a hurricane. All entrenchments were simultaneously destroyed, and in the contiguous sections of the first-line entrenchments, shelters and communication trenches were destroyed mostly by concentrated mortar fire.

From 1200 to 1400 hours the enemy tried three times to leave some sections of his entrenchments and advance against our position, but each time he was forced back by our rifle, machine-gun, and artillery fire. After each unsuccessful attempt the enemy fire (predominantly mortar) was renewed with the previous force along the first line of our entrenchments.

At 1500 hours the first line of our entrenchments and the wire entanglements in front of them were for the most part destroyed. Many defenders of this line (officers and lower ranks) were by this time pulverized or had taken to the surviving refuges and dugouts; surveillance of the enemy was weakened considerably.

Using these developments, the enemy between 1400 and 1500 hours began a new attack on the entire section; during this attack they used flamethrowers for the first time.

The initial outflow of flamethrower operators from the enemy entrenchments and their initial motion differed in no way from the usual start of infantry into the attack, so that it was not always possible to distinguish between flamethrower operators and grenadiers from a distance. Against some contiguous sections the flamethrower operators immediately showed themselves, emerging directly from their entrenchments. Thus, against the section of the 6th Company of the 217th Regiment, where the distance between the entrenchments was 30 paces, German flamethrower operators stood on the parapet of their entrenchment and from there they attempted to pour flame on our entrenchments, but the jets did not enter; several drops fell through only one loophole, which burned one lower rank. In 2-3 minutes the flamethrower operators were driven away by our fire. Similarly several Germans left their entrenchments and went against the 3rd Company of the 218th Gorbatovsky Regiment, where the distance between the entrenchments was about 25 paces; one was in front with the lance, from which the flame directly reached our entrenchment and set it ablaze.

For further offensives the flamethrower operators were usually gathered in groups of 5, 7, or 10 men; each such group was apparently composed in some organizational way around one flamethrower. From the statements of some eyewitnesses, in these groups there were grenadiers and men with light machine guns or automatic rifles. Sometimes grenadiers advanced in front, sometimes beside the flamethrower operators, or sometimes behind them. Infantry came after the flamethrower operators (but in some sections of the 217th Infantry Regiment, the enemy infantry did not).

Within 150 paces from our entrenchments, and sometimes where the distance between the entrenchments was less, flamethrower operators created a smoke screen in front of themselves immediately after they left their trenches. For this purpose they directed jets from the apparatus toward the earth, the consequence of which was thick smoke, the greater part black and in some places bluish, which almost completely hid the flamethrower operators from the sight of the defenders: using this curtain, the flamethrower operators moved several paces and then again repeated the same action, until they reached our entrenchments. Some eyewitnesses noted in this case that the flamethrower operators seemed to circumvent the recently doused places, since their motion was not linear. Many lower ranks (217th Regiment) mistook the smoke screen for the discharge of gas and hurried to put on masks; only after a time did they consider that the wind blew toward the enemy, and they tore away their masks. Obviously, the flamethrower operators managed to advance considerably while our troops were putting on and removing their masks.

Having reached our entrenchments, flamethrower operators usually went along them, dousing the entrenchments and the remaining defenders. The presence of flamethrower operators was discovered in the entire area under attack; however their continuous circuit in regular intervals distributed on the entire front was not observed.

Neither the flamethrower apparatuses used by the Germans on October 27 nor the noxious jets exuded by them appeared to have been uniformly applied along the entire front of attack.

According to the properties of the jets the apparatuses are distinctly divided into two forms: a) the apparatuses which project jets of flame, and b) the apparatuses which project jets of some kind of caustic liquid.

The first type of apparatus was used against the 218th Infantry Regiment, against the right flank of the 217th Regiment and against the 322nd Regiment; the second type of apparatus was used at the remaining front of the 217th Regiment…

From the statements of participants in the battle the impression made by flamethrowers is negligible in comparison with artillery, mortar, machine-gun and rifle fire, especially after everyone ascertained that the jet reached altogether only 15, 20, or 25 paces and that the flamethrower operators could move only at a walk. They did not have a decisive influence on the success of the German attack. Artillery and mortar preparation did everything. However, it is undeniable that flamethrowers had a significant negative effect on the degree of perseverance of the surviving defenders of the attacked entrenchments, and also on the immediate reserves. The wounded of the 218th Gorbatovsky Infantry Regiment departing to the rear shouted that "The Germans are spraying fire," "All the entrenchments are burning," and they made the remaining men extremely nervous with these exclamations...

Based on a detailed study of the application in combat on October 27 this year, of the attacking enemy's apparatuses that emit fiery jets or streams of caustic liquid, the commission reached the following conclusions:

> 1. The flamethrowers and the apparatuses which project caustic liquid are means of close combat at a distance not more than 30-40 paces; consequently, they can present a direct danger only to the defenders of entrenchments located at this distance from the enemy entrenchments. In all other cases the flamethrowers must be preliminarily delivered to within this distance, and only then they can be used for battle.
>
> 2. Flamethrowers as a result of their insignificant range cannot completely replace either artillery preparation, or machine-gun and rifle fire, or even hand grenades. They are only an auxiliary means used under the indispensable condition of the application of all other kinds of fire.
>
> 3. The effect produced by flamethrowers on defenders of entrenchments and the impression and spillover effect of their action are considerably inferior to all other kinds of fire and poisonous gases.
>
> 4. The successful application of flamethrowers is possible only for completing the defeat of the enemy who is shaken and demoralized by the previous battle, when his resistance is to a considerable degree broken, and when the number of flamethrower operators is significant.
>
> 5. Flamethrower operators can begin under a smoke screen.
>
> 6. Without the support of grenadiers, machine guns, and the infantry, flamethrower operators are unable to engage the enemy and hold that which they have seized.
>
> 7. Fire of all types is the most reliable means of protection against flamethrowers...

Signed:
Chairman of the Commission: Major-General Iskritskiy.
Members: Councillor of State Boguski, Colonel Eyden, Lieutenant Colonel Novikov, Captain Antonov.

Notes

[1]Using the Russian calendar.

[2]De-Lazari, pp. 132-134. The Russian and German accounts of the mass flamethrower attack at Skrobova are remarkably consistent except in their assessment of the effectiveness of the devices. Both the commander of the *Garde-Reserve-Pionier-Regiment, Major* Reddemann, and the German divisional commander at Skrobova, *Generalleutnant der Infanterie* von Woyrsch, concluded that flamethrowers were decisive. Also, no German reports of using flamethrowers to spray acid have yet been discovered. See Thomas Wictor, *German Flamethrower Pioneers of World War I* (Atglen, Pennsylvania: Schiffer Publishing, Ltd., 2007) pp. 112-115.

[3]Reddemann deployed an entire flamethrower battalion of four companies, armed with 24 *Grof* and 216 *Kleif*. This was the largest mass-flamethrower attack in history.

Endnotes

Introduction Notes

[1]Bernhard Reddemann, *Geschichte der deutschen Flammenwerfer-Truppe* (Berlin: Verein ehem. Angehöriger der Garde-Reserve-Pionier-Regiments, 1933), p. 8.

[2]Ibid., pp. 9-10.

[3]K. H. Karagodin, "Ognemetnoe Delo: Podozhenie Voprosa ob Ognenetanii do 1914 g. i Primenenie Ognemetov v Voĭnu 1914-1918 gg," in K. I. Velichko, ed., *Voenno-inzhenernyĭ Sbornik: Materialy po Istorii Voĭny 1914-1918 gg.*, Volume 2 (Moscow, 1919), pp. 1-90.

Chapter One Notes

[1]Reddemann, *Geschichte,* p. 8.

[2]Bernhard Reddemann, "Die Flammenwerfer," in Otto Riebicke, ed., *Unsere Pioniere im Weltkriege* (Berlin: Kyffhäuser Verlag, 1925), p. 195.

[3]Francis A. March, *History of the World War: An Authentic Narrative of the World's Greatest War* (Philadelphia/Chicago/Toronto: United Publishers of the United States and Canada, 1919) p. 92.

[4]*Current History: A Monthly Magazine of the New York Times,* Volume 11, October 1919-March 1920 (New York: New York Times Company, 1920), pp. 75-76.

[5]Hans Tröbst and Artur Leipold, *Das posensche Pionier-Bataillon Nr. 29 und seine Kriegsforationen* (Berlin: Kolk, 1932) p. 56. See also Jean-Joseph Rouquerol, *La Guerre en Argonne* (Paris: Payot, 1937), p. 53.

[6]Adolf Deutelmoser, *Die 27. Infanterie-Division im Weltkrieg 1914-18* (Stuttgart: Bergers Literarisches Büro, 1925), pp. 24-25.

[7]Tröbst and Leipold, page 33.

[8]Ministère des Affaires Étrangères, *Les Violations des Lois de la Guerre par l'Allemagne* (Paris/Nancy: Librairie Berger-Levrault, 1915), pp. 171-172.

[9]Although this document, Order No. 365/11. 14. A6, is found in the German Bundesarchiv-Militärarchiv, the file number is not known. It cannot be easily traced because there are no precise lists for the contents of each file in the archive.

[10]Reddemann, *Geschichte,* p. 10.

[11]Charles Theune, *Sturmtruppen und Flammenwerfer* (Berlin: Landes-Verlag, 1921) p. 248.

[12]Reddemann, *Geschichte,* p. 16.

[13]Bruce I. Gudmundsson, *Stormtroop Tactics: Innovation in the German Army, 1914-1918* (Westport, Connecticut: Praeger Publishers, 1989), p. 44.

[14]Reddemann, *Geschichte,* p. 11.

[15]Hermann Cron, *Imperial Germany Army 1914-18: Organisation, Structure, Orders-of-Battle* (Solihull, West Midlands, England: Helion and Company, 2002), p. 168.

[16]Reddemann, *Geschichte,* p. 12.

[17]Hauptmann von Schaewen, "Der erste Flammenwerferangriff," in Paul Heinrici, ed., *Das Ehrenbuch Der deutschen Pioniere* (Berlin: Verlag Tradition Wilhelm Rolf, 1931), pp. 524-525.

[18]Reddemann, *Geschichte,* p. 14.

[19]Oberstleutnant Clausius, *Erinnerungsblätter Deutscher Regimenter, Band 176: Infanterie-Regiment von Wittich (3.Kurhessiches) Nr. 83* (Oldenburg iO/Berlin: Verlag Georg Stalling, 1926), pp. 50-52. See also Prof. Dr. Hartenstein, *Das Kurhessische Pionier-Bataillon Nr. 11 im Weltkriege 1914-1918* (Zeulenroda in Thüringen, Germany: Verlag Bernhard Sporn, 1936), p. 26.

[20]Cron, *Imperial Germany Army,* p. 168.

[21]*Dem Andenken unserer gefallenen Kameraden: Garde-Reserve-Pionier-Regiment (Flammenwerfer)* (Berlin: Kameradschaft der Flammenwerfer im NS.-Reichskriegerbund, 1931), p. 32.

[22]Bernhard Reddemann to Brigadier General Amos A. Fries, Chief, Chemical Warfare Service, Thru: Major Herman H. Zornig, U.S. Army, Military Attaché, U.S. Embassy, Berlin, February 29, 1928, Record Group 175, File #470.71/32, U.S. National Archives, p. 5.

[23]Reddemann, *Geschichte,* p. 14. See also Cron, *Imperial Germany Army,* p. 168.

[24]"Liquid Fire Guns Russia's Terror," *Oakland Tribune* (March 28, 1915), p. 2, col. 2.

[25]Wilhelm Balck, *Entwickelung der Taktik im Weltkriege* (Berlin: R. Eisenschmidt, 1920), p. 73.

[26]Reddemann, *Geschichte,* p. 17.

[27]Hartenstein, pp. 34-36.

[28]Reddemann, *Geschichte,* p. 19.

[29]Philip Gibbs, *Now It Can Be Told* (New York and London: Harper and Brothers, 1920), p. 103. Private A. P. Hatton, "First Use of Liquid fire," *The Great War: I Was There!* Part 11 (December 13, 1938): 439-441.

[30]Reddemann, *Geschichte,* p. 19, and War Diary of *1. Landwehr-Pionier-Kompagnie XIV. Armee Korps,* Generallandesarchiv Karlsruhe 456 EV 105/98.

[31]Kriegsministerium Nr. 355.10.15 A6II, October 17, 1915, Generallandesarchiv Karlsruhe 456 F3/966.

[32]Graf Eberhard von Schwerin, *Königliches preussisches Sturm-Bataillon Nr. 5 (Rohr)* (Zeulenroda in Thüringen, Germany: Drud und Verlag von Bernhard Sporn, 1939), p. 18.

[33]Reddemann, *Geschichte,* p. 15.

[34]Ibid.

[35]Ibid., pp. 19, 50-51.

[36]Ibid., pp. 20-21.

[37]Ibid. See also Cron, *Imperial Germany Army,* p. 169.

[38]Records of Pioneer Regiment 23, Bundesarchiv-Militärarchiv PH 14/218.

[39]Oberleutnant Dürning, "Die Kriegsformationen der Pionierwaffen," in *Das Ehrenbuch Der deutschen Pioniere,* p. 63.

[40]Hermann Cron, "Übersicht der Behörden und Truppen in der Kriegsformation, Band 8," 1918, Bundesarchiv-Militärarchiv PHD 6/181.

[41]Cron, *Imperial Germany Army,* p. 168.

[42]Alexander Schwencke and Martin Reymann, *Die Tragödie von Verdun 1916. II. Teil: Das Ringen um Fort Vaux Reichsarchiv* Band 14 (Oldenburg, Germany: Drud und Verlag von Gerhard Stalling, 1928), pp. 15, 97, 108, 109, 111-112.

[43]Reddemann, *Geschichte,* p. 24. See also *Dem Andenken unserer gefallenen Kameraden,* pp. 32-33.

[44]Reddemann, *Geschichte,* pp. 31-32.

[45]Jean-Louis Larcade, *Deutsche Sturmtruppen: Troupes d'assaut allemandes (1914-1918),* (Les Jonquerets de Livet, France: Editions des Argonautes, 2002), p. 46.

[46]Friedrich Müller, *Brandenburgerisches Jäger-Bataillon Nr. 3* (Oldenburg, Germany: Verlag Gerhard Stalling, 1922), p. 51.

[47]Reddemann to Fries, p. 21.

[48]Larcade, p. 123.

[49]Reddemann, *Geschichte,* p. 24.

[50]Gudmundsson, p. 84.

[51]Larcade, p. 80.

[52]Reddemann, *Geschichte,* p. 26. See also Reddemann, "Die Totenkopf Pioniere," *Das Ehrenbuch der Deutschen Pioniere,* p. 523.

[53]"Vypiska iz Akta Komissii po Obsledovaniyu Sposobov Primeneniya Germantsami Ognemetov v Boyu 9 Noyavrp v Raĭone Skrobovskogo Ruchyya," in Aleksandr Nikolaevich De-Lazari, *Khimicheskoe Oruzhie na Frontakh Mirovoĭ Voĭny 1914-1918 gg,* edited and annotated by Mikhail Vasilyevich Suptotnitskiy (Moscow: Vuzovskaya Kniga, 2008), pp. 132-134.

[54]Theune, *Sturmtruppen und Flammenwerfer,* pp. 229-233.

[55]Reddemann, *Geschichte,* pp. 25-26.

[56]Reddemann, *Geschichte,* pp. 35-36. See also Theune, *Sturmtruppen und Flammenwerfer,* p. 149.

[57]Von Schwerin, p. 48. See also "'Stosstruppen' Battalion is Repulsed by Forty Frenchmen," *Warren Evening Times* (September 5, 1917), p. 1, col. 1.

[58]War Diary of *Sturmabteilung Marinekorps,* Bundesarchiv-Militärarchiv RM 120/324. See also Reddemann, *Geschichte,* pp. 34-35.

[59]Colonel W. W. Murray, *The History of the 2nd Canadian Battalion (East. Ontario Regiment) Canadian Expeditionary Force in the Great War 1914-1919* (Ottawa: The Historical Committee, 2nd Battalion, C.E.F., 1947), pp. 199-201.

[60]Reddemann, *Geschichte,* pp. 36-37.

[61]Ibid., pp. 32-36.

[62]Reddemann, *Geschichte,* pp. 37-38.

[63]Ibid., pp. 38-45.

[64]Maxwell Hundleby and Rainer Strasheim, *The German A7V Tank and the Captured British Mark IV Tanks of World War I* (Sparkford, Nr Yeovil, Somerset: Hayes Publishing Group, 1990), p. 34. Also Rainer Strasheim, letter to the author, April 16, 2005, quoting Erich Petter, *Kampfwagenabwehr im Weltkriege 1914-1918* (unpublished typewritten study, Berlin: 1932. Bundesarchiv-Militärarchiv Freiburg W10/50769), p. 107.

[65]Reddemann, *Geschichte,* p. 46.

[66]War Diary of *Infanterie-Division Nr. 29,* Bundesarchiv-Militärarchiv PH 8-I/205, 206, and 374.

[67]Emmett J. Scott, *Scott's Official History of the American Negro in the World War* (Chicago: Homewood Press, 1919), p. 234.

[68]Hermann Cron, *Geschichte des deutschen Heeres im Weltkriege 1914-1918* (Berlin: K. Siegismund, 1937), p. 174. War Ministry Order No. 1672. 18. G. A6.

[69]War Diary of Reserve-Division Nr. 76, Bundesarchiv-Militärarchiv PH 8-II/86 and PH 8-II/87.

[70]Reddemann, *Geschichte,* pp. 50-51.

[71]*Dem Andenken unserer gefallenen Kameraden,* pp. 32-33.

[72]Von Schwerin, p. 165.

[73]Reddemann, *Geschichte,* p.46. See also *Dem Andenken unserer gefallenen Kameraden,* p. 32, and Theune, p. 15.

Chapter Two Notes

[1]M. C. Ortner, *Österreichische Militärgeschichte 1998 □Folge 6. Die k.u.k. Sturmtruppen 1916-1918: Elitesoldaten Der Monarchie* (Vienna: Verlagsbuchhandlung Stöhr, 1998), p. 47.

[2]Ibid.

[3]Filippo Cappellano, "Lanciafiamme italiani 1915-1918," in *Studi Storico-militari 1999* (Roma: Stato Maggiore Dell'Esercito Ufficio Storico, 2000), p. 87.

[4]Ortner, *Die k.u.k. Sturmtruppen,* p. 47.

[5]Ignatius Phraye, "Liquid Fire as a German Arm. Terrors of the 'Flame Projector,'" *The War Budget* Volume VI, Number 11 (January 27, 1916): 329.

[6]Christian Ortner, *Storm Troops: Austro-Hungarian Assault Units, Commandos in the First World War: Tactics, Organisation, Uniforms and Equipment* (Vienna: Verlag Militaria, 2005), p. 64.

[7]The information on flamethrower platoons is found in *Anleitung für Flammenwerfer* (Vienna: Druckerei des k.u.k. Kriegsministeriums, 1916), pp. 5-10.

[8]Francis J. Reynolds, Allen J. Churchill, Francis Trevelyan Miller, eds., *The Story of the Great War: History of the European War from Official Sources,* Volume 5 (New York: P. F. Collier and Son, 1916), pp. 235-236.

[9]Ibid., p. 177.

[10]Ortner, *Storm Troops,* p. 64. See also *The Story of the Great War,* p. 177.

[11]Ortner, *Storm Troops,* pp. 64-65.

[12]Ibid., p. 67.

[13]Ortner, *Die k.u.k. Sturmtruppen 1916-1918*, p. 24.

[14]Peter Jung, *The Austro-Hungarian Forces in World War I (2), 1916-18,* Osprey Men-at-Arms Series No. 397 (Oxford: Osprey Publishing, 2003), p. 11.

[15]Ortner, *Die k.u.k. Sturmtruppen 1916-1918*, pp. 47, 51.

[16]Ortner, *Storm Troops,* p. 268.

[17]"The Battle of Ortigara, June 1917," by Richard Galli, http://www.worldwar1.com/itafront/ortnew.htm (accessed September 8, 2008).

[18]Ortner, *Die k.u.k. Sturmtruppen*, pp. 32-34.

[19]Unless otherwise noted, the remainder of the information on Austrian flamethrower troops is found in Ortner, *Storm Troops,* pp. 266-269.

[20]Perceval Gibbon, "Fight for Gabriele Rages Fiercely," *The New York Times* (October 6, 1917), p. 2.

[21]Alessandro Massignani, *Le Truppe d'assalto autro-ungariche nella grande guerra* (Valdagno, Italy: Gino Rossato, 1999), p. 101.

[22]"New Austrian Attack on Monte Corno Fails," *The New York Times* (May 19, 1918), p. 3.

[23]Francis A. March, *History of the World War: An Authentic Narrative of the World's Greatest War* (Philadelphia, Chicago, and Toronto: The United Publishers of the United States and Canada, 1918), p. 585.

[24]Charles M. Bakewell, *The Story of the American Red Cross in Italy* (New York: The MacMillan Co., 1920), pp. 78-79.

[25]Ortner, *Storm Troops,* p. 266.

[26]*Anleitung für Flammenwerfer,* pp. 5-10.

Chapter Three Notes

[1]Helmuth Gruss, *Die deutschen Sturmbataillone im Weltkrieg: Aufbau und Verwendung* (Berlin: Junker und Dünnhaupt, 1939), p. 70. According to von Schwerin, p. 34, the German training command consisted of 2 officers and 40 NCOs and men.

[2]Gruss, p. 71.

[3]V. N. Krapchanski; D. D. Vazel; G. R. Hristov; and I. K. Skachokov, *Kratak Obzor na boynia sastav, organizatsiyata, popalvaneto i mobilizatsiyata na balgarskata armia ot 1878 do 1944g* (Sofia: Darzhavno voenno izdatelstvo, 1961), p. 106.

[4]Gruss, pp. 169-171.

[5]Unless otherwise noted, the information on the Bulgarian Assault Battalion was acquired from an interview with Dobrin Todorov Dobrinov, staff member of the National Museum of Military History, Sofia, conducted by Ventsislav Gramatski on May 26, 2008.

[6]Krapchanski, p. 118.

[7]Bozhidar Dimitrov, *Voinite za Natzionalno Obedinenie 1912-1913, 1915-1918* (Sofia: Ul Sv. Kliment Okhridski Publishing, 2001.)

[8]Gruss, p. 71.

[9]Bozhidar Dimitrov, "Chervenata stena e makedonskata Shipka," http://www.bg-history.info/?p=statia&statiaid=949 (accessed February 11, 2008).

[10]Nikola Nedev, *Les opérations en Macédoine. L'Epopee de Doiran, 1915-1918.* Traduit par le Commandant Goetzmann (Sofia: Imprimerie Armeyski Voeno-Isdatelski Fond, 1927), pp. 194-195.

[11]Lyuben Eshtove, *Doyranskata epopeya. Boyata pri v "Duba" podvigata na svishtovtsi* (Sofia: Boyna biblioteka), pp. 22-24.

[12]Arthur Crookenden, *The History of the Cheshire Regiment in the Great War* (Chester: W. H. Evans, Sons and Co., Ltd., 1938), pp. 215-216.

[13]Bozhidar Dimitrov, "85 godini ot Doiranskata epopeya: Otblyasuk zhiv ot bitka velichava," *Bulgarski Voin* Issue 9-10, 2003, http://www.bgsoldier.eamci.bg/Scripts/isapiVWB.dll/doc?THEMEID=30340 (accessed March 24, 2008).

[14]Nedev, pp. 256-257.

Chapter Four Notes

[1]S. S. McClure, *Obstacles to Peace* (Boston: Houghton Mifflin Company, 1917), p. 340.

[2]Peter Downham, ed., *Diary of an Old Contemptible* (Barnsley, South Yorkshire: Pen and Sword, 2004), p. 136.

[3]Ersin Kalkan, "Son Kahramanlar," *Hürriyet* (October 28, 2003), http://arama.hurriyet.com.tr/arsivnews.aspx?id=180048 (accessed September 9, 2008).

[4]Edward J. Erickson, *Ordered to Die: A History of the Ottoman Army in the First World War* (Westport, Connecticut: Greenwood Press, 2001), pp. 139-141.

[5]Cihat Akçakayalıoğlu, *Birinci Dünya Harbi: Avrupa Cepheleri, Galiçya,* Vol. 7, Section 1, (Ankara: Genelkurmay Basımevi, 1967), p.84.

[6]Gruss, p. 70.

[7]Erickson, *Ordered to Die,* pp. 139-141.

[8]Necmi Koral et.al., *TSK tarihi Osmanlı Devri Birinci Dünya Harbi, İdari Faaliyetler ve Lojistik,* Vol.10, (Ankara: Genelkurmay Basımevi, 1985), p. 753.

[9]Edward J. Erickson, *Ottoman Army Effectiveness in World War I: A Comparative Study,* Cass Series: Military History and Policy (London & New York: Routledge, 2007), p. 133.

[10]Erickson, *Ordered to Die,* p. 233.

Chapter Five Notes

[1]Unless otherwise noted, the information on French flamethrowers is taken from *Lectures of the French Army Chemical Warfare School, First and Second Lectures,* File #MID 2314-C-90, Record Group 165, U.S. National Archives, and Ministère de la Défense, *Mémoire des Hommes: Journaux des Unités (1914-1918),* http://www.memoiredeshommes.sga.defense.gouv.fr/jmo/cdc.html, war diaries of the Schilt Companies (accessed April 29, 2009).

[2]"Une arme nouvelle sur la butte, le lance-flammes," http://pages-perso-orange.fr/vauquois.sno/vauquois/site/HTML/flammenwerfer.htm (accessed July 12, 2008).

[3]"French Using Fire on flanders Front," *Fairbanks Daily Times* (June 8, 1915), p. 1, col. 2.

[4]Grand Quartier Général des Armées de l'Est, État Major, *Instruction Relative À L'Utilisation Des Compagnies Schilt: Projection Des Liquides Inflammables* (Paris: Imprimerie Nationale, 1916), pp. 35-40.

[5]Grand Quartier Général des Armées du Nord et du Nord-est, *Instruction Relative À L'Utilisation Des Compagnies de Lance-flammes* (Paris: Imprimerie Nationale, 1918), pp. 17-19.

[6]Arthur B. Ray, "Incendiaries," Chemical Warfare Monographs Volume 43, Part 3 (Washington, D. C.: Chemical Warfare Service, AEF, 1919), p. 160.

[7]Ibid.

[8]Ibid., p. 159.

[9]Ibid.

[10]Edward Wright, "The Victory of Craonne and the Battle Along the Ladies' Walk," in H. W. Wilson and J. A. Hammerton, eds., *The Great War,* Vol. 9 (London: The Amalgamated Press Limited, 1917), pp. 239-240.

[11]Eric L., "Le nettoyage des creutes par les compagnies Z," *Souterrains & Vestiges,* http://souterrains.vestiges.free.fr/spip.php?article35 (accessed February 20, 2009).

[12]Laurence Stallings, *The Doughboys: The Story of the AEF, 1917-1918* (New York: Harper and Row, 1963), p. 65.

[13]Alan Palmer, *Victory 1918* (New York: Grove Press, 1998), pp. 215, 218.

[14]Ministère de la Guerre, Direction de l'Infanterie, *Instruction Provisoire sur l'Utilisation des Appareils Lance-flammes Portatifs et des Engins Incendiaires du 1er Février 1921* (Paris: Imprimerie Nationale, 1921), pp. 9-11.

[15]Ray, pp. 158-159.

Chapter Six Notes

[1]Unless otherwise noted, the information on Italian flamethrowers is from Filippo Cappellano, "Lanciafiamme italiani 1915-1918," in *Studi Storico-militari 1999* (Roma: Stato Maggiore Dell'Esercito Ufficio Storico, 2000.) pp. 87-148.

[2]Angelo L. Pirocchi, *Italian Arditi: Elite Assault Troops 1917-20.* Osprey Warrior Series No. 87 (Oxford: Osprey Publishing, 2004), p. 53.

[3]Pirocchi, p. 53.

[4]Ibid.

[5]Austin West, "Ardor of Italians Too Much for Foe," *The New York Times* (July 8, 1918), pp. 1, 3.

[6]Colonel Arthur Latham Conger, "Army: Part V. Italian Army," in *The Encyclopædia Britannica, 12th Edition. The New Volumes,* Volume 30 (London: The Encyclopædia Britannica Company, Ltd., 1922), p. 226.

Chapter Seven Notes

[1]Donald Richter, *Chemical Soldiers: British Gas Warfare in World War I* (Lawrence, Kansas: University Press of Kansas, 1992), p. 150.

[2]"Brief Record of Flame Projector Work at Wembley Experimental Station," WO142/250, British National Archives, p. 1.

[3]"Peter T. Scott, "An Awful Job," *Military Illustrated* Number 98, July 1996, pp. 36-37.

[4]J. F. C. Fuller, *Tanks in the Great War: 1914-1918* (New York: E. P. Dutton and Company, 1920), p. 28.

[5]"Flame Projectors," WO142/250, British National Archives, p. 2-3.

[6]"Ibid., pp. 2.

[7]"Scott, p. 36.

[8]"Brief Record of Flame Projector Work," p. 2.

[9]Ibid.

[10]Ibid., pp. 2-3.

[11]Scott, p. 37.
[12]Brief Record of Flame Projector Work," p. 3.
[13]Anthony Saunders, *Weapons of the Trench War 1914-1918* (Stroud, Gloustershire: Suton Publishing, 1999), p. 146-147.
[14]"Flame Projectors," pp. 7-11.
[15]Scott, p. 38.
[16]Charles. H. Foulkes, *"Gas!" The Story of the Special Brigade* (London: William Blackwood and Sons, 1934), pp. 95-96, 259.
[17]"Flame Projectors," p. 5.
[18]"Brief Record of Flame Projector Work," p. 3.
[19]Saunders, pp. 150-151.
[20]Richter, p. 153.
[21]Ibid., p. 154.
[22]Ibid., p. 154-155.
[23]Ibid., p. 155-156.
[24]Scott, p. 40.
[25]Richter, p. 153.
[26]Foulkes, p. 164.
[27]War Diary Special Sections, Royal Engineers, WO 95/122, British National Archives, p. 8.
[28]Ibid., p. 13.
[29]Ibid., p. 7.
[30]Scott, p. 40.
[31]War Diary Special Sections, p. 15.
[32]Ibid., p. 16.
[33]Richter, p. 156.
[34]Scott, p. 40.
[35]"Flame Projectors," pp. 3-4.
[36]War Diary Special Sections, pp. 20-21.
[37]Ibid., p. 24.
[38]Richter, pp. 156-157.
[39]Scott, p. 40.
[40]Foulkes, p. 164.
[41]War Diary Special Sections, p. 48.
[42]A. E. Byrne, *Official History of the Otago Regiment, N. Z. E. F. in the Great War 1914-1918* (Dunedin, New Zealand: J. Wilkie and Company, 1921), p. 137.
[43]Scott, p. 40.
[44]"Brief Record of Flame Projector Work," p. 4.
[45]"Flame Projectors," pp. 19-20.
[46]Richter, p. 157.
[47]"Flame Projectors," p. 16.
[48]J. M. Bruce, *RAF FE8,* Windsock Datafile 74 (Berkhamsted, Hertfordshire, Great Britain: Albatros Productions, Ltd., 1999), pp. 11-12.
[49]"Brief Record of Flame Projector Work," p. 4.
[50]Richter, p. 259.
[51]"Flame Projectors," p. 13.
[52]Major Charles Francis Atkinson, "Flamethrowers," in *The Encyclopædia Britannica, 12th Edition. The New Volumes,* Volume 31, p. 79.
[53]Foulkes, pp. 216-217.
[54]Richter, pp. 157-158.
[55]"Brief Record of Flame Projector Work," pp. 4-5.
[56]Military Attaché, American Embassy, London, to Chief Ordnance Officer, AEF France, December 7, 1917, File #T70268/7, Record Group 175, U.S. National Archives.
[57]Ibid.
[58]A. F. B. Carpenter, *The Blocking of Zeebrugge* (Boston and New York: Houghton Mifflin Company, 1922), pp. 186-194.
[59]C. Sanford Terry, ed., *Ostend and Zeebrugge: April 23: May 10, 1918: The Dispatches of Vice-admiral Sir Roger Keyes* (London: Oxford University Press, 1919), p. 148.
[60]Reports, Zeebrugge and Ostend, 23 April and 10 May 1918, ADM 137/507, British National Archives.
[61]General C. M. Wagstaff to Colonel Amos A. Fries, May 6, 1918, File #T70628/36, Record Group 175, U.S. National Archives.
[62]"Brief Record of Flame Projector Work," pp. 5-6.
[63]"Flame Projectors," pp. 15-17.
[64]War Diary Special Sections, Various Lists/Summaries of Casualties.
[65]Richter, p. 214.
[66]Foulkes, p. 111.

Chapter Eight Notes

[1]Vladimir N. Ipatieff, *The Life of a Chemist* (Stanford: Stanford University Press, 1946), pp. 213-214.
[2]De-Lazari, Commentary 16 by Supotnitskiy, pp. 188-189.
[3]Nathan M. Brooks, "Munitions, the Military, and Chemistry in Russia," in Roy MacLeod and Jeffrey Allan Johnson, eds., *Frontline and Factory: Comparative Perspectives on the Chemical Industry at War, 1914-1924.* Archimedes 16 (New York: Springer-Verlag, 2007), p. 86.
[4]Evgeniĭ Zakharovich Baruskov, "Glava VI: Sredstva Khimicheskoĭ Boryby," in *Artilleriya Russkoĭ Armii (1900-1917 gg.)*, http://militera.lib.ru/h/barsukov_ez2/12.html (accessed October 30, 2008).
[5]De-Lazari, Commentary 16 by Supotnitskiy, pp. 188-189.
[6]Baruskov.
[7]E-mail to the author from Dr. Mikhail Vasilyevich Supotnitskiy, July 30, 2008. Dr. Supotnitskiy (b. 1956) is a microbiologist and a colonel in the Russian reserves. From 1979 to 2006 he held several posts in the scientific research establishments of the Defense Ministry of the Soviet Union and Russia. He is the author of *Microorganisms, Toxins and Epidemic* (2000, 2005), *Descriptions of the History of Plague* (2006), and *The Dictionary of Genetic Terms* (2007). He is also the editor and commentator of the book *Khimicheskoe Oruzhie na Frontakh Mirovoĭ Voĭny 1914-1918 gg.*, by A. N. De-Lazari (2008). One of his fields of interest is the history of the development and application of weapons of mass destruction in the first half of the 20th century.
[8]De-Lazari, Commentary 38 by Supotnitskiy, p. 216.
[9]Brooks, p. 89.
[10]M. V. Krasilynikov, "Voenno-khimicheskoe Delo Russkoĭ Armii v Pervoĭ Mirovoĭ Voĭne (Obraéovanie i Raévitie). Chasty II. Kampaniya 1916 g." (Doctor of Science thesis, Moscow State University, 1952), pp. 14-15.
[11]Ibid., pp. 89-90.
[12]"Russian Offensive Spreads Over Front," *Lincoln Daily News,* March 24, 1916, p. 1, col. 6.
[13]"Flame Projectors," pp. 3-4.
[14]Atkinson, p. 79.
[15]Brooks, pp. 90-91. See also Supotnitskiy on De-Lazari, pp. 75-77.
[16]Information on the organization of the Flame-Chemical Training Battalion and Chemical Companies is extrapolated from Yuri Grigorevich Veremeev, "Voennaya Istoriya: Shtat Sapernoĭ Roty, Korpusnogo Sapernogo Batalyona, Russkoĭ Armii 1914 g.," http://tewton.narod.ru/history/saprota1914.html (accessed December 4, 2008).
[17]E-mail from Dr. Mikhail Supotnitskiy, July 30, 2008.
[18]Baruskov.
[19]Ipatieff, page 233.
[20]"Flame Projectors," pp. 15-16.
[21]Nik Cornish, *The Russian Army and the First World War* (Stroud, Gloucestershire: Spellmount, 2006), pp. 71, 240.
[22]Karagodin.
[23]Krasilynikov, pp. 210-212.
[24]De-Lazari, Commentary 16 by Supotnitskiy.
[25]Ibid. See also Baruskov.
[26]L. G. Beskrovnyĭ, *Armiya i Flot Rossii v Nachale XX v.: Ocherki Voenno-ékonomicheskogo Potentsiala* (Moscow: Nauka, 1986.), p. 101.
[27]E-mails from Dr. Mikhail Supotnitskiy, February 9 and 14, 2009.
[28]Ipatieff, page 233.
[29]Krasilynikov, pp. 14-15.
[30]"Flame Projectors," pp. 6, 15-17.
[31]Krasilynikov, pp. 210-212.

[32]Ibid.
[33]"Flame Projectors," pp. 15-17.
[34]De-Lazari, pp. 54-58.
[35]Krasilynikov, pp. 210-212.
[36]Nik Cornish, *The Russian Army 1914-18*. Osprey Men-at-Arms No. 364 (Oxford: Osprey Publishing, 2001), p. 12.
[37]Krasilynikov, pp. 210-212.
[38]Ibid.
[39]Baruskov.
[40]Krasilynikov, pp. 14-15.
[41]Baruskov.
[42]De-Lazari, Commentary 16 by Supotnitskiy.
[43]Ibid. See also Baruskov.
[44]Ipatieff, page 233. See also Cornish, *The Russian Army and the First World War,* page 240, and *Two Thousand Questions and Answers About the War* (New York: George H. Doran Company, by arrangement with the Review of Reviews Company, 1918), p. 97.
[45]Cornish, *The Russian Army 1914-18,* pp. 17-18.
[46]Wilhelm Balck, *Development of Tactics – World War,* translated by Harry Bell (Fort Leavenworth, Kansas: The General Service Schools Press, 1922), p. 86.
[47]"Flame Projectors," p. 13.
[48]Atkinson, p. 79.
[49]De-Lazari, Commentary 16 by Supotnitskiy.
[50]Baruskov.
[51]Kurt Braun, *Das Reserve-Infanterie-Regiment 104 im Weltkriege 1914-1918* (Leipzig: Emil Freter, 1921), p. 96.
[52]Nikolai Podvoisky, "Lenin – Organizer of the Victorious October Uprising," in Mark Jones, ed., *Storming the Heavens: Voices of October* (London: Zwan Publications, 1987), p. 109.
[53]Baruskov.
[54]Alexander Fyodorovich Ilyin-Zhenevsky, *The Bolsheviks in Power: Reminiscences of the Year 1918* (London: New Park Publications, 1984), p. 20.
[55]Cornish, *The Russian Army 1914-18,* p. 11.
[56]Ibid.
[57]Information on Russian flamethrowers in the postwar period is found in "Khimicheskaya Sluzhba Vremen Grazhdanskoĭ Voĭny 1918-1921gg," http://himvoiska.narod.ru/1918-1921.html (accessed June 16, 2008).
[58]Cornish, *The Russian Army 1914-18,* p. 11.
[59]De-Lazari, Commentary 16 by Supotnitskiy.
[60]Ipatieff, p. 237.
[61]Ronald I. Kowalski, *The Russian Revolution 1917-1921* (New York: Routledge, 1997), p. 116.
[62]Karagodin. See also M. J. Sukharevskiĭ, *Osnovy Ognemetnogo Dela* (Moscow: GAU, 1924).

Chapter Nine Notes

[1]Edward S. Farrow, *Gas Warfare* (New York: E. P. Dutton and Company, 1920), pp. 6, 8.
[2]Colonel de Chambrun and Captain de Marenches, *The American Army in the European Conflict* (New York: The MacMillan Company, 1919), p. 239.
[3]Henri Chapal to Colonel Bradley, July 19, 1917, File #T7033/1, Record Group 175, U.S. National Archives.
[4]James Thayer Addison, *The Story of the First Gas Regiment* (Boston and New York: Houghton Mifflin Company, 1919), p. 1.
[5]Leo P. Brophy and George J. B. Fisher, *The Chemical Warfare Service: Organizing for War* (Washington, D.C.: Office of the Chief of Military History, Department of the Army, 1959), pp. 5-6.
[6]Brooks E. Kleber and Dale Birdsell, *The Chemical Warfare Service: Chemicals in Combat* (Washington, D.C.: Office of the Chief of Military History, United States Army, 1966), p. 17.
[7]Amos A. Fries to Chief of Staff, AEF, August 24, 1917, File #T7033/2, Record Group 175, U.S. National Archives.
[8]Brophy and Fisher, p. 6.
[9]Ibid.
[10]Kleber and Birdsell, p. 18.
[11]Brophy and Fisher, p. 6.
[12]Kleber and Birdsell, p. 18.
[13]Addison, pp. 4-7.
[14]Farrow, pp. 126, 131-132.
[15]Brophy and Fisher, pp. 8-9.
[16]Leo P. Brophy, Wyndham D. Miles, and Rexmond C. Cochrane, *The Chemical Warfare Service: From Laboratory to Field* (Washington, D.C.: Office of the Chief of Military History, United States Army, 1959), p. 12.
[17]Brophy and Fisher, p. 9.
[18]Harvey Broun, *America in the War: Our Army at the Front* (New York: Charles Scribner's Sons, 1919), pp. 118-119.
[19]Colonel Amos A. Fries to Chief Ordnance Officer, AEF, January 30, 1918, File #F7186/114, Record Group 175, U.S. National Archives.
[20]Record Group 156, Records of the Office of the Chief of Ordnance, U.S. National Archives. As of August 2008, the entire chemical-warfare liaison file of the Trench Warfare Section, 1917-18, from Record Group 156.6.5, Records of the Engineering Division, was missing. Only descriptions of the reports remained.
[21]Description of report in missing chemical-warfare liaison file of the Trench Warfare Section, 1917-18, from Record Group 156.6.5, Records of the Engineering Division, U.S. National Archives.
[22]Addison, p. 213.
[23]Description of report in missing chemical-warfare liaison file of the Trench Warfare Section, 1917-18, from Record Group 156.6.5, Records of the Engineering Division, U.S. National Archives.
[24]Addison, pp. 10, 15.
[25]Lieutenant Salisbury to Chief of Gas Service, February 25, 1918, File #T70628/17, Record Group 175, U.S. National Archives.
[26]Lieutenant Percy H. Lawrence to Lieutenant D. W. Salisbury, February 2, 1918, File #T70628, Record Group 175, U.S. National Archives.
[27]Addison, p. 213.
[28]*History of Trench Warfare Material 1917-1919,* (Washington, D. C.: Army Ordnance, Government Printing Office, 1920), p. 218.
[29]Colonel Amos A. Fries to Officer in Charge of Gas Service, London, March 26, 1918, File #T70628/25, Record Group 175, U.S. National Archives.
[30]*History of Trench Warfare Material,* p. 218.
[31]Addison, p. 213.
[32]Ibid., p. 215.
[33]Lieutenant L. I. Shaw to Chief of Gas Service, May 5, 1918, File #T70628/39, Record Group 175, U.S. National Archives.
[34]Lieutenant L. I. Shaw to Colonel E. J. Atkisson, May 6, 1918, File #T70628/28, Record Group 175, U.S. National Archives.
[35]General C. M. Wagstaff to Colonel Amos A. Fries, May 6, 1918, File #T70628/36, Record Group 175, U.S. National Archives.
[36]Colonel Amos A. Fries to General C. M. Wagstaff, May 8, 1918, File #T70628/37, Record Group 175, U.S. National Archives.
[37]*History of Trench Warfare Material,* p. 215.
[38]"Flame Projectors: Record Card, Engineer Department, U.S. Army," File #T70628/2, Record Group 175, U.S. National Archives.
[39]Description of report in misplaced Chemical warfare liaison file of the Trench Warfare Section, 1917-18, from Record Group 156.6.5, Records of the Engineering Division, U.S. National Archives.
[40]Brophy, Miles, and Cochrane, pp, 12-13.
[41]*History of Trench Warfare Material,* p. 216. See also *Handbook of Ordnance Data, November 15, 1918* (Washington, D.C.: Government Printing Office, 1919), p. 295.
[42]Lieutenant Higbee and Colonel Fries to Lieutenant Salisbury, June 19, 1918, File #T70628/68, Record Group 175, U.S. National Archives.
[43]Brophy and Fisher, p. 12.
[44]"Flame Projectors: Record Card, Engineer Department, U.S. Army," File #T70628/2, Record Group 175, U.S. National Archives.
[45]Brophy and Fisher, pp. 11-12.

[46]Amos A. Fries and Clarence J. West, *Chemical Warfare* (New York: McGraw-Hill, 1921), pp. 35, 47.

[47]Kleber and Birdsell, pp. 19-20.

[48]Lieutenant L. I. Shaw to Colonel Johnston, June 29, 1918, File #T70628/76, Record Group 175, U.S. National Archives.

[49]Fries and West, p. 38.

[50]Addison, p. 213.

[51]"Flame Projectors: Record Card, Engineer Department, U.S. Army," File #T70628/3, Record Group 175, U.S. National Archives.

[52]Major Joel H. Hildebrand to Commandant of Experimental Field, July 2, 1918, File #T70628, Record Group 175, U.S. National Archives.

[53]Addison, p. 113.

[54]"Flame Projectors: Record Card, Engineer Department, U.S. Army," File #T70628/3, Record Group 175, U.S. National Archives.

[55]Ibid.

[56]Ibid.

[57]John W. Mountcastle, *Flame On! U.S. Incendiary Weapons, 1918-1945* (Shippensburg, Pennsylvania: White Man Books, 1999), p. 17.

[58]*History of Trench Warfare Material,* p. 218.

[59]Shipley Thomas, *The History of the A. E. F.* (New York: George H. Doran Co., 1920), p. 410.

[60]Addison, pp. 211-212.

[61]Ibid., p. 215.

[62]Fries and West, p. 352.

[63]*Field-service Printing: Quarterly Reports Submitted to the Joint Committee on Printing Under Authority of Section 11 of Public Act No. 314, 65th Congress, July 1, 1919, to June 30, 1920* (Washington, D. C.: Government Printing Office, 1921), p. 319.

Chapter Ten Notes

[1]Andrew Mollo, *Army Uniforms of World War I* (Poole, Dorset: Blandford Press, 1977), pp. 113-114.

[2]Cappellano, p. 136.

[3]Pirocchi, p. 11.

[4]Philip J. Haythornthwaite, *The World War One Source Book* (London: Arms and Armour Press 1993), p. 167.

Chapter Eleven Notes

[1]C. S. Grafton, *The Canadian "Emma Gees": A History of the Canadian Machine Gun Corps* (London, Ontario: The Canadian Machine Gun Corps Association, 1938), p. 75.

[2]*Canada in the Great War, Volume 4: The Turn of the Tide* (Toronto: United Publishers of Canada, Ltd., 1920), pp. 170-171.

[3]J. H. Boraston, ed., *Sir Douglas Haig's Despatches: December 1915-April 1919* (New York: E. P. Dutton and Co., 1919), p.110

[4]Tim Cook, *No Place to Run: The Canadian Corps and Gas Warfare in the First World War* (Vancouver and Toronto: UBC Press, 1999), pp. 142-143.

BIBLIOGRAPHY

Primary Sources

Government Documents and Public Records

Anleitung für Flammenwerfer. Vienna: Druckerei des k.u.k. Kriegsministeriums, 1916.

"Brief Record of Flame Projector Work at Wembley Experimental Station," WO142/250, British National Archives.

Cron, Hermann. "Übersicht der Behörden und Truppen in der Kriegsformation, Band 8," 1918, Bundesarchiv-Militärarchiv PHD 6/181.

Field-service Printing: Quarterly Reports Submitted to the Joint Committee on Printing Under Authority of Section 11 of Public Act No. 314, 65th Congress, July 1, 1919, to June 30, 1920. Washington, D. C.: Government Printing Office, 1921.

"Flame Projectors," WO142/250, British National Archives.

Grand Quartier Général des Armées de l'Est, État Major. *Instruction Relative À L'Utilisation Des Compagnies Schilt: Projection Des Liquides Inflammables.* Paris: Imprimerie Nationale, 1916.

Grand Quartier Général des Armées du Nord et du Nord-est. *Instruction Relative À L'Utilisation Des Compagnies de Lance-flammes.* Paris: Imprimerie Nationale, 1918.

History of Trench Warfare Material 1917-1919. Washington, D. C.: Army Ordnance, Government Printing Office, 1920.

Kriegsministerium Nr. 355.10.15 A6II, October 17, 1915, Generallandesarchiv Karlsruhe 456 F3/966.

Ministère des Affaires Étrangères. *Les Violations des Lois de la Guerre par l'Allemagne.* Paris/Nancy: Librairie Berger-Levrault, 1915.

Ministère de la Guerre, Direction de l'Infanterie. *Instruction Provisoire sur l'Utilisation des Appareils Lance-flammes Portatifs et des Engins Incendiaires du 1er Février 1921.* Paris: Imprimerie Nationale, 1921.

Ministero della Guerra. *Cenni Descrittivi degli Apparati Schilt.* Rome: Laboratorio Foto-litografico del Ministero della Guerra, 1916.

Petter, Erich. *Kampfwagenabwehr im Weltkriege 1914-1918.* Unpublished typewritten study, Berlin: 1932. Bundesarchiv-Militärarchiv Freiburg W10/50769.

R. Esercito Italiano, Comando Supremo, Ufficio Tecnico. *Cenni Discrittivi degli Apparecchi Lanciafiamme Portatili.* 1918.

Ray, Arthur B. "Incendiaries." Chemical Warfare Monographs Volume 43, Part 3. Washington, D. C.: Chemical Warfare Service, AEF, 1919.

Records of the Chief, Chemical Warfare Service, Record Group 175, U.S. National Archives.

Records of the Office of the Chief of Ordnance, Record Group 156, U.S. National Archives.

Records of the War Department General and Special Staffs, Record Group 165, U.S. National Archives.

Records of Pioneer Regiment 23, Bundesarchiv-Militärarchiv PH 14/218.

Reports, Zeebrugge and Ostend, 23 April and 10 May 1918, ADM 137/507, British National Archives.

Studi Storico-militari 1999. Roma: Stato Maggiore Dell'Esercito Ufficio Storico, 2000.

Sukharevskiĭ, M. J. *Osnovy Ognemetnogo Dela.* Moscow: GAU, 1924.

War Diary of *1. Landwehr-Pionier-Kompagnie XIV. Armee Korps,* Generallandesarchiv Karlsruhe 456 EV 105/98.

War Diary of *Infanterie-Division Nr. 29,* Bundesarchiv-Militärarchiv PH 8-I/205, 206, and 374.

War Diary of Reserve-Division Nr. 76, Bundesarchiv-Militärarchiv PH 8-II/86 and PH 8-II/87.

War Diary of Special Sections, Royal Engineers, WO 95/122, British National Archives.

War Diary of *Sturmabteilung Marinekorps,* Bundesarchiv-Militärarchiv RM 120/324.

Books

Auld, S. M. J. *Gas and Flame in Modern Warfare.* New York: George H. Doran Company, 1918.

Bertrand, Georges, and Oscar N. Solbert. *Tactics and Duties for Trench Fighting.* New York, G. P. Putnam's Sons, 1918.

Boraston, J. H. *Sir Douglas Haig's Despatches: December 1915-April 1919.* New York: E. P. Dutton and Co., 1919.

Byrne, A. E. *Official History of the Otago Regiment, N. Z. E. F. in the Great War 1914-1918.* Dunedin, New Zealand: J. Wilkie and Company, 1921.

Dem Andenken unserer gefallenen Kameraden: Garde-Reserve-Pionier-Regiment (Flammenwerfer). Berlin: Kameradschaft der Flammenwerfer im NS.-Reichskriegerbund, 1931.

Dion, S. A. *Tanks, Gas, Bombing, Liquid Fire.* New York: George U. Harvey Publishing Company, 1917.

Elliott, F. Haws. *Trench Fighting.* Boston and New York: Houghton Mifflin Company, 1917.

Foulkes, Charles H. *"Gas!" The Story of the Special Brigade.* London: William Blackwood and Sons, 1934.

Fries, Amos A., and Clarence J. West. *Chemical Warfare.* New York: McGraw-Hill, 1921.

Fuller, J. F. C. *Tanks in the Great War: 1914-1918*. New York: E. P. Dutton and Company, 1920.

Reddemann, Bernhard. *Geschichte der deutschen Flammenwerfer-Truppe*. Berlin: Verein ehem. Angehöriger der Garde-Reserve-Pionier-Regiments, 1933.

Terry, C. Sanford, ed. *Ostend and Zeebrugge: April 23: May 10, 1918: The Dispatches of Vice-admiral Sir Roger Keyes*. London: Oxford University Press, 1919.

Theune, Charles. *Sturmtruppen und Flammenwerfer.* Berlin: Landes-Verlag, 1921.

Articles

Hatton, Private A. P. "First Use of Liquid fire." *The Great War: I Was There!* Part 11 (December 13, 1938): 439-441.

Newspapers

"French Using Fire on Flanders Front," *Fairbanks Daily Times* (June 8, 1915), p. 1, col. 2.

Gibbon, Perceval. "Fight for Gabriele Rages Fiercely," *The New York Times* (October 6, 1917), p. 2.

"Liquid Fire Guns Russia's Terror," *Oakland Tribune* (March 28, 1915), p. 2, col. 2.

"New Austrian Attack on Monte Corno Fails," *The New York Times* (May 19, 1918), p. 3.

"'Stosstruppen' Battalion is Repulsed by Forty Frenchmen," *Warren Evening Times* (September 5, 1917), p. 1, col. 1.

"Russian Offensive Spreads Over Front," *Lincoln Daily News*, March 24, 1916, p. 1, col. 6.

West, Austin. "Ardor of Italians Too Much for Foe," *The New York Times* (July 8, 1918), pp. 1, 3.

Communications with the Author

Gramatski, Ventsislav. E-mails to the author, May 27-31, 2008. Interview conducted by Mr. Gramatski with Dobrin Todorov Dobrinov, staff member of National Museum of Military History, Sofia, on May 26, 2008.

Strasheim, Rainer. E-mails to the author, April 16, 2005. Updated information on the role of flamethrowers in the development of the German A7V tank.

Supotnitskiy, Dr. Mikhail Vasilyevich. E-mails to the author, July 30, 2008, and February 9 and 14, 2009. Information on the Imperial Russian Flame-Chemical Training Battalion and Russian flamethrowers.

Secondary Sources

Books

Addison, James Thayer. *The Story of the First Gas Regiment*. Boston and New York: Houghton Mifflin Company, 1919.

Akçakayalıoğlu, Cihat. *Birinci Dünya Harbi: Avrupa Cepheleri, Galiçya*, Vol. 7, Section 1. Ankara: Genelkurmay Basımevi, 1967.

Bakewell, Charles M. *The Story of the American Red Cross in Italy.* New York: The MacMillan Co., 1920.

Balck, Wilhelm. *Development of Tactics – World War.* Translated by Harry Bell. Fort Leavenworth, Kansas: The General Service Schools Press, 1922.

—. *Entwickelung der Taktik im Weltkriege*. Berlin: R. Eisenschmidt, 1920.

Beskrovnyĭ, L. G. *Armiya i Flot Rossii v Nachale XX v.: Ocherki Voenno-ékonomicheskogo Potentsiala*. Moscow: Nauka, 1986.

Braun, Kurt. *Das Reserve-Infanterie-Regiment 104 im Weltkriege 1914-1918*. Leipzig: Emil Freter, 1921.

Brophy, Leo P., and George J. B. Fisher. *The Chemical Warfare Service: Organizing for War.* Washington, D.C.: Office of the Chief of Military History, Department of the Army, 1959.

—; Wyndham D. Miles; and Rexmond C. Cochrane. *The Chemical Warfare Service: From Laboratory to Field*. Washington, D.C.: Office of the Chief of Military History, United States Army, 1959.

Broun, Harvey. *America in the War: Our Army at the Front*. New York: Charles Scribner's Sons, 1919.

Bruce, J. M. *RAF FE8,* Windsock Datafile 74. Berkhamsted, Hertfordshire, Great Britain: Albatros Productions, Ltd., 1999.

Canada in the Great War, Volume 4: The Turn of the Tide. Toronto: United Publishers of Canada, Ltd., 1920.

Carpenter, A. F. B. *The Blocking of Zeebrugge*. Boston and New York: Houghton Mifflin Company, 1922.

de Chambrun, Colonel, and Captain de Marenches. *The American Army in the European Conflict*. New York: The MacMillan Company, 1919.

Clausius, Oberstleutnant. *Erinnerungsblätter Deutscher Regimenter, Band 176: Infanterie-Regiment von Wittich (3.Kurhessiches) Nr. 83*. Oldenburg iO/Berlin: Verlag Georg Stalling, 1926.

Cook, Tim. *No Place to Run: The Canadian Corps and Gas Warfare in the First World War.* Vancouver and Toronto: UBC Press, 1999.

Cornish, Nik. *The Russian Army and the First World War.* Stroud, Gloucestershire: Spellmount, 2006.

—. *The Russian Army 1914-18*. Osprey Men-at-Arms No. 364. Oxford: Osprey Publishing, 2001.

Cron, Hermann. *Geschichte des deutschen Heeres im Weltkriege 1914-1918*. Berlin: K. Siegismund, 1937.

—. *Imperial Germany Army 1914-18: Organisation, Structure, Orders-of-Battle*. Solihull, West Midlands, England: Helion and Company, 2002.

Crookenden, Arthur. *The History of the Cheshire Regiment in the Great War.* Chester: W. H. Evans, Sons and Co., Ltd., 1938.

Current History: A Monthly Magazine of the New York Times, Volume 11, October 1919-March 1920. New York: New York Times Company, 1920.

De-Lazari, Aleksandr Nikolaevich. *Khimicheskoe Oruzhie na Frontakh Mirovoĭ Voĭ ny 1914-1918 gg*. Editing and commentary by Dr. Mikhail Vasilyevich Supotnitskiy. Moscow: Vuzovskaya Kniga, 2008.

Deutelmoser, Adolf. *Die 27. Infanterie-Division im Weltkrieg 1914-18*. Stuttgart: Bergers Literarisches Büro, 1925.

Dimitrov, Bozhidar. *Voinite za Natzionalno Obedinenie 1912-1913, 1915-1918*. Sofia: Ul Sv. Kliment Okhridski Publishing, 2001.

Downham, Peter, ed. *Diary of an Old Contemptible*. Barnsley, South Yorkshire: Pen and Sword, 2004.

The Encyclopædia Britannica, 12th Edition. The New Volumes, Volumes 30, 31. London: The Encyclopædia Britannica Company, Ltd., 1922.

Erickson, Edward J. *Ordered to Die: A History of the Ottoman Army in the First World War.* Westport, Connecticut: Greenwood Press, 2001.

—. *Ottoman Army Effectiveness in World War I: A Comparative Study,* Cass Series: Military History and Policy. London & New York: Routledge, 2007.

Eshtove, Lyuben. *Doyranskata epopeya. Boyata pri v "Duba" podvigata na svishtovtsi*. Sofia: Boyna biblioteka.

Farrow, Edward S. *Gas Warfare*. New York: E. P. Dutton and Company, 1920.

de la Gándara Marsella, Luis. *Moderna Técnica de Combate*. Madrid: Imprenta de Cleto Vallinas, 1921.

Gibbs, Philip. *Now It Can Be Told*. New York and London: Harper and Brothers, 1920.

Grafton, C. S. *The Canadian "Emma Gees": A History of the Canadian Machine Gun Corps*. London, Ontario: The Canadian Machine Gun Corps Association, 1938.

Gruss, Helmuth. *Die deutschen Sturmbataillone im Weltkrieg: Aufbau und Verwendung*. Berlin: Junker und Dünnhaupt, 1939.

Gudmundsson, Bruce I. *Stormtroop Tactics: Innovation in the German Army, 1914-1918*. Westport, Connecticut: Praeger Publishers, 1989.

Hartenstein, Prof. Dr. *Das Kurhessische Pionier-Bataillon Nr. 11 im Weltkriege 1914-1918.* Zeulenroda in Thüringen, Germany: Verlag Bernhard Sporn, 1936.

Hasselgrove, Michael J., and Branislav Radovic. *Helmets of the First World War: Germany, Britain, and their Allies.* Atglen, Pennsylvania: Schiffer Publishing, Ltd., 2000.

Haythornthwaite, Philip J. *The World War One Source Book.* London: Arms and Armour Press 1993.

Heinrici, Paul, ed. *Das Ehrenbuch Der deutschen Pioniere.* Berlin: Verlag Tradition Wilhelm Rolf, 1931.

Hundleby, Maxwell, and Rainer Strasheim. *The German A7V Tank and the Captured British Mark IV Tanks of World War I.* Sparkford, Nr Yeovil, Somerset: Hayes Publishing Group, 1990.

Ilyin-Zhenevsky, Alexander Fyodorovich. *The Bolsheviks in Power: Reminiscences of the Year 1918.* London: New Park Publications, 1984.

Ipatieff, Vladimir N. *The Life of a Chemist.* Stanford: Stanford University Press, 1946.

Jones, Mark, ed. *Storming the Heavens: Voices of October.* London: Zwan Publications, 1987.

Jung, Peter. *The Austro-Hungarian Forces in World War I (2), 1916-18,* Osprey Men-at-Arms Series No. 397. Oxford: Osprey Publishing, 2003.

Kleber, Brooks E., and Dale Birdsell. *The Chemical Warfare Service: Chemicals in Combat.* Washington, D.C.: Office of the Chief of Military History, United States Army, 1966.

Koral, Necmi et.al. *TSK tarihi Osmanlı Devri Birinci Dünya Harbi, İdari Faaliyetler ve Lojistik,* Volume 10. Ankara: Genelkurmay Basımevi, 1985.

Kowalski, Ronald I. *The Russian Revolution 1917-1921.* New York: Routledge, 1997.

Krapchanski, V. N.; D. D. Vazel; G. R. Hristov; and I. K. Skachokov. *Kratak Obzor na boynia sastav, organizatsiyata, popalvaneto i mobilizatsiyata na balgarskata armia ot 1878 do 1944g.* Sofia: Darzhavno voenno izdatelstvo, 1961.

Larcade, Jean-Louis. *Deutsche Sturmtruppen: Troupes d'assaut allemandes (1914-1918).* Les Jonquerets de Livet, France: Editions des Argonautes, 2002.

MacLeod, Roy, and Jeffrey Allan Johnson, eds. *Frontline and Factory: Comparative Perspectives on the Chemical Industry at War, 1914-1924.* Archimedes 16. New York: Springer-Verlag, 2007.

March, Francis A. *History of the World War: An Authentic Narrative of the World's Greatest War.* Philadelphia/Chicago/Toronto: United Publishers of the United States and Canada, 1919.

Massignani, Alessandro. *Le Truppe d'assalto autro-ungariche nella grande guerra.* Valdagno, Italy: Gino Rossato, 1999.

McClure, S. S. *Obstacles to Peace.* Boston: Houghton Mifflin Company, 1917.

Mollo, Andrew. *Army Uniforms of World War I.* Poole, Dorset: Blandford Press, 1977.

Mountcastle, John W. *Flame On! U.S. Incendiary Weapons, 1918-1945.* Shippensburg, Pennsylvania: White Man Books, 1999.

Müller, Friedrich. *Brandenburgerisches Jäger-Bataillon Nr. 3.* Oldenburg, Germany: Verlag Gerhard Stalling, 1922.

Murray, Colonel W. W. *The History of the 2nd Canadian Battalion (East. Ontario Regiment) Canadian Expeditionary Force in the Great War 1914-1919.* Ottawa: The Historical Committee, 2nd Battalion, C.E.F., 1947.

Nedev, Nikola. *Les opérations en Macédoine. L'Epopee de Doiran, 1915-1918.* Traduit par le Commandant Goetzmann. Sofia: Imprimerie Armeyski Voeno-Isdatelski Fond, 1927.

Ortner, Christian. *Storm Troops: Austro-Hungarian Assault Units, Commandos in the First World War: Tactics, Organisation, Uniforms and Equipment.* Vienna: Verlag Militaria, 2005.

—. *Österreichische Militärgeschichte 1998 – Folge 6. Die k.u.k. Sturmtruppen 1916-1918: Elitesoldaten Der Monarchie.* Vienna: Verlagsbuchhandlung Stöhr, 1998.

Palmer, Alan. *Victory 1918.* New York: Grove Press, 1998.

Pirocchi, Angelo L. *Italian Arditi: Elite Assault Troops 1917-20.* Osprey Warrior Series No. 87. Oxford: Osprey Publishing, 2004.

Reynolds, Francis J; Allen J. Churchill; and Francis Trevelyan Miller, eds. *The Story of the Great War: History of the European War from Official Sources,* Volume 5. New York: P. F. Collier and Son, 1916.

Richter, Donald. *Chemical Soldiers: British Gas Warfare in World War I.* Lawrence, Kansas: University Press of Kansas, 1992.

Riebicke, Otto, ed. *Unsere Pioniere im Weltkriege.* Berlin: Kyffhäuser Verlag, 1925.

Rouquerol, Jean-Joseph. *La Guerre en Argonne.* Paris: Payot, 1937.

Saunders, Anthony. *Weapons of the Trench War 1914-1918.* Stroud, Gloustershire: Suton Publishing, 1999.

Schwencke, Alexander, and Martin Reymann. *Die Tragödie von Verdun 1916. II. Teil: Das Ringen um Fort Vaux Reichsarchiv* Band 14. Oldenburg, Germany: Drud und Verlag von Gerhard Stalling, 1928.

Von Schwerin, Graf Eberhard. *Königliches preussisches Sturm-Bataillon Nr. 5 (Rohr).* Zeulenroda in Thüringen, Germany: Drud und Verlag von Bernhard Sporn, 1939.

Scott, Emmett J. *Scott's Official History of the American Negro in the World War.* Chicago: Homewood Press, 1919.

Stallings, Laurence. *The Doughboys: The Story of the AEF, 1917-1918.* New York: Harper and Row, 1963.

Thomas, Shipley. *The History of the A. E. F.* New York: George H. Doran Co., 1920.

Tröbst, Hans, and Artur Leipold. *Das posensche Pionier-Bataillon Nr. 29 und seine Kriegsforationen.* Berlin: Kolk, 1932.

Two Thousand Questions and Answers About the War. New York: George H. Doran Company, by arrangement with the Review of Reviews Company, 1918.

Velichko, K. I., ed. *Voenno-inzhenernyĭ Sbornik: Materialy po Istorii Voĭny 1914-1918 gg.,* Volume 2. Moscow, 1919.

Wilson, H. W., and J. A. Hammerton, eds. *The Great War,* Vol. 9. London: The Amalgamated Press Limited, 1917.

Articles

"Asbestos Shield Protects Firemen." *Popular Science* Volume 121 Number 4 (October 1932): 19.

"Asbestos Umbrellas for Firemen." *Modern Mechanix and Inventions* (January 1933).

Phayre, Ignatius. "Liquid Fire as a German Arm. Terrors of the 'Flame Projector,'" *The War Budget* Volume VI, Number 11 (January 27, 1916): 329.

Scott, Peter T. "An Awful Job," *Military Illustrated* Number 98 (July 1996).

Scholarly Works

Krasilynikov, M. V. "Voenno-khimicheskoe Delo Russkoĭ Armii v Pervoĭ Mirovoĭ Voĭne (Obraéovanie i Raévitie). Chasty II. Kampaniya 1916 g." Doctor of Science thesis, Moscow State University, 1952.

Online Sources

Barusov, Evgeniĭ Zakharovich. *Artilleriya Russkoĭ Armii (1900-1917 gg.).* http://militera.lib.ru/h/barsukov_ez2/index.html.

Dimitrov, Bozhidar. "85 godini ot Doiranskata epopeya: Otblyasuk zhiv ot bitka velichava," *Bulgarski Voin* Issue 9-10, 2003. http://www.bgsoldier.eamci.bg/Scripts/isapiVWB.dll/doc?THEMEID=30340.

—. "Chervenata stena e makedonskata Shipka." http://www.bg-history.info/?p=statia&statiaid=949.

Galli, Richard. "The Battle of Ortigara, June 1917." http://www.worldwar1.com/itafront/ortnew.htm.

"Istoriya Ognemetë." http://ss24.nnm.ru/istoriya_ognemjota.

Kalkan, Ersin. "Son Kahramanlar," *Hürriyet* (October 28, 2003). http://www.arama.hurriyet.com.tr/arsivnews.aspx?id=180048.

"Khimicheskaya Sluzhba Vremen Grazhdanskoĭ Voĭny 1918-1921 gg." http://www.himvoiska.narod.ru/1918-1921.html.

L., Eric. "Le Nettoyage des Creutes par les Compagnies Z." *Souterrains & Vestiges*. http://souterrains.vestiges.free.fr/spip.php?article35.

Ministère de la Défense. *Mémoire des Hommes: Journaux des Unités (1914-1918)*. http://www.memoiredeshommes.sga.defense.gouv.fr/jmo/cdc.html. War diaries of the Schilt Companies.

"Une arme nouvelle sur la butte, le lance-flammes." http://pages-perso-orange.fr/vauquois.sno/vauquois/site/HTML/flammenwerfer.htm.

Veremeev, Yuri Grigorevich. *Saper*. http://www.tewton.narod.ru.

INDEX